THE LIFE OF AFRICAN AMERICAN GIs IN BRITAIN IN WWII

THE LIFE OF AFRICAN AMERICAN GIs IN BRITAIN IN WWII

A WAR WITHIN A WAR

LIAM McCARTHY

Pen & Sword
MILITARY
AN IMPRINT OF PEN & SWORD BOOKS LTD.
YORKSHIRE – PHILADELPHIA

First published in Great Britain in 2026 by
PEN AND SWORD MILITARY
An imprint of
Pen & Sword Books Limited
Yorkshire – Philadelphia

Print ISBN 978 1 03619 550 2
ePUB ISBN 978 1 03619 552 6
ePDF ISBN 978 1 03619 553 3

A CIP catalogue record for this book is available from the British Library.

Typeset in Times New Roman 12/15 by
SJmagic DESIGN SERVICES, India.
Printed and bound in the UK by CPI Group (UK) Ltd.

The Publisher's authorised representative in the EU for product safety is Authorised Rep Compliance Ltd., Ground Floor, 71 Lower Baggot Street,
Dublin D02 P593, Ireland.
www.arccompliance.com

For a complete list of Pen & Sword titles please contact
PEN & SWORD BOOKS LIMITED
George House, Units 12 & 13, Beevor Street, Off Pontefract Road,
Barnsley, South Yorkshire, S71 1HN, England
E-mail: enquiries@pen-and-sword.co.uk
Website: www.pen-and-sword.co.uk

or

PEN AND SWORD BOOKS
1950 Lawrence Rd, Havertown, PA 19083, USA
E-mail: uspen-and-sword@casematepublishers.com
Website: www.penandswordbooks.com

MIX
Paper | Supporting responsible forestry
FSC www.fsc.org FSC® C013604

Contents

Preface

Eight decades after the Second World War ended, it is still an inspiration for historians, film-makers and journalists. In British popular memory, the regular anniversary celebrations and commemorations about the war act as a pivot in twentieth-century history around which contemporary events such as Brexit ('Britain against Germany') and terrorist attacks ('the Blitz spirit') are situated by the press. Even though it is within living memory, the war has become imbued with a mixture of myths and legends: 'Britain alone', 'the Blitz spirit', 'the Few' and of course 'the Yanks'.

The accepted narrative of the Americans in Britain is of white, well-paid and sometimes brash GIs, their generosity to local civilians … 'got any gum, chum' … their bravery in battle and the tens of thousands of GI brides they took back to America. The redolent images in Britain of 'the Yanks' are of B-17 Flying Fortress and B-24 Liberator bombers taking off on dangerous missions from East Anglia, paratroopers and glider troops based in the English countryside and hundreds of thousands of infantry GIs all leaving to take part in the D-Day landings. All of this took immense courage, placing it understandably at the forefront of the memory of the Americans in Britain during the war. But scratch below the surface and there are different and less heroic stories of the war with the capacity to surprise and shock. Stories of imported American racism, rioting and hostility on British streets, largely due to the surprisingly warm welcome given to African Americans by British civilians. In the segregated American military, many white GIs found it hard to accept the lack of segregation when they were off base, something accentuated by the blossoming relationships between Black GIs and British women. What ensued in Britain was a fight for equality by many Black GIs and a realisation that relationships with white people could be built on simple fairness, something they took with them back to America after the war. Of course, it would be wrong to assume that every white GI let racism play out on British streets. Similarly, it would be too simplistic to suggest that every African American GI became radicalised by their time in Britain to later join the fight for civil rights. Nevertheless, the experiences in Britain of Black GIs did have an impact on the civil rights movement that picked up pace in post-war America.

Setting out to write this book and uncover the experiences of the Black GIs in Britain, a major question stood out for me: is it still relevant after decades of military integration and civil rights legislation? The answer is a resounding yes. Understanding the difficulties and opportunities that Black GIs faced in Britain is core to understanding their desire for equality when they returned to the United States after the war. In the eight decades that have passed, although everything has changed, it can also be argued that in some areas of life very little has changed. During the Second World War, African Americans were segregated and relegated by the military to largely service roles, from laundry to logistics and, as this book shows, for top military officers the ideal fighting man was white. That African Americans in the military were discriminated against is accepted across the political divide. In 2024, Pete Hegseth, the future secretary of state for defence, wrote:

> African Americans fought in World War II before our armed forces were integrated, because their home country came first. America didn't deserve the humble devotion these incredible patriots displayed … Had African Americans and other marginalised citizens not considered themselves of use to defending our nation at war, we may not have won … there would have been no civil rights movement.[1]

What has changed in the military since 1945? In the mid-2020s, African Americans make up 13 per cent of the US population and while they are over-represented in every branch of the military, they are still seriously under-represented in terms of officers, especially senior ranks. In the US Army, just 6.5 per cent of generals are Black and there are even fewer three- and four-star generals.[2] It is a similar position in the US Air Force, where 17 per cent of enlisted personnel identify as Black but they account for 6 per cent of officers.[3] According to an NPR (National Public Radio) article on discrimination in the US Navy, only 10 of the 268 Admirals are Black. The article featured Keith Green, a retired Navy officer speaking about his book *Black Officer / White Navy* in which he argued that discrimination was still rife in the navy: 'It is not simply just unconscious bias … [Some in the Navy] don't like working for a Black person or a minority, and they don't like having one be their supervisor.'[4]

Eight decades after the end of the Second World War there is still an ongoing need for integration at the highest levels in the American military. Therefore an understanding of the lives of African American GIs in Britain during the conflict is an important lesson from history for the military of today.

A number of people have been influential in the ten-year process of bringing this book to print. I am indebted to Associate Professor Sally Horrocks and Professor George Lewis, both at the University of Leicester, and film-maker Jonathan Beamish. I am also honoured that Terry Harrison, Kerry Edmead, both sons of Black GIs and British women, and Edward Carroll, the son of a Black chaplain serving in Britain, allowed me access to their family archives; I hope I have done them justice. Finally, thanks go to my own family and especially my wife Helen for her encouragement during this project.

Liam McCarthy

Cover photographs. GIs playing Baseball, *Illustrated Leicester Chronicle*, 'American servicemen watching a baseball match at Abbey Park', University of Leicester Special Collections. The pictures of Louis and Patricia Venn on the front and back cover are courtesy of the Edmead family Archive.

CHAPTER ONE

Introduction

Three graves in the American military cemetery at Madingley near Cambridge in the English countryside bear witness to American racial violence on the streets of Britain during the Second World War. The white Latin cross headstones of Private William Crossland and Private First Class John L. Hendricks, together with the Star of David headstone of Corporal Arthur A. Abrams stand as part of a sweeping curved pattern of almost 4,000 graves in the beautifully manicured grounds of the cemetery.[1] Crossland, Abrams and Hendricks are just three of the GIs who met violent deaths in Britain at the hands of fellow Americans. Private Crossland, an African American from Virginia, was shot in the back in June 1943 in a fight with a white military police officer (MP) during a riot in Bamber Bridge, Lancashire. Private First Class Hendricks, an African American from Florida, was shot and killed at a routine traffic stop by a white US Navy Shore Patrol officer in the dock area of Cardiff, Wales, in April 1944. Corporal Abrams, a white MP from New York, died after being stabbed in the neck by a Black GI outside a pub during a disturbance in Leicester in the Midlands in May 1944. They were not the only GIs to lose their lives to racial violence in Britain; the bodies of others were returned home for burial after the war at the request of their families. This was part of a repatriation process by the American Battle Monuments Commission (ABMC) during the moving and reburying of American dead in the new cemetery at Madingley in 1947.

Those repatriated to the United States include Privates Robert Stafford and Curtis Phares. Stafford, who served in the 390th

Engineers Regiment (Colored), was murdered in March 1944 by two white MPs near Rugeley in Staffordshire after they had seen him dancing with a white girl. Phares was an MP in the 82nd Airborne Division and was stabbed to death in the incident that saw Corporal Abrams from the same unit murdered in Leicester. The families of these five young Americans who were sent to Britain by the US military could not have foreseen that their sons would die in such violent circumstances at the hands of their fellow servicemen. British civilians who witnessed the constant and visceral fighting between African American and white GIs found it difficult to understand the levels of animosity between them. Given the number of incidents right across the United Kingdom between 1942 and 1945, it is not surprising that deaths occurred, nor that it has faded from the collective public memory. Under wartime censorship rules, British newspapers were not allowed to report on the racial nature of violent incidents involving American troops and therefore it is not a major strand in the public memory of the war. In America, the Second World War is often seen as the last 'good war' and little is known about the wartime racial violence in the military – something that tarnishes the memory of the war against fascism.[2] After the war, there was a concerted effort by some politicians, especially from the southern states of America, to undermine the role of African Americans in the military and push back against the growing clamour for civil rights.[3]

In both Britain and America, problems with race predate the Second World War and continue to the present day. But what makes the hidden history of African Americans in Britain during the war remarkable is the manner in which they were welcomed by large swathes of the British population. They were accepted as equals and most British civilians refused to institute American colour bars and Jim Crow laws – laws that were introduced from the late 1870s in Southern States to enforce and legalise the segregation of white and Black people. The reception offered to these Black GIs marks a surprising pause in Britain to the animosity that was shown to people of colour before and more widely after the war. This is especially so as the estimated 240,000 African Americans who passed through

Britain between 1942 and 1945 were the largest community of people of colour seen in the country up to that point.[4]

The demonstrable problems with race in inter-war Britain include race riots in the great port cities of London, Cardiff and Liverpool after the First World War. Some of the worst of the racial violence occurred in 1919 in Liverpool, including the murder by drowning in the city's Queen's Dock of young Black sailor Charles Wootton. In the several days of intense rioting that followed, hundreds of other Black people in Liverpool were taken into protective police custody and three Black Americans were also stabbed.[5] The complex reasons behind the racial violence in these British port cities in 1919 included the issue of mixed relationships and marriages with local white women.[6] Local newspapers in Liverpool were quick to offer the populist suggestion that this miscegenation was the major reason for the violence. In June 1919, the *Liverpool Courier* argued in an opinion column:

> one of the chief reasons of popular anger behind the present disturbances lies in the fact that the average negro is closer to the animal than is the average white man, and that there are women in Liverpool with no self-respect.[7]

This racist tone builds on that taken by the British press at the turn of the century when immigration of Jews from Eastern Europe took centre stage in 'shock' reporting. Headlines from the national newspapers in the early twentieth century highlight these Jewish immigrants as 'The World's Riff-Raff' (1903) and an 'Alien Horde' (1906), with comments such as 'nobody has a word to say about the unrestricted admission of this rubbish' (1901).[8] This style of reporting built up resentment to immigrants among the British population and coupled with the post-First-World-War race riots makes the welcome that Black GIs received from a majority of British citizens more remarkable. It contrasts with the policies of the British Government, which in 1940 launched a campaign in the United States for military personnel and doctors to help the war effort but failed to select any African American volunteers. Similarly, after an urgent British call for blood stocks from America, blood offered by African Americans was turned down by the American Red Cross, who said they were operating on British instructions, something that historian Marika Sherwood describes as the 'duplicity, mendacity and racism of the British'.[9] African Americans who served in Britain were offered a measure of official ambivalence that contrasted with their surprising public acceptance.

The aim of this book, therefore, is to examine the life of African Americans in Britain during the war. It will argue that American racial violence on British streets should be viewed as a 'war within a war'. Many white GIs in Britain aimed to retain a measure of supremacy through the imported Jim Crow policies in the segregated military, while Black GIs resisted this pressure and enjoyed their new sense of equality and freedom 'off base'. The real battle for white Americans in the military and politics was how to prevent this equality – in whatever nominal form – shown to Black GIs in Britain from following them back across the Atlantic. Despite the desperate attempts to shore up and restore white supremacy after the war, historian Neil Wynn argues 'it is now widely accepted that the war years were crucial in the emerging civil rights movement'.[10] The experience of African Americans in Britain and their friendly mixing with white civilians was important in building the consciousness of Black troops towards equality. Historian Sarah Barksdale agrees with Wynn that it formed a 'critical connection between the Second World War and the civil rights movement'.[11]

This book locates the experiences of ordinary African American GIs in the non-combat zone of Britain, where they discovered that new, different, and sometimes vibrant relationships with white people were possible. The problems this caused within the segregated American military was monitored as a key indicator of troop morale – especially so in the long build-up to D-Day in June 1944, when the number of Americans in Britain reached its peak. The interception of personal mail from GIs back to family and friends in the United States helped to build a series of 'Morale Reports' for the American military. These reveal that a majority of white American GIs and their officers were concerned about racial equality in Britain, although their concern was that Black GIs on British streets had too much of it. They mostly feared the development of friendships and relationships between Black GIs and British women as a precursor to what might happen in America after the war.

The reception given to Black GIs by British civilians was a phenomenon that was largely unforeseen by both American and British authorities, and for much of the war in Britain, they were dealing with the fallout. Each of the chapters in this book attempts to reflect life as it was lived by African American GIs across Britain. They include details of riots, murders and the racism suffered by Black GIs from white Americans, also highlighting the new relationships that were possible with white British civilians and the babies that sometimes followed. While this book might seem to present a relentless catalogue of racism in the American military, it is important to remember that it did not involve everyone. This book also includes positive stories of senior officers weeding out subordinates guilty of racism and other white officers standing up for the rights and equality of Black GIs under their command. In the same vein, none of the evidence in this book points to Black GIs all behaving impeccably – some were just as capable of criminal activities from minor infractions to serious crimes, including rape and murder, as their white compatriots. Nevertheless, it is important to highlight the daily grind of racism that made many Black GIs feel like second-class Americans and contrast it with their reception by British civilians. That is not to say the British people were imbued with anti-racist feelings; it might be argued that their warmth towards Black GIs was more an animosity towards white Americans and just a feeling of wanting to see fair play. Historian Gavin Schaffer argues that the visibility of American racism on British streets during the war did make the British rethink their attitudes to race. But it was not enough to erode longstanding and racist British 'concerns about black intelligence and reliability', and a belief that mixed relationships could 'lead to the contamination of British racial stock'.[12] Following the departure of African American GIs after the war, these attitudes rapidly resurfaced with the arrival of immigrants from the Caribbean – the so-called Windrush generation, who are still fighting official British racism.

A Word About Sources

Primary research for this book was assisted by the increased digitisation and accessibility of American military records. The U.S. Army Heritage and Education Center in Carlisle, Pennsylvania, and the Air Force Historical Research Agency in Montgomery, Alabama, have both provided important new digitised records such as Unit Histories. The U.S. National Archives and Records Administration in Maryland provided excellent assistance during a personal visit to view files featuring African Americans in the military. However, some of the most valuable material for this book came from the personal family archives of Terry Harrison and Kerry Edmead, both sons of African American GIs who served in Britain during the war, and Edward Carroll, whose father was an army chaplain and served in Canada, Britain and France. To add depth to the stories, a number of strong local sources across Britain were accessed. For example, in exploring the impact of American GIs on British women in the city of Leicester, the records of the Leicester Corporation Health Board together with the minutes and annual reports of the Leicester Diocesan Moral Welfare Association allow this impact to be tracked.[13] In Leicester, these records show the increase in the number of illegitimate births, adoption and sexually transmitted diseases as the war progressed, with a strong correlation between the peak numbers of American GIs from early 1944 and the rise in births in 1944 and 1945, when over 1,100 illegitimate babies were born in the city. They also show that while both Black and white soldiers fathered babies, with the birth of 'Brown Babies' creating a more sensitive problem, especially for official adoption authorities.

In addition to primary research in British and American archives, this book draws on the academic history of the Second World War and the role of African American service men and women. The pre-war background of segregation in the Southern United States is covered in general surveys of civil rights and white supremacist politics; works by Newman, Fairclough, Litwack and Ward set out the established American social order of the time and chart the civil rights movement.[14] Studies by Morehouse, MacGregor, Motley, and Mershon and Schlossman cover the segregation in the military and explore the issue with an African American perspective. Each brings further nuances to the picture of Black GIs who felt they were written out of what was portrayed as a 'white war'. Morehouse is particularly strong in covering the post-war impact on Black GIs of the relative equality they experienced while posted overseas.[15] Latty and McGuire cover the personal experiences of African Americans in their work; Latty publishes letters home from Black GIs that highlight the racism they faced in the military, while McGuire shares a collection of interviews with Black veterans.[16]

In terms of crime, Lilly uses military statistics to review the cases of rape in the European Theatre of Operations (ETO) and his details of cases in England do show a disproportionate number of Black GIs being charged and convicted.[17] For Webb, the fact that some African American GIs received harsher treatment for the same crimes has no bearing in his analyses of the eighteen American GIs executed in Britain for murder and rape. In each case, the evidence shows that Black or white, those executed had committed heinous crimes and were executed at Shepton Mallet prison in England.[18] It was possible, though, for British public opinion to overrule military law, as in the case of Leroy Henry, accused of rape in the run-up to D-Day but freed by General Dwight Eisenhower after the intervention of local people and the national press in what was portrayed as an unsafe conviction.[19]

Around 2 million GIs passed through Britain on their way to Europe, and there are many general surveys that cover this period.[20] The comprehensive *When Jim Crow Met John Bull* by Graham Smith concentrates on the racial issues from a British and American perspective; from the reluctance of the British Government to accept Black GIs; worries about the sexual implications of their presence in Britain; the rioting between Americans that ensued; and the post-war integration of American forces.[21] A number of historians have highlighted serious racial disturbances across the country in multiple places ranging from small towns and villages, such as Launceston in Cornwall and Bamber Bridge in Lancashire, to larger cities, such as Cardiff in Wales, Bristol in the South West of England, and Leicester in the Midlands.[22] The story of the estimated 2,000 babies born to African American GIs and British women – the 'Brown Babies' – remained hidden for decades and is becoming more widely known thanks to the publicity around the use of DNA in tracing families in the United States. The work of Professor Lucy Bland has been critical in bringing the history of the 'Brown Babies' further into the light.[23]

Conclusion

This book adds important new strands to the history of African Americans in Britain during the Second World War and brings into sharp focus the everyday racism and abuse they encountered from some of their fellow Americans. We know that membership of groups actively pushing for civil rights in the United States, such as the National Association for the Advancement of Colored People (NAACP), received a boost after the war. This history shows that the British experience of Black GIs was an important part of the post-war civil rights fight in America; however, it is probably a stretch to claim it was the 'starting point' for the movement in the 1950s and 1960s.[24]

It would also be wrong to assume that all Americans took part in, or suffered from, the racial violence that unfolded in Britain, but it was very visible to civilians on the street, and each new wave of GIs brought their own personal prejudices with them. In the same way, not all British civilians welcomed African American GIs with warmth and affection, and for those that did, there were new 'moral' questions over the mixed relationships that ensued. This dilemma is highlighted by the wartime observation that British civilians might welcome the Black GIs as 'brothers in arms', but perhaps not as 'brothers in law'. This British contradiction can be seen in the post-war treatment of the 'Brown Babies', many were given up for adoption and others brought up by grandparents. The mothers who kept their children faced family 'shame' and abandonment, while many of the children themselves talk of facing racism growing up in the socially conservative Britain of the 1940s and 1950s.

Eight decades on from the end of the Second World War, this is a history that is becoming more widely known, still has relevance and is growing in importance.

CHAPTER TWO

American Segregation Fails in Britain, Creating a 'War within a War'

British and American racial attitudes and experiences clashed in the United Kingdom during the Second World War when civilians throughout Britain, to the shock of many in the British Government and US military, warmly welcomed African American GIs. The context of why and how this happened is important in understanding the racial antipathy that often developed into running battles between Black and white GIs on British streets. British people, especially those with exposure to the Empire, were every bit as capable as some Americans of holding white supremacist views. However, most people living in Britain had never met a Black person before and were willing to accept Black GIs and their courteous disposition at face value as new allies in the war. Indeed, British civilians often took the side of Black GIs in disputes over attendance at dances and entrance to public houses (pubs). Compared to the Jim Crow segregation practised in many American states, British racism had largely been 'off shored' to the Empire, while back at home, the general population viewed matters in terms of simple fairness.

The policy of the British Government was preferably that no African American GIs should be stationed in the United Kingdom. It hoped instead to persuade the US government to send them straight to the European continent and North Africa once those campaigns became active. However, President Roosevelt, having implemented the Selective Training and Service Act of 1940 through which African Americans were to represent one in ten of the military, was unwilling to bend to British pressure. Yet, even as the first African American soldiers arrived in the United Kingdom in the late summer of 1942, the British Government was still running an active rearguard campaign to convince the US Army that no more should be sent. The Foreign Secretary Anthony Eden offered one of the last and weakest arguments against their arrival when he 'helpfully' suggested to John Winant, the American ambassador to the United Kingdom, that the British weather was the real problem, as 'it was the damp which did the injury to negro health'.[1] This seemingly altruistic recommendation was brushed aside by Winant, and their terse encounter was set out in a 'most secret' memorandum written by Eden to Viscount Halifax, the British ambassador in Washington. Winant had countered Eden's argument by suggesting there were many white soldiers from the American South who would serve in Britain 'and it would not do to suggest that they could not stand the climate'.[2] Nevertheless, Eden persisted and urged Halifax to speak again to Winant in Washington as he still believed the American 'would do what he could to help us'.[3] Perhaps predictably this particular battle was never going to be won and President Roosevelt confirmed, through Winant, that the Black presence in Britain would match the overall targeted percentage of one in ten of the US military.[4] American politics and the pressure to include African Americans in the military during the war eclipsed any British efforts to restrict their presence. British Government ministers might have had silent allies in the senior US military who grudgingly accepted Black personnel and placed them into service rather than fighting units, but the military had little political influence in the matter.

Having failed to keep African Americans out of the United Kingdom, the remaining imperative for the British Government was to minimise the impact that their arrival in large numbers might have on the British population. In a briefing paper for the British cabinet in October 1942, Sir Percy Grigg, the secretary of state for war, pointed out the potential problem of the US Army policy of segregation that was built on the current social order in the Southern States:

> This policy which may perhaps be fairly described as the combination of equal rights and segregation practised in the Southern States is not generally known to the population of this country who with little experience of a colour problem at home are naturally inclined to make no distinction between the treatment of white and coloured troops and are apt to regard such distinctions as undemocratic.[5]

In a country where few civilians had ever met a person of colour, Grigg was right to be concerned that there would be friction between British civilians and white American troops. He argued that the government was therefore 'on a razor's edge' between the American and British outlook on racial matters.[6] He urged that every discouragement should be used to dissuade British women, especially those in the armed forces, from associating with African American soldiers. The advice he offered to his cabinet colleagues concluded that British Army personnel should be educated to 'adopt towards the USA coloured troops the attitude of the USA Army Authorities'.[7]

The Grigg briefing paper shows the fears of the British government were twofold; first, the need to avoid upsetting their American ally, especially given the attitudes that the British public might show to segregation and colour bars; and secondly, the probability of mixed relationships as Black GIs encountered English women. The outlook of the government towards African Americans being based in Britain perhaps represented existing political thinking, especially as the country was at the centre of an Empire that was home to more than 330 million people of colour who were often treated no better – or even worse – than Black people in the United States.[8] In comparison to the diverse nature of the Empire, there was only a tiny number of some 8–10,000 Black people living in Britain in 1940, with most centred on port cities such as London, Liverpool and Cardiff.[9] Therefore, for the vast majority of the British population, meeting a Black person was just not in their everyday experience, let alone a well-dressed and polite African American GI with an accent straight from Hollywood casting. It was perhaps natural that the government might be concerned about the impact of up to 240,000 African American service troops passing through or being stationed across Britain as they built airfields, camps and delivered military supplies. Nor did this seem a promising prospect for those African Americans who had either volunteered or been drafted into the US Army or Navy and now faced navigating daily life in Britain when they were off base.[10] As Reynolds argues, the question under consideration by the British government in 1942 was: should there be a 'discreet colour bar' in Britain for African American troops?[11]

This chapter will examine three key factors that would determine the type of wartime welcome and experience that African Americans would receive in Britain. First, it will outline how the advent of war had already brought unsettling change to the everyday lives and the existing social and economic reality of many African Americans; second, it will examine how the crossing of an 'American color line' by Black GIs as they enjoyed relationships with white British women became the major cause of the fighting with white American GIs; and third, it will focus on how the control of information in the press became key for the British and American governments as they tried to minimise the impact of the American racial conflict in Britain and the threat posed by Black GIs returning to America after enjoying a sense of equality in Britain.

America at War: Unsettling Change Begins

The Grigg briefing paper 'Notes on Relations With Coloured Troops', prepared for the British Cabinet by the Secretary of State for War, reads as though it was heavily influenced by a white perspective of daily life in the Southern States of America. If so, it is not surprising that it came to the conclusions it did, as the era between 1910 and 1950 was the 'heyday of white supremacy' in the segregated South.[12] As a way of dealing with the effect segregation had on their daily life, African Americans opted to develop parallel institutions, creating 'havens of security' that included churches and Black-owned businesses.[13] In the South, the doctrine of 'separate but equal' masked the huge disparities between the opportunities afforded to African Americans and whites in areas such as education, health, employment and voting rights. In addition, African Americans faced humiliating forms of everyday segregation in everything from lunch counters to buses, cinemas and public toilets, all enforced by often violent local police. This strengthened a Southern white supremacy that in reality marked a period of 'separate but unequal treatment of blacks'.[14] The most violent and visible image of this supremacy was the practice of lynching as a method of controlling the Black population and upholding Jim Crow laws by fear. The Equal Justice Initiative has recorded more than 3,500 cases of lynching (3,592) in the Southern States between 1877 and 1950, with over 500 cases each in the states of Mississippi, Georgia and Louisiana.[15] As late as 1939, lynching, though reduced, had not disappeared and the NAACP's *The Crisis* magazine drew attention to seven cases that occurred in 1938. Use of editorials in *The Crisis* by the NAACP saw active lobbying for a Federal anti-lynching law, arguing that individual states could not protect the lives of their Black citizens.[16] The slow decline of lynching was only partially due to Black activism as the practice was increasingly portrayed in the white press as the work of lawless 'lynch mobs', and was therefore rejected by many in 'polite' middle-class white society, and mass support for lynching began to wane.[17]

During the depression, economic change was sluggish and the slow recovery in the 1930s saw African Americans disproportionately suffering from poverty and unemployment. Despite the barring of racial discrimination in President Roosevelt's New Deal programmes, the work schemes were often administered by 'the same white people who had overseen the patterns of racism and segregation they were now supposed to reject', Greenberg suggests it was more 'Raw Deal than New Deal'.[18] Nevertheless, the New Deal was still an important initiative for African Americans as in 1930 an estimated four in ten of the Black population could not support themselves and were in need of assistance.[19] By the end of the decade, the closeness of the war in the Pacific and in Europe made it clear that even in a prevailing atmosphere of isolationism, America needed to rearm and modernise its military forces – if only for self-defence. This provided an opportunity for African American organisations such as the NAACP, the Black press and political activists to lobby for change, especially as the Federal Government was about to make huge investments in the military. Defence spending grew almost threefold from $1.8 billion in 1940 to $5.2 billion in 1941, kick-starting American manufacturing – especially in the Northern States. The accompanying growth in new jobs was a pull factor for a dramatic shift in the distribution of the African American population from rural to urban and from south to north. The US census shows that by 1950, the number of Black people in the Northeast and East North Central States had grown from 1.2 to 4.6 million to represent three in ten of the Black population.[20] This mass internal migration and the increasing discrimination that flowed from it provided civil rights organisations such as the NAACP with a bargaining chip as it lobbied the Federal Government to introduce legislation outlawing racist treatment in defence industries and the military. Companies bidding for Federal contracts came under the jurisdiction of the new Fair Employment Practices Committee (FEPC) established in May 1941. Through the FEPC, African Americans were able to get jobs in defence industries for which they had previously been rejected through the application of Jim Crow rules, and as a result, the FEPC was contested bitterly by Southern politicians.[21] The Selective Training and Service Act of 1940 introduced peacetime conscription and banned discrimination by race in the draft, leading to a million African Americans joining the military. While this movement towards equality did not go far enough to satisfy organisations such as the NAACP, it did lay down a marker for the future.

At the outbreak of the war in Europe, however, African Americans were still under-represented and undervalued in the armed forces. Of those who were in the military, an overwhelming majority were in non-combat service roles such as construction, trucking and laundry. In 1939, American military strength stood at around 350,000 troops, a number which grew to almost 2 million by the time of the Japanese attack on Pearl Harbor and would see around 12 million people in uniform by the time of the Japanese surrender.[22] Bringing African Americans into the military was a huge task as in 1939 only 1 per cent of personnel, just 3562, were Black.[23] Research for the Wilson Center established just how under-represented African Americans were in the US Army, finding that at the American entry to the war in 1941, there were just five Black officers, of whom three were chaplains.[24] The poor education standard of new recruits, especially African Americans as a result of the low level of education spending on Black children, was also a significant problem that would dog the military throughout the war, especially in an era of more sophisticated weaponry and equipment. The war therefore saw the American military take on a huge education programme from basic literacy through to higher technical courses.[25]

New African American recruits found themselves subject to military segregation in huge training bases set up across the country, with many bases set up in Southern States, where land was cheaper. Volunteers and draftees alike found the conditions on and off bases to be intolerable in terms of racism and Jim Crow rules. Their suffering was still raw in 1949 when Joseph Schiffman used contemporary material to record the disbelief of Black recruits as they reflected on the racism they suffered. Schiffman featured a letter from what he described as a 'Northern Negro' to his mother from an army hospital in El Paso, Texas:

> The parts of Mississippi and Louisiana that I visited were so revolting I can't see how people live there … there was all the segregation, Jim Crow and race problems you and I have heard of. This is supposed to be a war for democracy, freedom and equality … While in the hospital at Ft. Knox I've seen German P.W.'s [Prisoners of War] given more equality than I received.[26]

For this Northerner who was based in the South in his army service, there was a certain shock at the treatment he received. And yet, conditions in the South at this point were such that even the opportunity to offer any common courtesy to African Americans might be spurned. In Arkansas, the president of a local school board suggested to a researcher:

> No one down here calls a nigger Mr., Miss or Mrs. You just can't do it. You mustn't. Another thing don't say 'Thank you' to a nigger. You can say 'that is fine' or 'I like that' but never say 'thank you'. You must make him feel like you are superior … If you go around 'mistering' a nigger he will have less respect for you than if you cuss him and order him around.[27]

These oppressive attitudes and conditions led to rioting as many Black GIs fought back against the imposition of Jim Crow rules. Finkle argues that rioting took place 'at nearly every base in the South and many in the North'.[28] In an attempt to placate civil rights groups about the poor conditions in the armed forces, journalists from the NAACP were given access to military bases to highlight the work of African American personnel. The subsequent edition of the NAACP magazine *The Crisis* in February 1942 was rare as it was one of only five editions during the war to feature Black service personnel on the cover. The cover star is Air Cadet Lee Rayford from Washington DC, who is pictured sitting in the pilot's seat of a training aircraft. Rayford would go on to become a lieutenant colonel and fly 150 combat missions in Europe as one of the Tuskegee Airmen.[29] Above his photograph was a highlighted strapline pointing readers to '20 Pages of Army Pictures'. However, the unprecedented access that saw the magazine featuring African American recruits using the latest weaponry was undercut by other coverage of racial trouble both on and off military camps in the United States. The feature pages of army mechanics and engineers, liberally sprinkled with action shots, became lost in the accompanying and damning copy. The editorial argued, 'the US Army has meekly handed over control of its negro troops to any white Sherriff, constable or mayor in

Dixie that wanted to take over'. It goes on to point out the irony of fighting Nazi white supremacy while imposing Southern white supremacist views in the army: 'The 1942 negro resents and rebels against 1842 regulations. These must be rooted out whether they exist in the Mein Kampf of a Hitler, or in a memorandum in the adjutant general's office of the United States Army.'[30]

It is equally negative in its conclusion and the irony of fighting Nazi racism abroad: 'We believe this inescapable feeling of inferiority, and the shame and resentment of Negro soldiers and civilians that their government should force it upon them as a national policy in a war against racial bigotry and barbarity.'[31]

Black newspapers were equally aggressive in their demands for equality and an end to segregation in the military. The *Pittsburgh Courier* ran a 'Double V' campaign calling for victory against the Nazis and victory against racism in the United States.[32] In response to this and other criticism, the Adjutant General in Washington felt he should point out in a February 1942 letter to all commanders a range of army regulations with regard to the treatment of Black soldiers, including this exhortation: 'In this connection the use of any epithet deemed insulting to a racial group should be carefully avoided.'[33] Nevertheless, as the NAACP kept up pressure on the government, its own membership grew tenfold to around 600,000 by the end of the war.[34] The level of disappointment at how Black soldiers felt they were treated is perhaps exemplified by one African American officer home on leave: 'I hate it because every day since I've been in the Army some white person has reminded me through some word or act, although I wear the uniform of an officer of the United States Army, I'm still nothing but a 'nigger'.'[35]

While the NAACP campaigned against ongoing segregation in the military, white soldiers from the South felt pressure in the opposite direction, that somehow the lack of segregation abroad was all a Federal plot to end segregation at home. As Litwack argues, 'all in all Jim Crow didn't travel well, particularly in the United Kingdom'.[36] Segregation in the military was rigorously enforced and African American GIs even travelled to England in segregated ships, as Black war correspondent Roi Ottley noted in his diary.[37]

Before the war had begun in 1939, the NAACP commissioned editorial copy for *The Crisis* magazine from George Padmore, a Black journalist and activist who had spent time in America but was based in London. Padmore wrote:

> As long as Britain and France reserve the right to rule over 500 million colored peoples and exploit their labor in the interests of plutocracy, they cannot expect Germany to be satisfied. Empire and Peace are incompatible. And it is precisely for this reason we say that if peace is to be achieved, imperialism must be abolished.[38]

Padmore gave voice to doubts he and the NAACP had about British views on race. This was partly based on many cases of potential African American volunteers such as doctors, pilots and even blood donors who were keen to assist the British war effort but had been rejected on the basis of their colour.[39] The rearguard action by British Foreign Secretary Anthony Eden to minimise the number of African American troops in Britain, or exclude them completely, makes sense when considering the approach the Americans took to some British dominions. In Australia, for example, the 'White Australia' immigration policy of the government meant that after an initial deployment that saw clashes between American Black and white soldiers, 'General Brett recommended the withdrawal of all Negro troops'.[40]

The question for many African Americans as they crossed the Atlantic to Britain was: what sort of welcome would they receive? The answer lay in a British Ministry of Information Intelligence Report for August 1942 that suggested that the public 'have little, if any conception, of the attitude of US white to coloured men and a disinclination to accept their views when known'.[41] The seeds had been sown for conflict as American racial attitudes came up against those of the British public who had little, if any, contact with Black people in their everyday lives. This was particularly the case when it came to African American GIs mixing with white British women.

Crossing the 'American color line', Black GIs and British Women

It is difficult to understate the difference in attitudes to mixed-race relationships between the United States and Great Britain during the Second World War. In Britain, marriage between men and women of different ethnicities has never been against the law, even though it may have been frowned upon and not actively encouraged. With such a small Black and Asian population, numbering no more than 10–12,000 and mainly centred in larger port cities, it was simply not a major issue across the country as a whole before the war. However, in the United States, mixed marriages between different 'races' were illegal in 19 states, mostly in the South. In Virginia, legislation was enacted as late as 1924 to ban interracial marriage. The Virginia Racial Integrity Act defined a white person as having 'no trace of the blood of another race', initially factoring this as less than one-sixteenth of non-white blood.[42] The act remained in force in Virginia until 1967 when it was overturned after the US Supreme Court ruled in *Loving v Virginia* that the ban was unconstitutional.[43] This difference in racial attitudes is why the sight – and cultural shock – of an African American arm in arm in the street or dancing with a white British woman was such an affront to white GIs and why this reaction was not understood by many British civilians. The segregation of the US military into separate units and bases in Britain accentuated the impact of the arrival of African American troops based in large numbers in small towns and villages, who found themselves welcomed as new allies in the war.

The British experience was not easily replicated elsewhere later in the combat areas of the European Theatre of Operations. On the Continent, in fast-moving battle zones, the sometimes feral sexual attitudes of some soldiers – both white and Black – in a liberating or conquering army played out badly, with rape of local women a constant threat.[44] By contrast, in Britain, without active combat zones or language barriers and with Black GIs posted to bases for months at a time, there was both the chance of building relationships with British women and the 'self-policing' knowledge that if accused of sexual crimes, there was every chance of being caught. There was fierce competition between GIs for the attention of local women and the segregation of American military units made it almost inevitable that groups of Black and white soldiers would come to blows in large numbers. When the 82nd Airborne Division arrived in Leicester in the English Midlands, one of the commanding officers, General James Gavin, highlighted this in his diary when he wrote about English women: 'they prefer the company of colored troops … many are living with English women. American whites resent very much seeing a white woman in the company of a colored soldier. Here they almost see them in bed with them.'[45]

This was a situation replicated across the country between 1943 and 1945, where there was a virtual war within a war between white and Black Americans that often escalated into brutal violence and rioting on British Streets. African American War Correspondent Roi Ottley identified the trigger for much the violence in a revealing conversation on board his troopship during the voyage from New York to England in 1944: 'I talked with a white major – from the South – who was amazed that there was no Jim Crow in England. He said the white Southern troops will be very disturbed when they find out. They assume that Jim Crow exists everywhere.'[46]

Roi Ottley did not arrive in Britain until after D-Day, disembarking into Liverpool on 15 July 1944. The reaction of his 'white major from the South' to the lack of Jim Crow shows one of the problems faced by the American military. The constant churn of troops arriving and leaving for the Continent brought a permanent refreshing of American attitudes by white soldiers new to Britain, creating a revolving door of new racism. As early as August 1942, the Home Intelligence Reports of the British Government were marking out potential future causes of friction between white and Black American troops: 'Comment is reported to be growing over girls who 'walk out' with coloured troops. Criticism is directed at the girls rather than the troops … At the same time the extremely pleasing manners of the coloured troops is commented on.'[47]

According to the American *Ebony* magazine, what gave Black GIs the edge with British women was not just their politeness but the jitterbug:

> In the scramble for girlfriends, the average Negro GI had one advantage over his white Army brother: he knew how to jitterbug. English girls love to dance. Result was they flocked to dances given by Negro units, were thrilled by jitterbug experts and hot music. Many an English girl found a Negro beau at such dances, dating him regularly thereafter.[48]

The competition for 'girls' by white and Black GIs had an effect on British women. Homing in on one British city, Leicester in the Midlands, shows the dramatic effects this had. From dancing to relationship difficulties, racism, unwanted pregnancies and violence, it is possible to track the 'American effect' in the pages of the local press and the records of local health bodies. If some British parents dreaded relationships with American soldiers, some had more fear where African Americans GIs were involved, as Leicester woman Audrey Cuttill explained: 'We had coloured men in Leicester, we'd never seen them at all, at Braunstone Park, five or six hundred coloured Americans came over, we were horrified.'[49]

Conversely, as these African American soldiers became established in the city, letters began to appear in the local newspaper the *Leicester Mercury* suggesting these Black soldiers should not be shunned. Under the title 'Colour', the following letter appeared under the pseudonym 'First Army Soldiers Wife':

> May I put in a plea for hospitality in this country for our coloured allies, in particular those with brown faces and

> white hearts? Many of these boys have left their homes and loved ones behind in the United States of America and volunteered to fight for us. Is it the case that some publicans refuse to serve them with a drink when talking to white girls? Many of us have husbands in the Middle East and hope our husbands and sons are hospitably treated and not snubbed because of their colour.[50]

The phrase in this letter 'brown faces and white hearts' is perhaps a metaphor for how some British people viewed African American GIs – almost, but not quite, equals. A reply by a Miss Winfield of Syston, close to the base of around 200 African Americans in the tiny Leicestershire village of Gaddesby, was printed two days later: 'I should like the thank 'Soldiers Wife' for her loyalty to our dark allies. If people would pause and ask themselves why they are here, they would realise that they are entitled to the same hospitality and courtesy meted out to our other allies.'[51]

Romantic liaisons between local women and African American soldiers happened, and happened often. According to one woman in Syston, the African American troops based at Gaddesby came in trucks to the local village hop: 'A convoy of trucks would stretch 300 yards from Brook Bridge to the Bakers Arms pub on a Saturday night.' She described them as 'immaculately turned out, louder than life and endlessly courteous'.[52] Another Syston resident, Hazel Rayns recalls the dances in Syston and the obvious tension between Black and white Americans: 'If you went into a dance room and a coloured one were there they'd go [the white soldiers] or get the black soldiers to go out. They didn't want to be together, we always noticed that.'[53]

Having a liaison with an African American soldier may have been difficult, but consideration of marriage was impossible. While an estimated 70,000 GI brides returned with their white husbands to America after the war, officers refused to give permission to Black GIs to marry their white girlfriends.[54]

Nevertheless, relationships did occur and – as will be seen in Chapter Three, which tracks the 1938th Quartermaster (QM) Truck Company (Aviation) across Britain – babies were fathered by men in the unit. Unwanted pregnancies became one outcome of relationships between local women and American soldiers but as abortion was illegal in Britain, many women tried to 'get rid' of the baby themselves and backstreet abortions were rife. These procedures were dangerous and not always successful, as Beatrice Chapman, a trainee nurse at the Leicester Royal Infirmary, told the BBC: 'Another tragedy of the War was the number of "incomplete abortions" after the GIs arrived. One whole ward was set aside for them, 24 hours a day.'[55]

Despite the rise in backstreet abortions, news of an increase in illegitimate births in Leicester reached the pages of the *Daily Mirror* in October 1944 in a story headlined 'Illegitimate baby births have risen to one in fourteen', where it was suggested 'the authorities are alarmed at this appalling increase in illegitimacy since the war began'.[56] In 1945, the health records of the Leicester Corporation indicate that of 4,907 births in 1944, 617 were illegitimate – a rate of one in eight.[57] Nationally, between 1941 and 1945 in England and Wales, illegitimacy rates ran at 6.9 per cent, while in Leicester the rate rose to 14.3 per cent by 1945.[58]

While there are no figures on abortion, we do know from official statistics that at least 1,070 local women gave birth to children 'out of wedlock' in 1944 and 1945 because this was the number of babies given up for adoption to the Leicester Diocesan Moral Welfare Association. The association had become a registered adoption agency in 1943 and was responsible for trying to place these babies into local families.[59] There was, though, a moral dilemma for this Church of England body, of how to deal not only with the unwanted babies but how to educate young local women about sex. In a pragmatic approach for a church organisation, in 1944, the Leicester Diocesan Moral Welfare Association engaged a full-time sex education worker to go into schools, factories and voluntary groups to give talks to young women. This new worker managed 202 lectures in 1944 and 243 in 1945, a prodigious rate of almost one every working day – showing both the ability of the churches' Moral Welfare Association to respond to requests and indeed the number of requests it received to give the talks.[60] In its annual report for 1945, the association concludes with a reference to babies fathered by African American

GIs and born to English mothers: 'there are however a number of healthy children for whom life offers little hope of security unless they are adopted'.[61]

Estimates of the number of these 'Brown Babies' born across Britain range from hundreds to thousands, but the number is difficult to pin down. In November 1946, *Ebony* magazine reported that the 'League for Colored Peoples' in England had announced there were 570, but the story goes on to suggest that 'the actual number is not less than 2,000, perhaps as high as 5,000'.[62] There is no way of calculating the actual figure but the suggestion of around 2,000 has stuck and been used regularly by historians.[63] The label 'Brown Babies' was first used in the Black press in America but has since been adopted by the children themselves in adulthood as a positive acceptance of their heritage. Many of the 'Brown Babies' born as a result of relationships between British women and African American GIs languished in children's homes. Others were more fortunate and were looked after by their mothers, and in some cases grandparents.[64] Jennifer was born on 5 December 1944 at the General Hospital in Leicester after her mother's relationship with an African American soldier based in the city. This was far from being a casual relationship or a one-night stand. Jennifer was told that her father:

> used to borrow somebody's buggy and he used to take me up the street and round Charnwood Street ... My grandma used to like him, she used to call him midnight and he didn't mind, that were a nickname for him ... they reckon I were like him in likeness, to look at ... the neighbours used to say, 'you look more like your dad everyday'.[65]

Her father, who came from Alabama, continued to write and send money to Leicester after the war, but when Jennifer found the letters and asked questions about her father, her grandmother burnt them, leaving her little chance of finding him. Jennifer was brought up by her grandmother, with both facing terrible post-war racism as a consequence. The phenomenon of the 'Brown Babies' was highlighted by the Black press in America when the *Pittsburgh Courier* 'found' the first adopted baby to be returned to the United States.[66] The *Ebony* magazine feature mentioned above suggested that British civilians 'had demonstrated their freedom from prejudice and accepted Negro GIs as equals', but went on to argue that 'the soaring illegitimacy rate strained British notions of equalitarianism and fair play'.[67]

As well as unwanted pregnancies, women in Leicester also suffered from an increasing prevalence of sexually transmitted diseases (STDs), which, according to the City Health Board, reached a wartime peak of 745 in 1944, coinciding with the highpoint of American forces in Leicester in the same year. From 1944 onwards, more women than men presented with symptoms at the Granby Halls clinic.[68]

Unfortunately, not every encounter between American soldiers and local women was consensual, and assaults and rape happened across Europe – including in Britain. Historian Robert Lilly suggests the difference in the number of rapes reported between Britain and the Continent is stark and was almost five times lower in England than in the combat zones in Germany. Official figures suggest there were 121 rapes in England compared to 552 in Germany.[69] Rape was a capital offence under US military justice and in many US states, but for many African Americans in Britain, military segregation also meant the same problems of racial bias in the justice system that they witnessed in America. A 1946 summary of court martials for the European Theatre of Operations shows that seventy soldiers were executed in Europe during the war, fifty-five of them Black and fifteen white.[70] This led to the possibility of an American soldier being executed for the crime of rape, which was not a capital offence under English law or that of his home state.[71] In Britain, nineteen Americans were executed at Shepton Mallet Prison in Dorset – ten were hanged for rape or rape and murder, of which six were African American.[72] This high proportion of Black soldiers executed for rape is part of what Roberts calls the 'racialisation of rape' by the American military that built on existing prejudices against African Americans.[73] However, in Webb's analysis of the trials that resulted in executions in Britain, the sentence of death appears to be justified. The following mail intercept from a white officer in a US Army Morale Report suggests the justice system was not impartial, and could be heavily stacked against Black soldiers:

> Today I sat in on the court-martial again, had 4 negro cases ranging from 'Assault with intent to kill' to 'AWOL'. All guilty as hell and all got the limit. I'm sure getting tired of these niggers … I still can't help hating the nigger as a group and as individuals.[74]

The question of how the military approached mixed relationships in Britain became a point of moral outrage for the NAACP. An editorial in *The Crisis* magazine titled 'Black and White Rape' argued that 'Negroes get the minimum defense required by law, and the maximum penalty.' It reported:

> a white Southern lieutenant in a Negro anti-aircraft company just could not stand to see his men enjoying any courtesies extended by the white women of a certain Eastern seaboard town. He posted a notice that *any* type of association with white women would be regarded as rape, and reminded his men that the penalty for rape during war time is death.[75]

Rape was part of a bleaker side of relationships between Americans and British women, along with other violent assaults. Leicester CID officer Jock Joiner recalls that prostitutes used to come to Leicester from Nottingham and Derby: 'it was a financial bonanza for them, the Yanks had got money to burn'.[76] Local woman Alice Hannah remembered: 'Prostitutes came from London. We used to meet a friend at the Clock Tower, but when they came they took their handbags and slosh you one. They thought you were taking their pitch.'[77]

The Americans were quite willing to pay to get what they wanted but some took things further, as is shown in several assaults on local women. Local crime statistics for this period in the City of Leicester police archives show that between January to June 1944, 914 crimes were recorded in the city including: one murder, one attempted murder, three rapes, one of 'carnal knowledge' and eight assaults on females. It was noted at the time that three prisoners were 'arrested and handed over to the American military authority', although we are not told for which crimes.[78] There is no question that many white and Black American soldiers in Leicester were looking for sex and they also knew that as 1944 progressed, they were getting nearer to D-Day and possible death. Historian Mary Louise Roberts suggests that 'once aroused, the GI libido proved difficult to contain'.[79] In November 1943, Constable Bull of the City of Leicester police recorded in his notebook: 'Accompanied by USA MPs re: Miss (*Name withheld*). Complaint of a coloured soldier assaulting her on Southampton Street.'[80] Detective Sergeant Lacy records on 6 March 1944: 'Patrolled City Centre and paid particular attention to assaults', then the following day: 'Enquiries re: Assault on Miss (*name withheld*)', and three days later: 'At American Police Office re Assaults'.[81] In March 1944, DS Lacy spent no fewer than seven days making inquiries about different assaults by American soldiers and two days at the American Police Office. The assaults were an ongoing problem – in August 1944, PC Bull records in an entry: '11.10 p.m. Woman on Evington Street accosted by very dark USA soldier who struck her. Reached home safely. Soldier ran off.'[82] Local woman Hazel Rayns still recalls a frightening experience with a friend after two Black soldiers offered them a lift home in an army truck after they had missed their last bus:

> Suddenly a lorry came up … they put us in the back of the van and we said, 'Are you going to Syston' and they said 'Yes' … but they weren't. We got to the Hall [Gaddesby Hall where African American soldiers were based] and they went up the stairs and said, 'Don't go girls, come and have a drink' … as soon as they got up there we ran straight out and off up the road.[83]

Hazel did eventually visit Gaddesby Hall and danced with some of the Black soldiers, who she described as polite and 'great dancers', though she says 'there were some very bad ones'. For the civilian population of Leicester, the relationships between local women and American soldiers were a revelation, and for African Americans, they were no less than a revolution.

Controlling the Message: Would African American 'Equality' in Britain return home?

For many African Americans who served in Britain, the semblance of equality was refreshing. Conversely, the question for white Americans was, could these 'freedoms' be reversed at home after the war? In an article about the racist tactics of Southern officers in Britain, titled 'Dixie Invades Britain' for *PM* magazine in 1944, Roi Ottley succinctly outlined their problem: 'The one hopeful aspect of this situation is the fact that the noose of prejudice has not closed. The reason may be found in the fact that many of the most rabid anti-Negro soldiers are now not sure of their positions. They do not have wide public support for any show of racial hostility.'[84]

From the first arrival of Black troops in Britain in 1942, the American military and British authorities tried to control and monitor any information about racial tension that might be useful to the enemy or politically embarrassing. The potential difficulties of American-imposed segregation and the question of Black soldiers dating white women were top of the list because of the effect they might have on morale in the segregated US Army. There was no political support from the British Government for their unarmed police force to manage American-style segregation, and Cabinet papers show the reluctance of the British to get involved in the issue: 'British authorities should not assist the US Army in enforcing segregation, the Cabinet agreed not to object to the policy and to caution Britons about becoming too friendly with black GIs.'[85]

Before African Americans arrived in Britain, the Ministry of Information acceded to American demands to limit press and radio coverage about any racial problems. A copy of the 'D' notice (Defence Notice) from 1942 that would restrict press coverage survives in the written archives of the BBC, which as a broadcaster was also subject to these strict wartime guidelines. The 'D' notice outlined the censoring of publication of issues by the press regarding the US Army and 'the question of Coloured Troops':

It may be stated that Negro troops are serving in this theatre. The US War Department requests that no stories should be published without submission to censorship which:

(i) describe incidents or behaviour likely to inflame racial prejudice either here or in the U.S.A.,
(ii) characterise coloured troops as 'labour troops',
(iii) suggests that a colour bar is exercised against U.S. Troops,
(iv) suggests that their presence here creates a problem.[86]

These press and broadcast restrictions show a recognition that friction between Black and white Americans on British streets was expected and therefore the restrictions codify the desire to keep to a minimum any news of problems that might leak out. What the American military 'PR machine' did not take into account was the appetite of the British press to actively circumvent restrictions placed on it by the government. During the course of the war, a raft of stories about colour bars, rioting and the treatment of African American soldiers appeared, much to the annoyance of American officers. British journalists tried circumventing the rules of the 'D' notice by using vague locations and not identifying specific units. A favourite method was to print a letter from a 'reader' to provide a stimulus for editorial comment on the issues raised by the letter – such as colour bars. Senior American officers in Britain resented these stories, and offending clippings from the main British national newspapers can be found attached to files on morale and relations between African American and white troops. Typical is a press cutting from the large-circulation *Daily Mail* in the administrative history of the 8th Air Force. Attached by clear sticky tape is a reader's letter suggesting that white officers were responsible for the poor treatment of African Americans by white GIs. This extremely well-informed letter even quotes the editor of the *Louisville Courier-Journal*: 'He (The Negro) must realise that there is no power in the world which could now force the Southern white people to abandon the principle of social segregation.'[87]

Underneath the cutting, Colonel W. Ganoe, who served for the US Army during the war as the head of the historical section of the European Theatre of Operations, was forthright in his condemnation of the letter: 'it is not only destructive, but contrary to the fact from my point of view'.[88] Attached to the same file is another cutting from the popular *Daily Sketch*, dated 19 February 1944, and is a typical example of the type of story run in the British national press that the Americans found difficult to accept. This story pointed out to readers that British civilians overruled an attempt at American segregation at a dance in the 'West Country' – the vague location was used to comply with the censor to not identify exactly where American units were based. Under the headline 'Colour Bar Barred At British Dance', the story tells of what happened when Americans ordered 'coloured American soldiers' out of the dance hall: 'Applause greeted the M.C.'s announcement that as the coloured Americans were ordered out, all white Americans were also requested to leave.'[89]

Given their knowledge of racism throughout the British Empire, many in the US Army found the prevailing public attitude in Britain to American segregation difficult to accept. However, for ordinary British citizens, this kind of behaviour was something that most had never come across before given that the non-white population of Britain was tiny. Dealing with the publicity around African American soldiers was therefore a crucial issue for the senior staff in charge of operations in Britain. This became a high priority when news of the June 1943 American 'mutiny' at Bamber Bridge in Lancashire was inferred to be a racial incident in the local newspaper, the *Lancashire Daily Post,* which described it as a fight 'between military police and a small group of Negro soldiers'. The story was then picked up and covered by the British national newspapers and the American press.[90]

Despite most press stories in the UK steering away from putting the stress on the racial tone of incidents such as Bamber Bridge, the prevailing view of the friction between Black and white Americans was seeping through into public opinion. As the national broadcaster, the BBC regularly carried out research into public attitudes and feedback to inform programme-makers. In 1943, a special 'Listener Research Project' was carried out across the country to gauge public reaction to the arrival of American troops. It found that the 'coloured troops are preferred because they appear to have better manners', something that might be ascribed to social conditioning in the Southern States. However, the report is clear about racism within the American forces: 'The attitude of white American troops to their coloured compatriots was mentioned only to be condemned and used as evidence against the reality of American democracy.'[91]

This was not a good look for the American leadership in Britain and by September 1943, the US Army began a twin-track public relations approach in trying to deal with the problem, firstly by trying to understand it better and secondly to keep it out of the British press. The first strand involved the recruitment of Brigadier General Alexander as 'an expert on the so-called Negro problem' to visit 'the colored units in the U.K.' and 'to help formulate public relations policies governing the release of material regarding negro troops'.[92] The second strand was to work with the British Controller of Censorship, to effectively muzzle the press:

> They have a certain method whereby a 'Press Guidance Memo' is issued by the Ministry of Information. This is a hallowed document which is the guidance and background for papers and correspondents, to enable them to have the reasons why the British Government wishes certain material either not to be run or to be run in a certain manner.[93]

In the surviving memos from his headquarters in England, it seems that Supreme Commander Dwight Eisenhower tried to ensure that, though segregated, the Black soldiers under his command should be given equal treatment and strong leadership. Reporting to Eisenhower in December 1943, General Thrasher of the Southern Command in England outlined a range of issues affecting the Black and white troops in his area and advised: 'White troops from states where strong control over the colored population is still maintained, must be instructed that, while they remain in the British Isles, colored troops must not be in any way molested when encountered in the company with white British civilians.'[94]

The issue was a constant fire-fighting operation with new challenges to senior officers and their orders on the treatment of African Americans. For example, the local Commanding Officer of the Eastern Base Section Headquarters in England circulated his own memorandum on the subject titled 'Leadership of Colored Troops'. It stated: 'Colored troops are akin to well-meaning but irresponsible children. Generally they cannot be trusted to tell the truth … The colored man does not look for work … The colored individual likes to 'doll up', strut, brag and show off. He likes to be distinctive and stand out from the others.'[95]

According to historian Allison Gough, this attitude 'is a resurrection of the "positive good" pro-slavery argument which viewed slaves as children and their masters as paternalistic caretakers'.[96] Within days, General Lee, on behalf of Eisenhower, issued an instruction to the Eastern Base Section to obtain all copies of the memorandum that were sent out, destroy them and in future submit all such memos and letters regarding Black troops to his office for approval.[97]

Public relations was an important consideration for the American forces. Major rioting and racial incidents could largely be kept from the press, and the ability to place sympathetic images of American soldiers was used to create a peaceful and harmonious image. In Bamber Bridge and Launceston, where Black GIs armed themselves and held 'shoot outs' with white MPs, the events were prosecuted as mutiny and not race riots, hiding the racial nature of the fighting.[98] However, mail intercepts of letters from American GIs in the European Theatre to their families showed the level of animosity on the ground. Examples from the mail intercept report issued for the period 16 to 30 June 1945, after the end of the war in the European Theatre, show a clear concern by white soldiers about what the experience of equality in England might do when Black soldiers returned to America. One soldier wrote about African Americans: 'they have built up a misguided sense of equality on the one hand and superiority on the other that may take very severe measures to readjust when they return to the States'.[99]

Another voiced his fears about the post-war era: 'I try to be optimistic about the post war racial problems but have not the confidence I did before I came to this theater.' Continual worries about relationships between African Americans and white women were also apparent, as expressed in this letter home to a sweetheart: 'I wish to remind you not to go around at night by yourself. With large groups of troops returning to the USA now, it is very dangerous, especially with colored troops having been with white girls here.'[100]

Written in 1945, the American 8th Air Force Command History suggested that the military had only been partially successful in dealing with racial matters and that it remained a major American social issue:

> The British civilian authorities made few complaints against negro troops. The inability of many white American troops to adjust themselves to the different social attitude vis a vis [*sic*] the negro in the United Kingdom was probably the chief factor in upsetting the balance of white-negro relations. The occasional 'chip on the shoulder' attitude of some negro troops, a bit intoxicated with the wine of equality, was a contributing factor in more than one fracas. Since the problem of white-negro relations is incapable of final solution by the Army, it was possible for VIII AFSC [Air Force Senior Command] only to meet and ameliorate those difficulties which arose from time to time.[101]

That the official historian of the 8th Air Force could blame African Americans encouraged by the intoxicating 'wine of equality' for causing 'more than one fracas' with white Americans points to wider worries about what would happen when Black troops returned to the South. It speaks to a mood by some in the United States to clamp down on thoughts of equality for African Americans, with segregationist politicians from the South beginning their own war of attrition against any lessening of Jim Crow. There were moves in the South for the Federal Government to row back equality legislation introduced during the war, such as employment rights under the FEPC. Senator James Eastland of Mississippi used his 1945 trip to the US Army in Europe as part of the Joint Senate Military-Naval Affairs Committee to attack the work of African American troops. In a speech to Congress on his return in June 1945, Eastland said: 'The Negro was an utter and dismal failure in combat in Europe … Negro soldiers disgraced the flag of their country.'[102]

Eastland's speech received widespread coverage in white Southern newspapers. An example is the front-page coverage in the *Tuscaloosa News* from Alabama under the headline 'Eastland Takes Up FEPC Fight', which includes quotes from his speech on African American troops with a subheading 'Claims Negro Soldiers Have Been Failures'. The story goes on to point out the heart of the matter for Southerners – the importance of racial politics. In reporting the Eastland story, it quotes him telling journalists: 'And we're asked here to set up an unfair preference against a white soldier because the Negro minority sells its votes to the highest bidder.'[103]

The article concludes by linking potential voting reform by the Federal Government in the minds of readers and urging them to back calls for individual states to retain control over such matters.

The Black press took the opposite view. In Jackson Mississippi, the front page of the *Jackson Advocate* carried two stories on the Senator Eastland statement about African American troops. At the top of the page under the headline 'War Undersec'y Patterson Refutes Senator Eastland', the story quotes Robert Patterson as saying: 'The War Department is proud of its troops and that includes Negroes.' Lower down the front page, a story under the banner headline in bold capitals 'AMERICAN VETERANS PROTEST EASTLAND SLUR' takes an unusual twist by quoting the American Veterans Committee in a subheading 'White Group Calls Remarks "Rank Calumny".'[104] Taking a similar line was the front page of the *Arkansas State Press* published in Little Rock on 13 July 1945, which had a large banner headline on the Eastland claims: 'SOMEBODY LIED about U.S. Negro Troops'. Below the banner headline was a secondary bold title that left the reader in no doubt of the editorial view of the Eastland comments:

'AMERICAN GENERALS AND FRENCH ARMY DENOUNCE SEN. EASTLAND SLANDER'.[105]

There was a mood among Black soldiers that they would have more opportunities for jobs and education after the war. As the conflict ended, polls conducted by the army found that while white troops largely thought their rights and privileges in society would stay roughly the same, African American soldiers were more optimistic, with four in ten (43 per cent) expecting things to improve.[106] Black veterans were to be disappointed. As they returned home, they found their work went unrecognised, particularly in the South, where they found themselves written out of a 'white' war. African American GI Thomas McPhatter, who later became a marine sergeant, noted when recalling D-Day: 'When you talk to white people they will swear up and down that there were no black people in the first wave. But I went in without my unit. I was put on another LST [Landing Craft].'[107]

After being wounded, McPhatter stayed on the beach under fire to treat the more seriously wounded:

> There was no other medic around here on Omaha Beach. It was just about ninety minutes after the start of D-Day. I had pulled a tent roll out of the water and so I set up a first aid station. It was the only one on the beach. It seemed like everyone was either dead or screaming, 'Doc. Doc. Help me.' I took a bullet from the shoulder of one and dressed a gaping hole in the shoulder of another. I even amputated a right foot.[108]

The white American press in the South was particularly keen to play down the role of Black veterans and to cover the segregationist policies of local politicians through the late 1940s and 1950s. It played an important part in trying to shore up white supremacy.

Conclusion

For African Americans, the Second World War opened the door to the possibility of genuine change in civil rights in America. The

FEPC and the Selective Service Act (SSA) introduced by the Federal Government brought new rights to Black citizens, and the United States did see some change. However, both the FEPC and SSA were fiercely resisted by politicians in Southern States who wanted to retain their segregated social system and its Jim Crow laws. Newly recruited Black GIs found out that an army uniform was no protection against violent racism on training bases and in local towns across the South. A segregated military system restricted Black GIs to service units in support of white troops, reinforcing white supremacy. The thought of serving in an Imperial Britain that controlled an Empire in which hundreds of millions of Black people were also treated unequally might not have seemed an enticing prospect.

However, African Americans who came in Britain enjoyed what the US 8th Air Force recorded in its administrative history as 'the wine of equality'. For almost all the Black GIs, this was their first time outside of the United States and they encountered a totally different social fabric in Britain. While their units and bases remained strictly segregated, there were no such restrictions off base and a simple jitterbug at a local dance could lead to relationships with British women which in turn led to the birth of an estimated to 2,000 'Brown Babies'. Black GIs must have felt they had stumbled into a parallel universe. The importance of this seminal experience of African Americans serving in Britain has been described as part of a turning point in the fight for equality in America. As early as March 1944, in *New Republic* magazine, the civil liberties campaigner Lucille B. Milner argued that serving during the war would create what she termed a 'new Negro': 'A new Negro will return from the war – a bitter Negro if he is disappointed again. He will have been taught to kill, to suffer, to die for something he believes in, and he will live by these rules to gain his personal rights.'[109]

After the war, membership of organisations like the NAACP surged and many Black GIs who served in Britain became active in the civil rights movement.

CHAPTER THREE

Life in an African American Unit: The 1938th Quartermaster Truck Company

Twins Terry and Susan Harrison were born on 9 June 1944 at the cottage hospital in Melton Mowbray in England, just a few miles from where the family lived in the small village of Gaddesby in Leicestershire. Terry and Susan were two of at least five 'Brown Babies' born in and around the village who were the result of relationships between African American GIs and local English women. Terry and Susan's mum Edna Harrison and their GI father met at one of the regular Saturday night dances in the local village halls. Edna was married and her husband was away serving in the British Army. Terry and Susan knew nothing about their biological father until their mother died and Terry, by then in his 60s, began searching for their American roots. It became clear from a photograph in Edna's personal possessions of a grave at the Cambridge American Cemetery that she believed the father of her twins was named John Hendricks. Private First Class John Lawrence Hendricks was from Orange County, Florida, and based in Gaddesby in the late summer and autumn of 1943 as part of the 1938th QM Truck Company (Aviation). He and Edna enjoyed a relationship while he was stationed in the village until the 1938th was moved from Gaddesby on 26 December 1943. By the time Terry and Susan were born, their father was dead, killed in April 1944 while on duty close to Cardiff docks in Wales. It would take another six decades before Terry found out about the death of his father in the American military personnel file for Hendricks that he was sent in 2010. This file and the newly digitised Unit History of the 1938th QM Truck Company (Aviation) form the spine of the research for much of this chapter.

This chapter follows the progress of Black GIs in the 1938th from their enlistment in the United States, through their time in Great Britain, and on to the end of the war in Europe. The GIs in the 1938th would witness conflicts with white Americans and have experiences of connecting with British civilians in a manner that would have been unimaginable in the United States. Terry and Susan were just two of the estimated 2,000 'Brown Babies' born to British women and Black GIs during the war across the United Kingdom.[1] The story of the 1938th partly explains why some, but by no means all, Black veterans, having enjoyed new freedoms in Britain, would return home after the war and become engaged in the struggle for civil rights.

The journey of Private First Class John Hendricks and his GI buddies in the 1938th through Britain was not just physical, but also psychological, one of new social horizons tempered by their experience of violence and racism from some of their white American compatriots. On joining up, they were sent to segregated military bases in the United States, crossed the North Atlantic in segregated troop ships and served in segregated units in Britain providing service functions from trucking to laundry and labouring for their white counterparts.[2] The 1938th QM Truck Company had five white officers and a changing core of between ninety and a hundred Black GIs operating up to sixty trucks in each of three platoons. It was a small, tight-knit unit that, according to its official history, was used to operating independently: 'The 1938th has nearly always been detached, even in England and has profitted [*sic*] greatly thereby. This outfit has made many contacts not normally made by a Company and is, therefore, self-sufficient.'[3]

This independence, operating from small bases right across England, makes the 1938th an interesting case study. John Hendricks was one of three soldiers in the unit who died on active duty, though none were killed as a result of enemy action. The surviving records show that at least eight of his colleagues were part of various court martial trials in which the American military justice system seem stacked against them. When sentences were handed down in the field, these Black GIs were more likely to receive demonstrably longer custodial sentences with hard labour for lesser charges than white soldiers.

The non-combat service roles of Black GIs reinforced the stereotype of 'blacks' serving 'whites', mirroring America's racially segregated society.[4] Senior officers in the armed forces argued that this lowly station reflected 'the position attained by the negro in civilian lives'.[5] A typical advert for the US Marines seemed to openly perpetuate this prevailing military thinking in its call for African American recruits: 'Negroes having training as barbers, cooks, bakers, clerks and truck drivers have been urged to enlist immediately.'[6]

The military might have argued it was 'not a sociological laboratory', but the experiences of African Americans in the United Kingdom was to be exactly that – a sociological experiment.[7] The sense of 'equality' that Black GIs enjoyed when off base is what made Britain problematic for the American military authorities and ordinary white troops – especially those used to Jim Crow restrictions in the Southern States. Outside of American military bases, Britain offered Black GIs new accessible experiences in their daily lives in a relatively safe and English-speaking non-combat zone. The only threat came from their white American colleagues zealously guarding what they regarded as the established American social order.

Joining Up

The first taste of military life for the 1938th QM truckers was in huge training bases in the United States. Those joining the unit included the five GIs that were in a truck with Hendricks in Wales on the night he died. Corporal William Walker was a 27-year-old college-educated artist, sculptor and art teacher from Duval County in Florida. Private First Class Lewis Carter, a 23-year-old farm hand from Nottoway County, Virginia, enlisted at Fort Meade, Maryland, in February 1942. A day after Carter had enlisted, 23-year-old Private First Class Reginald Calloway, who was from Washington County,

Pennsylvania, also enlisted at Fort Meade. Booker T. Owens, a 20-year-old from Prince George County in Virginia, and already a trained driver, enlisted in New York City in January 1942. Columbus Hill from Jasper County in Georgia joined the army in 1942.

The 1938th QM Truck Company was activated on 6 March 1941 at Dale Mabry Field in Tallahassee, Florida, and recruits from across the country, including Hendricks and his soon-to-be buddies, joined as the company was built up to strength. In February 1942, the unit moved to Wilmington, North Carolina, and then to Key Field in Meridian, Mississippi, to continue training and to make preparations for their transfer to Britain.[8] In their training camps in the South, they not only received their basic sixteen-week infantry training but also learned to drive trucks the army way – in close formation at high speed – and studied basic truck maintenance courses. The segregated camps were prone to racial violence, which carried over into the nearest local towns. For example, there are many reports of fighting and deaths in Tallahassee both at Dale Mabry Field and in the town itself right through the war.[9] The local newspaper, the *Daily Democrat*, carried an editorial aimed at calming the fear of local white business owners worried about the influx of Black GIs to the base, in which it pointed out that 'war department policies forbidding discrimination between white and negro personnel' did not apply to local businesses. The view of the paper and local townspeople was that 'segregation was not a problem to be solved' but was 'the answer to the question of the African American's place in society'.[10] Most of the military camps in Mississippi suffered from racial friction – including the killing of a Black soldier by the military police – when African Americans from the North fought against Jim Crow segregation.[11] The oral histories of Black veterans who were based on Southern training camps recall the racism they faced from their own officers and local people. Leroy Reese from Monticello in Virginia, who became an army construction engineer, experienced racist attitudes in Alexandria – the nearest town to Camp Claiborne in Louisiana:

> Well, they treated you like you was black. You couldn't go into a liquor store and buy a decent bottle of liquor.

> I went to one place and asked for a Coca-Cola. This guy told me 'Niggers don't buy enough ice to keep cokes cold'. And he didn't sell it to me.[12]

At the end of training, Reese was moved to Camp Shanks, the embarkation point in New York. He recalled how his unit was hastily shipped off to England after trouble flared up between Black and white GIs in the city:

> Some guys got unruly, they ripped a lot of things up there. So they called us all out at about three in the morning, fully dressed and everything, loaded us into cabs and brought us down to 42d Street. I thought we were going into a warehouse … and you go into a room and there are bunks in there! Which I didn't know was a ship.[13]

The ship that Reese and his fellow GIs had boarded was the RMS *Queen Mary*, one of the many segregated troop ships that ferried American service men and women across the North Atlantic during the Second World War. On their crossing, Walker, Owens, Hendricks, Hill, Calloway, Carter and their fellow Black GIs in the 1938th must have had some apprehension about the reaction they would get from local people when they arrived in Britain. They may have wondered if they would be welcomed in Britain with its long colonial history and links to the Atlantic slave trade that had brought their forbears to the United States. If they had read any of the Black newspapers before their departure, they would have seen the editorials warning them that the British had the colonial blood of Black people on their hands. The *Pittsburgh Courier* had been arguing since 1939 that there 'was little to choose between the rule of the British in Africa and the Germans in Austria'.[14]

The first glimmer that things might be different in Britain came to most as they watched the joint US/British information film titled *A Welcome to Britain* on board ship. Included in the general information on how the British had endured food rationing and bombing, or how GIs should behave in a British pub, the film makes clear in the gentlest way possible that there was no enforced colour bar in England. Buried deep in the film is an understated introduction to the subject of Black GIs meeting white women in Britain. It features no scenes of Black GIs dancing or socialising with young British women in dance halls or pubs, nor does it linger on the subject. Instead *A Welcome to Britain* features a gentle scene in which an elderly British woman is leaning out of a train window at a railway station and shaking the hand of a Black GI. While she is still holding his hand, the woman smiles at the GI and asks him home to tea, telling him how it seems strange that they both come from Birmingham – she in the English Midlands and he from Alabama. At this point, the presenter of the film, Meredith Burgess, the well-known Hollywood actor dressed in army fatigues, conspiratorially beckons the camera close to him. Looking straight at the lens to make direct eye contact with the viewer, he says in a low but cautioning voice:

> Now look, men … let's be frank about it, there are coloured soldiers as well as white here and there are less social restrictions in this country. That's what you heard – an English woman asking a coloured boy to tea. She was polite about it and he was polite about it. Now, look, that might not happen at home but the point is we're not at home and the point is too if we bring a lot of prejudices here, what are we going to do about them?

The message was clear for both Black and white American GIs watching the film that their time in Britain was going to be very different, especially for anyone used to Jim Crow segregation. This point is underlined in the film by General John Clifford Lee, who is standing on the station platform and introduced to the viewers by Meredith Burgess. Lee was in charge of the Services of Supply operation in Britain and therefore most African American soldiers were under his command. Burgess tells the viewers that Lee is 'from Kansas and I happen to know that his family fought for the Confederacy'. The Black soldier from the train and Burgess are summoned to his side and Lee addresses a personal message directly to the camera. In his obvious Southern drawl, which seems accentuated to appeal to white Southern troops, Lee calls for respect between white and Black GIs:

> America has promised the Negro real citizenship, and a fair chance to make the best of himself. When the Army needs Americans to fight for the country, it takes Niggras [*sic*] along with whites – everyone is treated the same when it comes to dying. And so the Army wouldn't be true to America if it didn't try to live up to the promises about an equal chance … You don't get over a prejudice that easily … but we can try to live up to our American promises … that's one of the reasons that makes our world worth fighting for. But you're all together in this small country … [with] the same amount of pay to spend and the same sort of places to spend it. And we are all here as soldiers. Everything we do, we do as American soldiers, not Niggras [*sic*] and white men, rich or poor, but as American soldiers. It's not a bad time, is it, to learn to respect each other both ways?[15]

These warm words may seem to come from a political rather than military lexicon, but to be fair to General Lee, there are many written examples in the archives of him pushing his subordinates to live up to these ideals and admonishing them when they fell short – as they often did. For African American GIs, this short film segment must have looked like the opening of a new world of opportunity, something beyond the life experience of those raised in the South, so long as they were to be allowed out of their segregated bases. As service troops, African Americans were mobile and were sent to where the work was. It was this mobility – the 1938th QM had eight different bases in the two years they were in England – that offered them many contacts with British civilians and the opportunity to spread news, information and rumour across the Black military establishment. The spreading of rumour between troops became an important social currency and as it was not controllable by the army, it represented a dangerous problem for commanding officers.

Arriving in Liverpool in August 1942, the first bases of the GIs in the 1938th QM Company were two transit and familiarisation camps in Poynton and Glazebrook in Lancashire. Their experiences as they criss-crossed the country were not exceptional but they were exposed to serious violence in a number of their postings. They moved from Lancashire and Yorkshire in the north of England to Suffolk and Norfolk in East Anglia, to Leicestershire and, from mid-September 1942, Northamptonshire in the Midlands, where they settled for six months at an American camp at Kettering.[16] They also moved to Gloucestershire in the South West, and Hampshire on the south coast before they crossed to France after D-Day.

Kettering, Northamptonshire.
18 September 1942 – 1 March 1943

Kettering, located in the centre of England, was ideally suited for a truck company running a distribution point for the US Air Force. The 1938th were based at Wicksteed Park in the town and became a common sight for local people during the winter of 1942 into 1943. There is a marvellous *Movietone Newsreel* film of African American soldiers from Company 'B' of the 529th QM Battalion 'jive marching' through Kettering town centre in 1943. The film is titled *The Cook-house Shuffle* and reveals the very noticeable sight of the unit's clearly embarrassed white officers not sure how to march alongside them. Some of the parade footage in the film was shot at Wicksteed Park. The unison with which they marched was the result of hours on the parade ground and is revelatory to watch.[17] Local film-makers have also found footage and outtakes of the film being shot by a *Movietone News* crew with excited crowds of local people lining the streets to watch the Black GIs march.[18] While in Kettering, the GIs would have had the opportunity to spend off-duty time in the nearby city of Leicester, where they would have witnessed hostility between white and Black Americans in the dance halls and pubs. The Unit History, written by Captain Clarence Raine – the white officer in charge of the company – records the welcome they received in Kettering:

> The English people have been very cordial to members of this organisation and the men have appreciated this fact. The English girls have been very friendly, which has been a decided asset in most cases, in as much as there are no girls of the Colored race in this country.[19]

Mixing with English women would prove to be the major point of friction with white Americans and some of their senior officers from Southern States as the build-up of US troops in England was stepped up in preparation for D-Day. It would come to a head in their next posting.

Lancashire, Bamber Bridge. 1 March 1943 – 30 June 1943

In March 1943, the 1938th QM Company were moved from Kettering to Camp Adams Hall on the outskirts of Bamber Bridge, a village close to Preston in Lancashire in the North West of England. Known by the military as United States Army Air Force Station 569, it was a huge staging post for troops arriving from America. The role of the 1938th was to transport these newly arrived soldiers and their kit to bases across the North West. This gave them an opportunity to tell the new GIs what life was like for Black soldiers in England, especially off base. Adams Hall was the first point for newly arrived African American GIs to express their new-found 'freedom' and experience the lack of a colour bar as they mixed off base with the locals in nearby pubs such as 'Ye Olde Hob Inn' in the centre of Bamber Bridge village. This was also an opportunity for overzealous MPs, particularly in the 234th US Military Police Unit, and white GIs to try to re-impose their American racial values on British streets. The recorded memories of local residents about the Americans during the war suggests that white soldiers found it difficult to accept that British citizens treated the African Americans as their equals.[20]

A major outbreak of racial violence took place in the village on 24 June 1943 and has been a constant source of academic interest since the war. Bullet holes from the fighting can still be seen across the village from its aftermath. In 1975, military historian Kenneth Werrell described the night of violence as the 'Mutiny at Army Air Force Station 569'.[21] For Werrell, the aftermath of the Bamber Bridge incident was an important moment that he argued became part of a wider movement for civil rights as 'one of a number of incidents in the black's [*sic*] and America's continuing crusade for freedom'. Indeed, the Bamber Bridge 'mutiny' brought about changes in the management of Black service troops and an improvement in the quality of their white officers.[22] Writing about the same incident a quarter of a century later, Pamela Walck notes that the fighting at Bamber Bridge took place just two days after the accidental broadcast by CBS from London on the fledgling American Forces Network (AFN) of news about the Detroit race riots and the declaration of martial law in the city.[23] Walck argues that rumours circulating about the Detroit riots among the Black troops in Britain may have played a part in the fierceness of the battle at Bamber Bridge between newly arrived African American troops and the military police. Examining contemporary press coverage of the rioting, Walck notes that local people often took the side of and defended African American troops, growing wary of 'white Americans who were foisting Jim Crow laws on Britain … reinforcing discriminatory practices within the armed services'.[24]

The fighting at Bamber Bridge, or rumours about what had happened, would have been known about by the GIs in the 1938th Truck Company, who were at their base at Adams Hall on the outskirts of the village at the time. We do not know if they played any part on the periphery of the riot, but certainly none in the unit was put on trial. The trouble began at the Hob Inn, a thatched-roofed pub in the centre of the village on the night of 24 June 1943. An altercation took place in which the MPs assaulted and shot two Black soldiers. Colleagues of the African Americans who had been shot returned to their base, broke into an arms store, stole rifles and a truck and when they returned, a 'shoot-out' took place with MPs in the centre of Bamber Bridge village. During the riot 'a white officer and three black GIs were shot, one fatally, and several Black GIs and MPs were injured'.[25] The transcripts of the resultant court martial portray the fear that Black soldiers felt when dealing with MPs who were ready to use weapons with little provocation, as in this description of how Black GI William Crossland met his death:

> The military policeman who had spoken to him at the Hob Inn approached him and said: 'You are the one I am looking for let's go'. Nunn refused. The Policeman commenced striking him with a club. The three other policemen approached and Crossland, Jackson and other colored soldiers came to Nunn's assistance. The fight commenced. Nunn saw a policeman who had been injured with blood on his forehead and face, the same one who had shot the two soldiers. Nunn thought he was going to shoot them again. He ran to him and tried to take his gun. The policeman hit him with his club, pushed him away and shot him. Then Nunn kept knocking the gun up to keep it from being fired at other soldiers.[26]

It was in the ruckus that Crossland was fatally shot in the back, starting the subsequent fighting in the village. Many of the those who took part in the riot were never identified, but those Black soldiers who were tried received sentences of up to ten years' hard labour. An Office of the Judge Advocate General (JAG) review of the case found the original court martial was flawed, highlighted the poor leadership of Black troops and the overreaction of the MPs. At a retrial, held away from the area the sentences were substantially reduced or commuted. After Bamber Bridge, the US Army Air Force reviewed the command of all its African American units and in the autumn of 1943, Colonel S. Grubb was appointed to take on the role of the direct management of Black QM troops. Grubb was white but believed that most of the racial trouble 'was provoked by white troops', and that 'negro troops are more courteous and well-mannered than white troops'.[27] He quickly identified the need to weed out weak white officers and employ the cream of new officers coming to Britain. In October 1943, orders were circulated from the office of General Lee to HQ Units authorising a '25% overstrength of officers serving with colored units' in an effort to 'provide the closer supervision necessary for proper control' of African American units.[28] Grubb went on to reorganise the QM Truck Units, including the 1938th, into a new Combat Support Wing, in an effort to try to make his men feel that they were directly contributing to the war effort.[29] This paid dividends as by February 1944, records show that Grubb had cut the crime rate of his new Combat Support Wing by half.[30] The work of Grubb reinforces the point that with poor leadership from white officers who would rather not lead Black troops, discipline in the units broke down and the crime rate had risen.

In August 1944, a year after the killing of William Crossland, the Black war correspondent Roi Ottley wrote about Bamber Bridge in his regular column in the *Pittsburgh Courier*. Using details he had gleaned from British and American press sources, he described the incident as the 'Battle of Bamber Bridge' and went on to suggest that white American MPs in England were now 'regarded by Negroes as their mortal enemy'.[31] In his diary, Ottley outlined the official position of the military – set out by General Lee in *A Welcome to Britain* – to offer Black service men and women equality of 'treatment, wages, rations as white troops … and equal opportunity for recreation'. However, he also wrote that instructions to this effect were often ignored by white officers: 'there is ample evidence to prove that racial prejudice' was encouraged 'by such officers, a group often dominated by Southerners'.[32]

Was Ottley being melodramatic in describing MPs as the 'mortal enemy' of African American GIs? Consider the case of Black technician Robert Stafford of the 390th Engineer Regiment, who was murdered by two white American MPs at Rugeley, Staffordshire, in March 1944. Stafford was intercepted by a group of five white MPs in a jeep while he was walking back to camp along a country lane. He was brutally beaten and left for dead in the middle of the road, partially hidden by newly fallen snow and left to be run over by passing traffic. Only the intervention of British civilians trying to help Stafford and their subsequent evidence saw two of the MPs, Forester and Bryant, brought to trial. In a written statement to the court martial, civilian Evan Savage said that as he moved Stafford to the side of the road, he was admonished by one of the MPs, who said:

> Leave him alone. I put him (this dam nigger) in the middle of the road for the goddam truck to run over him as he is no good. He's been out with a white girl, and in the States we don't have anything to do with them. We treat them like dogs.

Both were found guilty, discharged and sentenced to hard labour for life at a military camp in the United States. Unlike other GIs executed for murder in Britain, Forester and Bryant were not executed for the deliberate murder of Robert Stafford, and none of the other three MPs who witnessed but failed to stop the attack were criticised in the court martial proceedings.[33] So perhaps Ottley's observations about MPs being the enemy of Black GIs were not too far from the mark.

At the beginning of July 1943, and just seven days after the rioting at Bamber Bridge, the 1938th were moved some 250 miles to rural East Anglia in the east of England.

East Anglia. Summer 1943

Hingham, Norfolk, 30 June 1943 – 10 August 1943
Sudbury, Suffolk, 11 August 1943 – 28 August 1943

The counties of Norfolk and Suffolk jut out into the North Sea on the eastern coast of England, and their geography and generally flat topography made them an ideal place for launching air attacks on occupied Europe and Germany. The 1938th spent the summer delivering munitions and war materiel to the bases of the American 8th and 9th Air Forces across East Anglia. The American presence in Norfolk and Suffolk built up rapidly after African American engineering units – including segregated Black units – had constructed thirty-eight airfields and smaller supply bases. By 1943, when the

1938th arrived, there were around 90,000 US personnel in the two counties and the truckers in the 1938th would have found themselves very much in a minority compared to their postings in towns like Kettering, where they often found themselves in a majority of Americans.[34] The fact that so few African Americans were based in the region is why some local historians have questioned the racial nature of fighting between Black and white Americans. In his book *The Friendly Invasion*, about the US presence in East Anglia, historian Roger Freeman asserts that a 'prejudiced picture of the relationship between white and coloured US troops in Britain has been created by investigative journalists looking for injustices'.[35] However, African American troops faced the same racial problems with their white compatriots as they did in other parts of the country, it is just that there were fewer of them and therefore the incidents were less prevalent. The American airbase at Great Ashfield in Suffolk, which was home to the B17 Flying Fortress Bombers of the 385th Bombardment Group (Heavy), was a typical bomber base. One young English female worker on the base recalled how some bored white GIs entertained themselves:

> When the GIs on our base had nothing better to do, they got together in bands of twelve or even twenty, armed themselves to the teeth with razors, cut throats, and knives and would then go off on what they called nigger hunting … when we talked to the CO we were told to 'mind our own goddam business'.[36]

There was a casual nature to the violent attacks on African Americans by some white GIs, which went further when they attacked Black soldiers and airmen in British uniforms. The week before the 1938th arrived in East Anglia, Sergeant Arthur Waldron – a 'West Indian' volunteer in the RAF who served as a rear gunner in a Stirling bomber – was beaten up by a group of white GIs. His 'crime' was dancing with a white girl in a dance hall at Bury St Edmonds in Suffolk. Determined to make a formal complaint, Waldron wrote a letter to the colonial secretary demanding action. However, he was killed during a bombing raid over Germany soon after and his complaint was dropped, saving the government an embarrassing conversation with the Americans.[37]

To avoid such violence, the truckers in the 1938th would visit nearby Ipswich, the county town in Suffolk, searching for safety in numbers as they enjoyed their nights out. Here, with Jim Crow being in full flow, the American Red Cross (ARC) had set up separate service clubs for Black and white GIs. The 'ARC negro club' had fewer facilities and far less capacity for GIs to stay overnight in town – which was therefore discouraged.[38] The town itself was segregated by the American military and a small number of pubs close to the 'black ARC club' were designated as 'exclusively for coloured troops'.[39] The numerical dominance of the white Americans is shown by the fact that of the 160 pubs in Ipswich, only eight were designated as 'black' and together with the ARC 'negro club', they formed the nucleus of entertainment for African Americans.[40] Some British organisations followed the American example of segregation – the Women's Voluntary Service (WVS) set up a 'Silver Birch Club' for African American GIs and 'Welcome Club' for white GIs in Ipswich, adding to the limited offer in the town for Black GIs.[41] Self-segregation into their 'own' areas by American GIs avoided much of the trouble that afflicted many other British towns.

As elsewhere in Britain, the service troops in engineering and logistical roles were initially welcomed by local people in East Anglia, but this cooled somewhat as the number of white GIs and aircrew increased dramatically during 1943. If they were not already aware of the reluctance of some white girls to dance with African Americans, the men of the 1938th would have certainly found this out in Norwich, close to their base in Hingham. With such a large majority of white GIs and aircrew in the area, girls were often wary of dancing with Black GIs for fear of being shunned by white Americans at future dances. One girl from Norwich remembered a 'disastrous dancc' she was taken to only to find the Americans were Black: 'No one had the courage to say, "we don't dance with Blacks",' she recalled, 'but we filtered away one by one back to the cloakroom and walked half a mile up the dark country road to another 'drome, which sent us home in their truck.'[42]

The 1938th only stayed in East Anglia for a matter of weeks during the summer of 1943, hardly long enough to build up any romantic relationships with local women. This would change in their next posting, which would last for four months and include the Christmas season.

Leicestershire, Gaddesby. 28 August 1943 – 26 December 1943

By late August 1943, the 1938th QM Truck Company had been transferred from Norfolk and was based under canvas in the grounds of Gaddesby Hall. The hall was in the centre of the small, picturesque Leicestershire village of Gaddesby, with its population of under 500 people. The setting up and opening of the camp by the 8th Air Force Service Command close to the village in December 1942 had seen the ramping up of the number of Black GIs in the area. African Americans were also based a mile away in the even smaller village of Ashby Folville and in the city of Leicester eleven miles to the south west. Their arrival set the conditions for what would be some of the most violent American race riots in Britain in the nearby city of Leicester in 1944.

It was not long before the racial tensions between Black and white Americans spilled out onto the streets of the city. According to one local aircraft worker, Leicester pubs were zoned by the Americans as Black or white, but still violence occurred outside pubs: 'The American MPs would rope off the ends of the street and let them fight it out … Any passing GI could slip over the ropes and join in, after being frisked for knives etc, by the MPs.'[43]

It was into this febrile atmosphere that the 1938th QM came to Gaddesby in the late summer of 1943. Being aware, if only by rumour, of the fighting at Bamber Bridge, they would have now been attuned to the potential of violence and intimidation from white GIs. Having previously been based in Kettering just 25 miles to the south, the nightlife in Leicester was probably not new to the 1938th. As they settled in rural Leicestershire for the next four months, they were ready to fight to retain their off-base privileges in an unsegregated England. Certainly, altercations on the streets of Leicester continued and according to historian Graham Smith, 'a white American from Kettering had been stabbed by a black based in Gaddesby'.[44] The Unit History of the 1938th does not record if any of its soldiers were accused or charged with offences in Leicester, even when other records such as court martial reviews of incidents elsewhere show that they were charged with misdemeanours at other times. So we cannot say if this incident involved a member of the 1938th.

Popular memory of the arrival of the African Americans in a dreary and war-weary Gaddesby was set out in a *Leicester Mercury* newspaper feature in 2004: 'Soon, the whole sleepy backwater was bewitched by their razzle-dazzle spell. As far as the locals, particularly the girls, were concerned, these boys impossibly exotic, immaculately turned out, louder than life and endlessly courteous, were the best thing ever.'[45]

These 'impossibly exotic' African Americans proved to be irresistible to some young women, who found themselves sentenced to prison terms with hard labour or put on probation and fined for trying to spend time with them. The GIs in the 1938th would have quickly become aware of the popularity of the Gaddesby camp with young women from nearby Leicester. Lewd stories of teenagers breaking into the camp at Gaddesby were drip fed into the pages of the local newspaper, the *Melton Times*, through 1943 and 1944. One story from May 1943 was headlined in bold capital letters: 'ESCAPADES WITH COLOURED SOLDIERS', and according to the report, the magistrates were told 'coloured soldiers from the U.S.A. were, it was stated by police, found with the girls, some in a summer house and some in a laundry'.[46] The summer house was in the gardens of Gaddesby Hall and the laundry in its array of brick outbuildings. In another story titled 'Girls and Coloured Soldiers' from April 1944, a police officer told the magistrates court in Melton Mowbray that he 'saw the girls lying in a field with coloured troops all afternoon and later in the evening with other coloured troops'. The younger of the three girls was sent to a remand home in Leicester and the others were fined.[47] These court cases, with their stories of clandestine meetings, were not the normal manner in which soldiers and their girls first met. Dances in village halls, visits to local pubs and nights out in Leicester and Melton Mowbray provided more conventional meeting places.

The length of their stay in Gaddesby between September 1943 and December 1943 gave the GIs in the 1938th ample time to form more than passing relationships with local women. From his army personnel file, we know that Private First Class John Lawrence Hendricks from Florida had a relationship with a local married woman. Hendricks met Edna Harrison at one of the regular Saturday-night dances at Gaddesby Village Hall and though she was married to a British soldier away on active service, she had a relationship with him and became pregnant. Terry and his twin sister Susan Harrison were born on 9 June 1944 and after their birth, Edna wrote to the American forces to try to find the current location for John Hendricks, who she believed to be their father. The letter from Edna was found in the personnel file for Hendricks that was sent to Terry and confirmed his belief that he had found the identity of his father.

After four months in Gaddesby, the 1938th were moved again on Christmas Day 1943, severing any personal relationships they had built up in the local area.

Tetbury, Gloucestershire. 26 December 1943 – 19 July 1944

For John Hendricks, the Westonbirt American Air Force Base AAF529 at Tetbury was to be his last. During their time in England, especially at Bamber Bridge and in Leicester, the GIs in the 1938th had witnessed racism and violence from white Americans and this continued when they travelled for nights out in Bristol some 29 miles south of Tetbury in the spring of 1944. Files in the American Archives reveal a tranche of correspondence from 1943 onwards about the unease in senior circles of white and Black servicemen attending the same dances in Bristol. The result was a decision by the Deputy Theatre Provost Marshall in December 1943 that all such dances should be segregated in future.[48] This constant tension between Black and white Americans in Bristol culminated in a major riot breaking out in the city centre after D-Day. The Park Street riot in July 1944 involved 400 African American GIs and 120 MPs and resulted in numerous stabbings and the death of one Black soldier.[49] Multiple sources suggest the fighting in Bristol between American soldiers was so severe that the city remained under curfew for several days after the incident.[50]

According to the Unit History, entertainment while off duty was key to maintaining morale of the men and the 1938th joined a local dance in Tetbury organised by their battalion in March 1944:

> This type of entertainment is always well received, both by the men and also by local girls, who are learning the American 'Jitter bug' style of dancing and who apparently enjoy it very much. Refreshments were served following a short welcoming speech by Major E.M. ANDERSON, Battalion Commander.[51]

As he set off on his last journey with the 1938th QM Trucking Company to Cardiff Docks, John Hendricks did not know that Edna Harrison, who he had met at a similar dance in Gaddesby, was trying to contact him through the US Army to tell him that she was pregnant. His journey across Britain was to end in a dead-end street off Bute Street in Cardiff, when he was shot dead by a Navy Shore Patrol officer. Court martial papers from the trial of the two white Shore Patrol officers accused of shooting Hendricks are particularly special because the words of the African American witnesses are recorded verbatim in the written statements taken by their white commanding officer, Captain Clarence Raine.

On 11 April 1944, Corporal William R. Walker was in charge of five 1938th QM trucks as they set off on a regular journey to Cardiff to retrieve a load from the docks for delivery. He was accompanied by Private Booker T. Owens, Columbus Hill, Reginald Calloway, Lewis A Carter and John L. Hendricks. There was a delay in unloading the shipment at Cardiff Docks and Walker was instructed in a telephone call with his battalion sergeant to take his men in one of the trucks to spend the night at Camp Malpas in Newport. On the way to Newport, Walker took the men to the Colonial Club by the docks on Bute Street to get a sandwich, ordering Hendricks to stay in the back of the truck to guard it. Bute Street was in the centre of the Tiger Bay area of Cardiff, which, in the 1940s, was one of the most multiracial areas in Britain. In popular memory, Tiger Bay was the place where you could drink and dance all night:

> There were parties all the time, house parties and shebeens, and illegal drinking joints full of people having fun and letting off steam … This included lots of black GIs who had never seen black and white people mixing like this. The authorities tried to ban them from the pubs but the locals and landlords refused and welcomed the soldiers with open arms.[52]

Therefore, the American miliary police and shore patrols were constantly on the lookout for Black soldiers who had gone absent without leave (AWOL) in Tiger Bay. On this evening, two Shore Patrol officers found the seemingly abandoned QM truck on Bute Street and went to investigate. They woke the sleeping John Hendricks in the back of the truck, 'who could give no information regarding the driver'. They were later to acknowledge in their court martial that they were aware Hendricks was in the back of the truck when they fired their weapons at it.[53] When the Black GIs came out of the club, they showed their duty passes to the Shore Patrol and Corporal Walker's testimony to the court martial makes it clear that he understood he and his men were clear to leave the scene: 'Coming out of the club, we were detained by two S.P.'s [Shore Patrol]. Showing him the trip ticket and papers, Booker T drove off as I counted the men and closed the cab curtain, having already received the O.K. from the S.P.'s, we continued.'[54]

This was confirmed in the witness statement of Private Columbus Hill: 'Walker showed him the papers then gave them back to Cpl Walker and we got into the truck … and drove off.'[55]

The accounts of Walker and Hill were disputed by the Shore Patrol officers, McKenna and Ritchie, who were on trial. They said they had instructed the corporal (Walker) and his men to stay on Bute Street. When Walker instructed Owens to drive off: 'McKenna fired one shot in the air and three additional shots at the rear tires of the truck. Hardy fired two shots from a thirty eight revolver.'[56]

One of the shots fired by Stanley McKenna hit Hendricks, who was asleep in the back of the truck. On hearing the six shots, a clearly worried Walker said in his testimony that he feared for the safety of his men:

> We drove for a short distance, I heard shots so Booker T. Owens drove faster to avoid the rest of the men getting killed, suddenly we came to a dead-end street. The S.P. and, I think, a few M.P.'s stopped us. Calloway told them that John L. Hendricks was shot and someone returned, 'We'll take care of him'. Another said, 'We should kill all of those Dam Niggers'.[57]

The Shore Patrol ordered the soldiers out of the truck. Reginald Calloway takes up what happened next in his witness statement:

> One of the S.P.'s told us to get out of the truck with our hands up. He then lined us up beside the wall and searched us. The S.P. made the remark … 'What I should do is kill all of you black sons-of-bitches'.[58]

In his witness statement, Private Lewis A. Carter again made reference to the racial name-calling as they became surrounded by sailors from the Service Club:

> While we remained standing there with our hands still over our heads, they made bad remarks, 'We should kill all those black sons-of-bitches', some said, 'Black mother fuckers' and others said similar remarks. There was nothing we could do as it appeared to me that there were 35 sailors plus some M.P.'s.[59]

The soldiers were right to be concerned about the presence of white American sailors, who proved to be an aggravating factor in driving up the tension between the Shore Patrol and Walker and his men. According to Brigadier General Alexander, the provost marshal, sailors new to Britain were not being instructed by the navy about the 'racial conditions in the United Kingdom, such as negro soldiers going with white girls and this is causing trouble'. Alexander noted that 'Sailors, white and negro, are allowed to go on shore leave wearing their knives', something he wanted to stop.[60] The sailors who had been attracted by the shooting and shouting in the street outside the club found the Shore Patrol holding the five Black GIs at gunpoint against a wall. As Hill testified, it was 'about 30 minutes' before the SP looked in the back of the truck 'to see whether the man was dead or alive':

> When they moved the truck and Pfc. John L Hendricks' body, they went and got a weapon Carrier with a Sub machine gun mounted on it, and then made the remarks 'I should kill all of the black sons-of-bitches'. He cocked the gun, but instead of shooting, he then took us away and locked us up'.[61]

According to Walker, he and his men were locked up where they 'remained and suffered for three days' before their witness statements were taken.[62] Questioned in the court martial, SP officer Stanley McKenna was quick to refute the allegations made by Walker and his soldiers as the trial transcript shows:

> **Q** Did you hear at this time any references to colored men, and shooting them?
>
> **A** No Sir.
>
> **Q** No derogatory remarks hurled at them?
>
> **A** The soldiers did as they were told. I didn't hear any remarks.[63]

The testimony from McKenna was accepted by the court and despite being accused of an 'aggravated and grossly careless act' in shooting at the truck, it was recommended that no action be taken against him.[64]

When Terry Harrison, a former British Royal Marine and who believed himself to be the son of John Hendricks, first read the court martial transcripts, the lack of discipline showed by McKenna and Richie angered him:

> When I was in the Marines one of the important things was team spirit, we all fought for each other … Having read the story I know the man that shot Hendricks was a very young 21-year-old man … when I read that he had been found not guilty that sowed seeds in my mind about the deep prejudice at that time in American society, because you would never shoot at a truck with your own forces. That is ridiculous in wartime.[65]

However, at the time, the 1938th Unit History from 1 May 1944, written by Captain Raine, agreed with the findings of the court martial that Hendricks was shot accidentally while 'moving away against Shore patrol orders' and concluded that one of the shots 'ricocheted from the street surface, striking Pfc. Hendricks and killing him instantly'.[66] There is no mention of the reckless nature of the shooting by McKenna in the summing up of the case, nor the 'mock execution' by cocking the machine gun on the weapons carrier.

Hendricks was clearly a popular figure in the 1938th and in the narrative history of the unit he received fulsome praise:

> The entire Company was saddened by the death of Pfc. John L. Hendricks. Pfc. Hendricks was one of the most popular men in the organisation, beloved by his fellow soldiers and respected and trusted by his officers. He was an excellent soldier with an unblemished record.[67]

In death, Hendricks did discover a true American equality in his first burial at Brookwood Cemetery in Woking near London, as the Unit History records:

> A military funeral was held on 18 April 1944. Fifteen other deceased American Soldiers were buried at this ceremony. The dead were saluted by a flight of American P-38s in addition to the traditional procedure. Approximately thirty members of this organisation were able to attend the funeral services … 'God Bless you, John Hendricks, Fine Friend, Fine Man, Fine Soldier'.[68]

John L. Hendricks is now buried at Plot C, Row 1, Grave 39 in the Cambridge American Cemetery in England to where his remains were transferred in the late 1940s. No distinctions of rank or colour were made by the American Battle Monuments Commission between soldiers buried in their cemeteries. For the Hendricks family in Florida, the news of his death came first by telegram and then a more formal letter. In neither were there any details of how or why he had died in Cardiff, the army suggesting: 'initial casualty reports are very limited due to the conditions under which they are prepared, the limited facilities available for their transmission and the fact that all the circumstances are not known at the time the initial report is released'.[69]

This was followed a month later with more details about how their son had died:

> Private Hendricks died almost instantly in the early morning of 12 April in Cardiff, Wales as the result of a gunshot wound accidentally received when the truck in which he was sleeping was fired upon by an armed guard while the driver was attempting to escape after being caught in an off-limits area. Private Hendricks was on a duty status at the time of his death.[70]

The letter concludes by implying no blame was attached to their son: 'The tragic and untimely death of your son is deeply regretted and my heartfelt sympathy is with you in your sorrow. May the knowledge that he served honorably and faithfully in his country's cause be a source of sustaining comfort to you.'[71]

With no charges brought against any of the troops in the truck that night, they all returned to duty in Tetbury. While the 1938th were stationed in Westonbirt, a report was commissioned from a British liaison officer about the supposed 'terror and alarm' that existed in the local vicinity. According to a local farmer, after a rape had been committed nearby, he felt compelled to sit up at night armed with his shotgun. The local MP and lord lieutenant of the county pressed for an investigation, although this found no evidence of major trouble, stating all was 'calm and peaceful' in this 'pleasant area of Gloucestershire'.[72]

A pleasant area or not, the men of the 1938th were keen to move on. D-Day on 6 June 1944 was recorded with enthusiasm in the Unit History, which noted that the men were eager to join the invasion: '30 June 1944: The organisation on this date is anxious to leave England, because of the fact that France beckons and because it means one more step towards the United States, home, and loved ones. Morale is high, condition of men and equipment is excellent.'[73]

The Unit History of the 1938th suggested that weapons training needed to be stepped up by 'ceasing operations' and having an opportunity to 'test equipment for combat'. As service troops, these men were taught basic infantry fighting during their initial training but clearly their officers felt they needed to build on these skills before heading into mainland Europe into an active combat zone.[74]

Nether Wallop, Hampshire. 1 July – 16 August 1944

The 1938th QM Truck Company moved to their base at Nether Wallop, between Salisbury and Winchester in Hampshire close the English south coast, three weeks after D-Day. Known as 'AAF Station 449' by the American Air Force, it was ideally placed for hauling loads to and from the ports supplying the invasion. Before the move to France, the 1938th truckers were kept busy, with the Unit History recording: '85 percent of our vehicles were on continuous hauls during the preceding fourteen days'.[75] From Nether Wallop, the 1938th travelled to Portland and crossed to France, landing on Omaha beach on 16 August.

France, Belgium and Germany. 16 August 1944 – 17 October 1945

The exploits of the 1938th in continental Europe add further evidence of both their abilities to fulfil their role and how they could still fall foul of American military prejudice. The unit was certainly efficient in its job of hauling materiel such as petrol, rations and ammunition to the front lines. In one twenty-seven-day period in September 1944, it carried '7,000 tons of battle supplies', equating to more than 100 truck movements per day on poorly maintained roads and sometimes under fire.[76] They also saw action in Paris on 30 August 1944 – five days after the liberation of the city – when men from the 1938th engaged in fighting as they assisted the Free French Forces (FFI) 'in an attempt to capture another sniper, who had been firing at moving vehicles from a building'.[77] The unit was part of the front-line evacuations during the Battle of the Bulge in the winter of 1944, where they were despatched to evacuate an Air Force unit, with the 1938th history recording 'it appeared to the officers and men of the company that they were going into battle while the fighting forces were retreating'.[78]

It is worth noting that the ongoing Unit History of the 1938th was compiled and written and/or approved by Commanding Officer Captain Clarence Raine, who was selective about what he entered. We know this as he failed to make any mention about a court martial in which two of his men received severe sentences for fighting with him in August 1944. The case was reviewed in Washington by the office of the JAG as the sentences seemed so out of step with similar cases that had been tried in the European Theatre of Operations. The court martial took place on 4 October 1944 in Creil in Northern France at the headquarters of the 2nd Advance Air Depot. The accused were Private Christopher L. Moore from Tennessee and Private John A. Jones Junior from Alabama, who were tried for disobeying an order, raising a gun and then striking Captain Raine, also from Alabama.[79] The evidence against Moore and Jones in the court martial transcripts shows that the two soldiers were under the influence of a 'quart of cognac' and did indeed strike their senior officer – but this was after Raine had struck one of the men first. The evidence presented to the court was heavily skewed to the prosecution with just one witness for the defence, who contradicted most of the evidence against Moore and Jones.[80] Three previous cases against Jones were introduced as evidence, including the striking of a civilian, leaving a truck convoy without permission and being absent without leave for five days.[81] This shows a lack of discipline in the unit for which Raine, as captain, would have been responsible. The sentences imposed on Moore and Jones show how harshly African American GIs could be treated by the military justice system in the field. Both soldiers received a dishonourable discharge and were sentenced to incredibly long stretches of hard labour – Moore for fifty years and Jones for life. When the case was reviewed by Brigadier General E.C. McNeil, the assistant judge advocate general in Washington in December 1944, he made it clear that compared to similar cases, the sentences given to Moore and Jones were excessive. Indeed, McNeil argued that the sentences should be 'considerably reduced', especially as he noted, 'the striking of Moore by Raine precipitated the offenses by Jones', and he asked for 'immediate clemency' to be considered.[82] There are no available records to show if the request for clemency was acted upon.

While on the Continent, there were two further deaths in the 1938th. Private First Class Abraham Wade from Kershaw County, South Carolina, died on 3 March 1945 and is buried in Epinal American Cemetery in France. Wade was one of the original members of the 1938th and died when his truck left the road and rolled down a railway embankment. He was described as 'a good soldier and performed faithfully well in his duties as a mechanic'.[83] Just days before the end of the war on 27 April 1945, Private Jack White from Atala County, Mississippi died in an accident and is buried in Luxembourg American Cemetery.[84] He was the last of his unit to die and the sadness of the 1938th at his death comes across in the Unit History:

> With the war so nearly finished here in Europe, it seems even harder for these men who must give their lives right

> up to the last day and the last hour against an enemy that must realise there is nothing to gain by this continued and useless resistance.[85]

As the war ended, the 1938th continued into Germany, with the first few soldiers being sent back to America on 14 May. The Unit History provided new evidence for Terry Harrison that his 'real' father had actually survived the war. During his long search for his roots, Terry had assumed that his mother was correct in her assumption that John Hendricks was the father of her twins. But new DNA evidence found that his biological father was in fact an African GI named Vander Lee Ellis, and the Unit History for the 1938th identified him as a staff sergeant in the unit. It shows that Ellis, who was unaware he had fathered twins in Leicestershire, was one of the GIs released from duty and sent back to America on 27 September 1945 when sixty-six men 'were put on the train to Frankfurt to start the long trip home'. In 2024, Terry Harrison would finally meet his half-sister and the rest of his American family, bringing to a close his lifelong search to find his father. On 22 October 1945, the unit was deactivated and the remaining men transferred to other duties or returned home.[86]

Conclusion

The experience of the African American soldiers in the 1938th QM Truck Company is neither untypical nor remarkable for Black soldiers serving in the United Kingdom. Their experiences may have radicalised some of them and convinced them to join the fight for civil rights on their return to the United States. Certainly, organisations such as the NAACP witnessed a rapid growth in membership and influence in this period.[87] However, it is easy to overstate the desire for most African American GIs to see the Second World War as a front line in the fight for civil rights, nor did all see it as an opportunity to forge a new post-war American equality. Bristol and Stur argue that these were young men, aged from 18 upwards, who much like their white equivalents, were not necessarily bogged down in questions about wartime policies and politics.[88]

Nevertheless, the hundred or so men in the 1938th had been on both a physically and socially expansive journey during their time in England. There are no records of the men in the truck with John Hendricks when he was shot in Cardiff in April 1944 taking up a high-profile role in the civil rights movement. When Private Lewis A. Carter, whose moving and shocking testimony about the shooting of Hendricks is recorded in the court martial transcripts, returned from Germany, he joined his two brothers – also Second World War veterans – on the family farm in the Piedmont region of Virginia. Today, the farm is still in the family and is an award-winning social enterprise growing organic African vegetables and holding seminars and events highlighting current issues facing Black farmers and historic subjects such as 'Liberty and Justice for All: The stories of the United States Colored Troops'.[89] Michael J. Carter, the great nephew of Private Carter, is a professor at the University of Virginia, where he teaches 'African-centered agricultural and farming practices', keeping African American heritage in the South alive.[90] He told me his uncle Lewis never spoke about his time in England, nor did he ever drive again in America – possibly still shaken by the shooting of John Hendricks in Cardiff and the trauma of the mock execution he suffered.

For Terry Harrison and his twin sister Susan, the DNA evidence pointing to Staff Sergeant Vander Lee Ellis of the 1938th as their father brought them close to their American family. They are now in contact with their half-sister in America, keeping the memory of the African American experience alive for future generations of these two families.

Despite their achievements during their time in England, France, Luxembourg and Germany, the 1938th – and their fellow African American GIs – received little credit in a post-war America keen to write them out of the war. In the official view of the 9th Air Force, of which the 1938th was a part, the contribution of African American troops was denigrated by suggesting African Americans were only fit to serve white troops in service units.[91]

CHAPTER FOUR

American 'Race Wars' on British Streets: Leicester, England, 1944

From the arrival of the first Americans in the city of Leicester in late 1942 and into 1943, white GIs were responsible for constant petty incidents of racism against Black GIs. This would explode into three separate full-scale riots in 1944 when the city became crowded with American paratroopers in the run-up to the invasion of Europe. Local people found it hard to accept the abuse that Black GIs suffered. In one such minor incident, Ray Elgood, a volunteer member of the local Home Guard, took matters into his own hands:

> We used to go to Stoughton aerodrome and guard things. One duty, us four Home Guards went into the canteen. There was only about two people in the whole place and in the corner was this Black chap. All of a sudden, in came these four white blokes and kicked his chair from under him and threw his dinner all over him. I looked at Johnno and Johnno looked at me and I thought 'this is not on' so I went up and belted this thug. There was 200 quids [pounds sterling] worth of damage done to the tables and I got a black eye and finished up in the police station at Charles Street.[1]

This one incident captures some of the prevailing attitudes of British people to the plight of African American GIs when faced with the violence of their white comrades and why they often took the side of the Black GIs. The arrival in Leicester of the 82nd Airborne Division in February 1944 saw an eruption of racial unrest and 'American race wars' were fought on the streets. This deadly fighting included the murder of American soldiers and has been highlighted by a number of historians. David Reynolds notes 'some particularly serious clashes in 1944 in Leicester between black GIs and white paratroopers from the 82nd Airborne Division'.[2] Local historian Vincent Holyoak describes the trouble in Leicester as 'an unprecedented explosion of violence'.[3] When asked to give their own examples of racial disturbances in official histories, senior officers of the American 8th and 9th Air Forces highlighted the city of Leicester in the English Midlands as the place where serious bouts of racial disorder occurred throughout 1944.[4] This chapter goes further, bringing new evidence showing that Leicester suffered some of the worst American violence in Britain.

Leicester in 1944 was a reasonably prosperous working city of around 250,000 people, renowned for its clothing, footwear and light industrial factories. Historically, a considerable proportion of Leicester's women worked in these factories and achieved independence within the traditional household, something that was accentuated with many men away at war.

African American GIs were the first Americans to be based in and around the city from the end of 1942, deployed to build the US military infrastructure of camps, munitions dumps and airfields in preparation for an eventual invasion of the European continent. For over a year, the number of Black GIs based in Leicestershire formed the majority of the American service personnel. Figures for December 1943 put the number of Americans based in the city and county at just 323.[5] However, with over 60,000 mostly white Americans based in neighbouring counties, Leicester, with its American Red Cross Service Club and its sleeping facilities for GIs on off-duty passes, became a popular destination for servicemen.

The arrival of the 82nd Airborne in February 1944 boosted the number of Americans in the city and county to 12,333 by April, completely overturning the existing African American majority.[6] Although branded as 'All American', the white paratroopers and glider troops of the 82nd Airborne included a high proportion of recruits from Southern States who were not about to share Leicester with the existing African Americans troops.[7] The serious nature of the fighting and rioting in the city has largely remained hidden when compared with other places in the United Kingdom where court martial records and contemporary press reports give an account of mutinies and riots. In Leicester, there are few courts martial records or press reports of the fighting. This can be partly explained by the need to keep the presence of the 82nd Airborne in the city secret given their impending part in the D-Day invasion of Normandy. However, through research and collation of dozens of official American sources, diary entries, memoirs, British police reports lodged in the American Archives and personal memories, a picture of the extent of the racial violence in the city has emerged. It shows a continual undercurrent of American racism from 1943 that built to a crescendo in three separate short but brutal bursts of unrest in February, May and September of 1944. When pieced together, these disparate records show that at least fifty American soldiers – both Black and white – were arrested and charged by the British and military authorities, and a number of senior officers of white and Black units were removed from their posts. The charges range from carrying concealed weapons, the stabbing and shooting of other Americans, through to the stealing of rifles and a truck to drive back to the city to continue fighting. The same records show that dozens of Americans were injured – mainly suffering stab and gunshot wounds, with at least two murders and other unexplained deaths. The 82nd Airborne are rightly celebrated in the city for their heroism in battle, but the blame for much of the racial violence in Leicester can also be laid at their door. The affectionate and abiding memory in the city is of the 'warm glow' of hundreds of 'GI brides' from Leicester starting new lives after the war in the United States. But behind the heroism of the 82nd and the story of GI brides, there is a darker side of a 'war within a war' on the streets of Leicester.

Thanks to entries in the personal notebook of the postmistress in the small Leicestershire village of Gaddesby – around 11 miles from the city – we know that what she called the first 'Dark Americans' arrived on 16 December 1942, and that the '2nd Darkies' arrived on 21 May in 1943.[8] The phrase 'Darkies' became a shorthand for African Americans that according to historian Norman Longmate, was used as a term of affection by local people to distinguish them from their white compatriots.[9] The Post Office notebook from Gaddesby lists the names of what must have been some of the best customers from the American camp over the road at Gaddesby Hall and at the village of Ashby Folville, just a mile away. The African Americans in Gaddesby and Ashby Folville were in QM truck companies and used their vehicles to travel into Leicester on their days off for recreation, gradually establishing themselves in the wider local area. As more white Americans arrived and tried to assert 'American norms', so the racial tension ramped up.

This chapter will examine the evidence of the all-American race riots in Leicester across three key themes: first, the impact of American racism in Leicester; second, the violence that saw the injury and murder of GIs in the city; and third, it will assess the public relations operation by the American military as it tried to mitigate the damage to its image caused by this overt racism. It will argue that while African American soldiers received much sympathy from the local population, they received little from their compatriots fighting the same war, in the same uniforms and under the same command.

American Racism in Leicester

As they became accepted and welcomed by the local population, a whole raft of new social possibilities opened up for African Americans based in Leicester. Most locals had no experience of African Americans other than what they had seen at the cinema and in newsreels, so this was a new experience for them as well. In 1942, Leicester had seen little in terms of Black or minority ethnic immigration, though it had witnessed migration from Europe and Ireland and had a small Jewish community.[10] There were so few

Black people living in the city at the outbreak of war that local man Trevor Peake, who grew up in the late 1930s and 1940s in his father's pub, The Woolpack on Catherine Street in the north of the city, can remember them by name:

> Where we lived there were only two West Indians, Harold Augustus and Flo Hardy, and Harold Augustus had about six or seven kids and his wife Ada was the nicest person you'd ever like to meet – and the kids. We never thought about the black and white business.[11]

He then recalled the friction between white and Black American GIs during the war and in particular one aggressive American GI in The Woolpack: 'I always remember the hostility and a white GI saying to my father, "We like to come down here Frank, but we ain't coming down if those goddam niggers are here", and my father said, "well in that case you're not coming then are ya".[12]

Pubs and dance halls became the lightning rod for racial violence, but in the early days of the American presence, the 'service troops' from Black units were in the majority. They were based either in rural camps such as Gaddesby Hall and Ashby Folville or on the edge of the city, building new military camps at Braunstone Park and in Evington to cope with the build-up of Americans for D-Day. Local woman Pat Pickering grew up in Evington, close to the site of the camp built on Shady Lane for the 82nd Airborne and remembers her first encounter with an African American soldier:

> It was quite scary for some people to see these soldiers, who were very polite and very nice. One day a black soldier knocked on our door and said: 'Excuse me I'm building the camp up at Shady Lane and I wondered if I could keep my bike here because I have had several pinched', and my mother said, 'yes you can keep it in the garage' and he said, 'Well that's very kind of you Ma'am'. So that was my first encounter with a Black man.[13]

This politeness was a deference to white people that African Americans developed as a social norm in America – a defence mechanism against bullying or even lynching, but it endeared them to people in Leicester. A photograph in the local newspaper *The Illustrated Leicester Chronicle* shows the warm, perhaps inquisitive, welcome they received, showing local spectators who turned out to watch them play baseball in Abbey Park in the city in August 1943.

Behind the bench of Black soldiers waiting to take their turn to face the pitcher is a crowd of local men and women fascinated in both the game and the soldiers themselves. The other side to the American presence was the constant underlying racism, especially when alcohol was involved. As a young boy, Michael Dally lived opposite the Cedars Hotel in Evington and recalled watching from his bedroom window as African American and white GIs came to the hotel and trouble flared:

> There was probably fifty, sixty to a hundred soldiers, it was a lot, and they all went piling in and within about half an hour the military police started to arrive. A cause of trouble would be their consumption of beer, which was on ration. The military sealed the doors and then dozens, literally dozens start coming over the pub garden walls into the car park to make their escape.[14]

Dally noticed an unusual aspect of the American military police for 1943 that there was some show of integration – or at least working together: 'Those that arrived in jeeps, there was usually one white military policeman and one black. There was probably around ten or twenty jeeps on the car park and then some lorries arrived to take away the soldiers that had been arrested.'[15]

The US Army had set up the first African American MP units in 1942 and some were based in London from 1943, so this action in Leicester is an early example of this integration. As early as January 1943, there had been 'a black white clash at the canteen at the railway station' and as Michael Dally had witnessed, 'there were various brawls in local pubs'.[16] The constant brawling and the simmering racial tension in the city led Oswald Cole, the chief constable of Leicester, to write to the North Midlands Regional Police Office to ask for approval to introduce a colour bar or 'alternate black and white nights for American troops' in Leicester.[17] This was in response to a complaint from the landlord of The Three Cranes hotel and public house in the city centre about African American soldiers bringing girls to the pub and being taunted by white Americans: 'the white troops are the cause of the trouble and they begin the taunting of the blacks, goading them into fights'.[18] In effect, Cole was asking to introduce Jim Crow-style segregation in Leicester but his attempt was unsuccessful. The Home Office, sticking to its policy of not managing or approving American segregation, refused his request. Nevertheless, even though it was not enforced or managed by the British police, there may have been some early American self-segregation in Leicester.[19] Local resident Tony Hurst recalled how the white and Black Americans seemed to frequent different areas of the city:

> The white Americans tended to stick around the Clock Tower area [The centre of the city]. But if you went down, let's say Humberstone Road, and you went into one of the outlying pubs, let's say on Brunswick Street, the coloured Americans used to go in that one. And that is what it was like around Leicester on the periphery, coloured Americans.[20]

This area immediately to the east of the city centre was a working-class neighbourhood with a mix of tightly packed terraced houses cheek by jowl with small factories. The increasing racial tension in Leicester saw the US military police presence in Leicester ramped up and in the summer of 1943, an American police station was opened in Saxby Street in the city under the management of an assistant provost marshal, who became resident in Leicester.[21] Strikingly, inside the front cover of every surviving police notebook in the Leicestershire archives is the number of the American Police Office, indicating it was used often.[22] Leicester man Kenneth West recalled the racist violence between American GIs that prompted the military police to boost their local presence in the city:

> The segregation of the American armed forces – it was vicious. They had the 'leave wagons' come in and they all parked in Humberstone Gate and it used to be a riot, especially on a Saturday night, all-out fights with the white Americans attacking the black Americans. It was unusual to us; we couldn't understand it. It was vicious; in the American army the divide was complete. They didn't mix.[23]

War on the Streets of Leicester: 1944

By early 1944, the atmosphere in Leicester was toxic and was stirred further between February and April with the arrival of paratroopers and glider troops of the 82nd Airborne. Locally, there were a total of 140 different units on twenty bases in and around Leicester, a situation that was recalled in the *Leicester Mercury* in a series of retrospective stories twenty years later in September 1964:

> There was a time in 1943 and 1944 when it seemed that Leicester had become the 49th state and the Stars and Stripes flying over a building facing the Midland Station must have reinforced that impression. You can't house more than a division of troops in a city the size of Leicester and not expect to have the city swarming with them. And swarm they did. They were everywhere.[24]

All those years later, the *Mercury* reporter William Kidd, who had been in Leicester during the war, was keen to differentiate between the Americans in the city, such was the impact they had on the local population: 'Americans were everywhere; coloured, white, near Indian, GIs, top sergeants, master sergeants, officers with a succession of ranks, WAACs and ebony hued drivers; the lot in fact.'[25]

Kidd went on to describe the valour of the 82nd Airborne in Europe and noted that 'between 400 and 500 Leicester girls became GI brides', helping to reinforce what is still the collective memory of the Americans in Leicester.

The arrival of the 82nd to their bases on the outskirts of the city on Valentine's Day in February 1944 meant the limited recreation facilities in Leicester became crowded, with unsegregated public houses and dance halls ripe for friction between Black and white Americans. Keeping the peace in this newly packed city with GIs looking to let off steam was an impossible job for the City of Leicester police as at the beginning of 1944, the force numbered only thirty-seven full-time officers.[26] Even the addition of special constables, some of whom carried out just three hours of duty a week, only took the nominal headcount up to 195.[27] As a consequence, there was a heavy reliance on the American military to keep control of their own troops through MP units actively out on the streets, something even they struggled with after the arrival of the 82nd Airborne. Memoirs by 82nd Airborne soldiers all describe with some warmth the welcome they received in Leicester and how, after the battle zones around Naples, where they had been based, they found England to be extremely hospitable and as close to home as they could get – and they wanted to enjoy themselves. Nevertheless, prior to their arrival in Leicester, their commanding officer General Matthew B. Ridgway expressed his trepidation over the friendliness shown to African American troops by local people:

> I had been there earlier, to look over the ground and what I found disturbed me a little. The only other U.S. troops in the area were service troops, most of them Negro units. They had been there for some little time and had established themselves with the friendly folk of England. Many had made pleasant liaisons with some of the young women of the towns, and I could foresee that I was really going to have a rough time when I brought my paratroopers into the area.[28]

Many local women continued to enjoy the company of African American soldiers despite the efforts of white Americans to discourage them. Braunstone Park in the city, surrounded by a sprawling social housing estate, became the local headquarters of the 82nd Airborne and several other central Airborne units. One of the new 'Braunstone residents', Kenny Knotts of the 307th Medical Unit of the 82nd, captured his sense of incredulity at the relationships between Black GIs and local women in his photo album. Now placed in the archives of the U.S. Army Heritage and Education Center, Knotts's album features a photograph of two mixed-race children in Braunstone Park whom he believed to have been fathered by African American soldiers. The caption underneath reads 'English girls are indifferent as to color', suggesting that Knott believed women in Leicester were colour blind to the merits of American soldiers.[29]

Ridgway's deputy General James Gavin also noted in his personal diary how African American troops had been welcomed into Leicester. Gavin, like Ridgway, rightly feared this was to be the cause of much of the fighting between African American and white GIs, as his diary entry for 21 February shows:

> Dinner at the house with Col. Grubbs this evening. He is in charge of all colored AC troops in the UK. Some Job. We had trouble with them downtown last night. Everyone is scared to death of the riot potentialities of the situation. Our troops are touchy about the problem … and tough enough to do something about it if anything starts, a bad combination.[30]

Gavin was right to describe his men as 'touchy' and 'tough enough' to deal with anything they saw as a 'problem', and that included African American GIs in Leicester. Soldiers of the 82nd Airborne were described as a breed apart by journalist Martha Gelhorn, who noted: 'They walk as if they know how good they are', and they certainly were ready to tackle Black GIs.[31] Looking back, parachutist Charles A. Harrington described his buddies as being rough as well as tough: 'The fine men I met in the 82nd were not all paragons of virtue.'[32] As they began to visit Leicester for recreation, these supremely confident, battle-hardened soldiers needed no excuse to enter into the fray in the 'trouble downtown' that Gavin wrote about in his diary. In fact, it marked the beginning of a week of serious fighting. The alarming nature of the trouble was revealed in a declassified document in the American archives. In a regular report titled 'Weekly Report No. 6', a British police liaison officer wrote to the Home Office about an incident in Leicester on Sunday, 20 February 1944:

> On the 20th. instant a number of white American Glider troops were attacked by coloured Americans in Leicester. Six white Americans received injuries necessitating Hospital treatment. Later the same evening the civil police received information that a number of American paratroops were about to assemble to attack coloured American troops. The civil police and the Military police succeeded in dispersing the soldiers. Four coloured soldiers were arrested by the American military police for having concealed weapons in their possession.[33]

It was the following evening, while Gavin was having dinner with Colonel Grubb, that things escalated further. In his diary, Gavin tried to put the racial fighting into some sort of context:

> Several near riots in town last night. English people, especially the lower classes, do not discriminate in any way. In fact, they prefer the company of colored troops. The colored troops have been in this community for almost a year and they are well intrenched [*sic*]. Many are living with local english [*sic*] women. With the advent of the white troops frays and minor unpleasant encounters have occurred in the local pubs and dance halls.[34]

Gavin then goes on to describe further violence that occurred, which had echoes of the Bamber Bridge riot in 1943. Gavin's entry for 22 February describes the Leicester incident:

> Last night the 505 had its officer patrols armed. The negroes resented this alleging that the white officers intended to get them. A group of negroes broke into an arms storeroom, secured arms, stole a truck and headed for town. They were intercepted on the way by one of their own officers and taken back to camp thus avoiding what might have been a disastrous situation … Placed Leicester off-limits until further orders, had all unit CO's make a shakedown for weapons and talk to their men personally … The colored problem took most of the damn day.[35]

This diary entry reveals that Gavin knew only too well that his paratroopers were going into Leicester armed with knives both to confront Black soldiers and to protect themselves. Superintendent May's 'Weekly Report No. 6', stamped 'SECRET', included further details of the violence:

> On the evening of the 21st. instant, a white American soldier was attacked and injured in Leicester by two coloured soldiers. The military police were reinforced as the coloured soldiers on their part had been reinforced. Shortly after this incident two shots were heard and the civil police on going to the scene found a number of coloured soldiers arguing with the Military Police and waving knives and flashing torches in the faces of the military police. A large number of soldiers gathered and it was necessary to call additional civil police who maintained a cordon at each end of the street concerned and the police managed to get the troops away.[36]

A scene emerges of unarmed British police officers forming two barriers to contain American soldiers as they fought on the street, with some firing guns. However, as May's report continues, it confirms that the African American troops that Gavin suggested had returned to barracks to steal arms were in fact based in Gaddesby, the base of some of the QM troops who had witnessed the 'shoot-out' at Bamber Bridge: 'Later the same evening 20 coloured soldiers broke into a storeroom at Gadsby [*sic*] and took away 20 rifles and with a stolen truck proceeded to Leicester about 11.40 p.m. and were then stopped and disarmed by American officers.'[37]

This new information adds some merit to an unpublished interview for the *Leicester Mercury* conducted with Home Guard Ray Elgood in 2003. Without the location of the base of the Black GIs, a story told by Elgood about a 'shoot-out' could not be verified, but the route from Gaddesby to Leicester towards the Palais de Danse where shooting had been heard earlier that evening would have brought the African Americans along Scraptoft Lane to its junction with Uppingham Road. Now the question asked by Elgood to journalist Austin Ruddy makes more sense:

> Just one thing – did you ever come across this battle that took place on Scraptoft Lane? It was hushed up. There was two actually. There was one in town. It was the Americans as usual. There is still some marks on the houses there from ammunition holes.[38]

In the interview, Elgood suggests the location of the shoot-out in town was outside the Palais de Danse – close to The Three Cranes pub – and the other on Scraptoft Lane at the junction of Uppingham Road. He goes on to say there were 200 to 300 MPs involved, that some soldiers – both Black and white – were killed and that the shootings were mentioned in a novel by Nevil Shute.[39] There is no evidence of deaths in the local press, American records or in burials at the American cemetery in Cambridge; however, it is mentioned in Shute's novel *The Chequer Board*, written in 1947. Shute's narrative is based around four soldiers on the run from the authorities and thrown together during the war, one of whom is an African American accused of rape in England, and as Elgood says, the Leicester event is mentioned: 'He learned of pitched battles with firearms between American white troops and American Negroes at Leicester and at Lancaster [Bamber Bridge], reports of which were censored from the newspapers.'[40]

Certainly, Elgood's account is more plausible given the new evidence in Superintendent May's report. His suggestion of shooting outside the Palais de Danse on Humberstone Gate ties in with later events at the Dixie Arms on Humberstone Road, suggesting this area of the city was a buffer zone between African American and white GIs. May reports that American officers disarmed twenty soldiers from Gaddesby, but there are no court martial records available for these arrests, nor for the four African American soldiers arrested for having concealed weapons on 20 February.[41] Considering the charges of mutiny for the Black GIs involved at Bamber Bridge, this is unusual. Ridgway and Gavin, as commanders of the 82nd Airborne, were not alone in characterising the racial situation in Leicester as disturbing. Superintendent May was clear in his assessment:

> A great deal of unrest and a dangerous undercurrent of ill-feeling exists between the 82d American Airborne Division and the coloured troops at Leicester. The question is being considered [by the American military] as to the advisability of white and coloured troops visiting Leicester for recreation purposes on the same nights. An effort is also being made to place Leicester out of bounds to coloured troops.[42]

On Wednesday, 23 February, Gavin noted in his diary: 'Presented the local colored situation to General Ridgway. He went to work on it this morning. Little can be done at the moment but talk and let the situation simmer down.'[43]

Ridgway's memoirs show he was clearly ready to deal with the trouble and that his fears about Leicester had been justified:

> The first night one of our combat units got in there, one of my men was stabbed in a fight with one of these service

> troops. He didn't die, but the rumor spread through the division that he had, and I knew the situation called for instant and energetic measures to prevent a serious outbreak. Immediately I visited every unit bivouacked in the area. I called the officers together and laid down the law to them. I told them that the troops who were there when we arrived were wearing the same uniform we were wearing; they were under the orders of competent authority. They were performing tasks just as essential to the war effort as we were performing. And though this matter of color might be one of the great problems that plagued our people at home, it was not our responsibility to try and settle it three thousand miles from home in the middle of a war.[44]

However, Ridgway's confidence about ending the violence was misplaced as the buddies of the paratrooper from the 505th Parachute Regiment who had been stabbed in Leicester plotted their revenge. The officer in charge of the 505th, Lieutenant Colonel Herbert Batcheller from South Carolina, was unhappy that one of his soldiers had been stabbed by an African American GI in Leicester. According to local historian Deryk Wills, he announced at lunch on the following day: 'Everyone is on a pass tonight', effectively declaring war on the African Americans in Leicester.[45] This account is corroborated in a letter from paratrooper John Ray of the 505th, based at Camp Quorn, to his wife in Louisiana, written on 28 February: 'Today was payday, and all the boys are going out and raise hell tonight [*sic*].'[46] A number of accounts outline what happened on these two nights at the end of February 1944 in Leicester, enabling a broader picture to be drawn. Deryk Wills suggests that on 28 February: 'War broke out on the streets of the city. There were dozens of fights and well over twelve servicemen suffered knife wounds. The interior of the American Red Cross Club on Granby Street was wrecked.'[47]

Military historian GH Bennett in his book on the Normandy landings suggests: 'That night the trouble escalated and it took strong intervention from Divisional officers over several nights to calm the city … racial trouble continued to be a feature of the 82d Airborne's stay in the English Midlands.'[48]

The 319th Glider Field Artillery, part of the 82nd Airborne, was based in the village of Lubenham, and came to Leicester on nights out. In a history of the unit, glider troops historian J.S. Covais backs up the accounts of the severity of the fighting in Leicester: 'Race riots with numerous injuries and some loss of life followed. In the morning one officer from the 505 [505th Parachute Regiment based at Quorn] noted "several" blacks hanging by their necks, dead, from the upper windows of the Bell Hotel in downtown Leicester.'[49]

This suggestion that lynching took place in the city became a strong rumour and was believed by many 82nd Airborne troops. However, it was dismissed by another trooper from the 319th, who told Covais:

> They didn't like whites and we didn't like blacks, it was as simple as that. They messed our men up, we paid them back the next night. We tore them a new ass … Nobody got lynched. Nobody got lynched. They got the shit kicked out of them with fists and beer bottles, but lynched – no, no, no. If somebody'd [*sic*] got lynched it would have been an all-out bloody war then.[50]

Another trooper confirmed that the American Red Cross had been wrecked and 319th veteran C. Lenton Sartain, a retired judge from Baton Rouge in Louisiana, told Covais he felt at the time that the discipline in the 82nd Airborne was poor: 'I just didn't care for the bravado attitude you know. Discipline wise they were always in trouble in town. They started more ruckuses in town. That's why they got Leicester and a couple of other towns put off limits to the 82d.'[51]

Lieutenant Colonel Batcheller, who had reignited the trouble in the city, was relieved of his command by Gavin and moved to another 82nd Airborne unit in Nottingham. Covais suggests that Batcheller was 'slated for a Court Martial', but he was killed in action on D-Day.[52]

There is certainly no mention of charges brought against white or African American soldiers in the account of the February riot in the official history of the American 8th Air Force. But it is clear in its assessment of the seriousness of the violence in Leicester:

> In February 1944 trouble occurred in Leicester between Air Force negro troops and white American paratroopers recently arrived from the Mediterranean, and again, the major part of the disturbance was the willingness of all concerned to believe unfounded rumors. The joint use of dance halls, pubs and the Red Cross by both white and colored troops led to altercations which resulted in the beating, stabbing and shooting of a small number of white and colored soldiers. Rumors concerning the kidnapping of paratroopers by negro soldiers and the mistreatment of negro soldiers in Leicester circulated freely among both groups and added fuel to the flames.[53]

This account again talks of the stabbing and shooting of 'white and colored soldiers' without explaining any disciplinary action that may have been taken. The incidents of violence on the streets of Leicester in February were so severe that Ridgway called meetings with local officials in Leicester and promised them he would keep the peace between the GIs. In an action confirmed by May's 'Weekly Report', Ridgway doubled the MP patrols in the city and according to his memoirs, 'spent the next few evenings riding and walking through the streets to make sure my orders were being carried out', suggesting: 'There were no more incidents of violence.'[54] We do not know which of the units of Black troops based in Gaddesby and Ashby Folville were involved in the fighting in February 1944, but the unit histories of the 1946th and 2034th QM Truck Companies (Aviation) and the 1514th QM Headquarters Unit perhaps provide some clues. The 1514th HQ Unit had been based in Bamber Bridge at the time of the riot in 1943 and on 12 March 1944, shortly after the trouble in Leicester, they received a new commanding officer but remained in Gaddesby.[55] Also, after the rioting in Leicester, the 1946th were moved 80 miles north to Brigg in Lincolnshire on 20 March, having been in Gaddesby since Christmas 1943.[56] The Unit History of the

2034th QM Truck Company (Aviation) shows that this unit also received a new commanding officer after the events in Leicester, but is rather more forthcoming:

> The morale of the men was very high through these first two weeks [of March 1944], especially through the several days of disorder in the Liberty Town [Leicester]. Words of praise for the company as a whole was [*sic*] passed down by the Commanding Officer for the station, Major Ernest Crego.[57]

This is the only reference to the Leicester trouble in records of African American units. The changing of commanding officers after the rioting is worth noting as discipline may not have been high. Two replacement Black QM units arrived in Gaddesby in March 1943 – the 2056th and 2057th QM Truck Companies (Aviation).

Throughout the spring, there was sporadic trouble between paratroopers and these newly arrived African American soldiers – despite an American attempt to 'zone' the city with the centre reserved for white troops and the area along Humberstone Road to the east for African Americans. Freda Parker, a local woman who had a white American GI boyfriend, recalls both the zoning and the next bout of serious violence in May 1944:

> You wouldn't have a public house with white troops and Black troops in. The places were either a white pub or a Black pub, and the one on the corner of street [*sic*] where I lived was 'the Dixie', and that was a black pub. The black soldiers used to go in there. One night there was a commotion going on, and we lived inside just down from the Dixie and I went to see what was happening. There was [*sic*] a lot of Black soldiers milling about and we heard that somebody had been murdered, but we weren't sure if it was a white one or a Black one. We found out afterwards it was a white MP who was murdered and it was all hushed up.[58]

The murder at the Dixie Arms happened on 1 May 1944. It appeared in heavily censored form on the front page of the *Leicester Evening Mail* on the following day. Under the headline 'MIDLANDS FRACAS: US SOLDIERS DIE', the one-sentence story read: 'Following a disturbance in a Midlands town, it is reported that two American soldiers have died of wounds.'[59]

This was hardly specific enough for anyone in Leicester who had not witnessed the disturbances to know it was a local event. The following day, the *Leicester Mercury* also ran the story – possibly after appealing to the censor and the American authorities. In the *Mercury* report, Leicester is named as the place of the killing, although only one death appears in the headline. There is no mention of the name of the pub at which it occurred nor any racial context. Under the headline 'U.S. Army Policeman killed in Leicester', the report reads:

> A Military Policeman was one of two American soldiers who received fatal injuries in Leicester on Monday (1st May). One of the victims died from a knife wound in the neck, the other is stated to have died from self-inflicted wounds. The affair occurred around closing time outside a public house in a main street near the centre of the city. The American Military Policeman received fatal injuries when trying to create order. The two men were dead when they were taken to the Leicester Royal Infirmary. Others received minor injuries. All the investigations are being made by the American military authorities, who state the matter was purely a military one, and had nothing to do with the civilian population. In the circumstances no inquiry will be made by the Leicester City Coroner.[60]

That the story appeared in the local press is quite unusual, which suggests that the censor was involved in approving this later version. The widespread violence in February 1944 had received no press coverage at all, but the visibility of this event in the residential streets of this working-class area around Humberstone Road and the anxiety of the Americans to downplay any racial aspects of the deaths may have trumped secrecy. A witness to one of the murders was Alan Boot from Thurnby Lodge in Leicester, who was 17 at the time. He recalled the incident while studying a photograph of the side entrance of the Dixie Arms:

> That doorway there is where the American snowdrop was standing [MPs had white helmets, hence the nickname of snowdrop], the pub was full and I stood with my girlfriend at the time on the opposite corner waiting for Mum and Dad to come out of the pub. No one was allowed into the pub and no one was allowed out of the pub. British policemen, American Military Policemen; bedlam. The snowdrop fell to the floor, I saw a Black man suddenly run up towards the town centre … as I say, the Black man that stabbed him ran right into the town centre.[61]

There are many unanswered questions arising from this incident, including how did a soldier die of 'self-inflicted wounds', how many others suffered minor injuries, and were they stabbed or shot? It is interesting to note that City of Leicester police officers were in attendance and shows how stretched they could become when incidents escalated. The MP murdered outside the Dixie Arms was Corporal Arthur A. Abrams of Wayne County, Alabama, who was serving with the 82nd Airborne Military Police HQ at Camp Braunstone. The soldier who died of 'self-inflicted' wounds was Private Curtis Phares, also of the 82nd Airborne.[62] In his book on the 82nd Airborne and their time in the East Midlands, Adam Berry has interviewed veterans about the murder at the Dixie Arms. One told him the incident did not go unavenged: 'Those bastards got what they deserved. We went and got four or five of them, and nobody saw them again – see what I'm saying son?'[63]

The 9th Air Force history highlights this event in Leicester as being a 'typical instance of tension and disorder':

> One serious incident involving white and negro soldiers occurred at Leicester, England, between while paratroopers

> of the 82d Airborne Division and negro soldiers of the 1514th Quartermaster Battalion Mobile (Avn). The paratroopers were very tense, it being prior to D-Day, and were in a very truculent and provocative frame of mind. When they saw negro soldiers escorting white women to pubs, and to dances, they made remarks which grew increasingly bitter as time went on, culminating in a mass fight and finally a riot which resulted in the death of a white military police of the 82d Airborne Division. Further trouble was avoided by the transfer of the Battalion from this vicinity.[64]

The 1514th QM Battalion had been based in Bamber Bridge at the time of the riot, so were no strangers to racial incidents. Fighting on this evening spread across the city and was recalled by local woman Hazel Rayns, who was the girlfriend of an 82nd Airborne paratrooper. She was out with her girlfriends in the city centre:

> Well, we were going to the dance at the Corn Exchange in Leicester … we heard music playing when we went in through the market and beyond the market was where it was happening, and there was some black ones there and that's when we saw them close up. One of them started fighting, it might have been with the Americans [white MPs] that were clearing them out, to stop them taking over and dancing with the girls. We stood outside because we didn't want to get into trouble … and then there was one who went flying through the window and he was lying on the floor. A policeman sent for an ambulance and the ambulance took two, and apparently, they died. It wasn't in the paper, but my dad learned about it, he knew. So, then he wouldn't let me and my friend go out on our own.[65]

Again, there are no recorded deaths of Black GIs in Leicester, so there is no way of telling if there were deaths at the Corn Exchange in Leicester – but Mrs Rayns believes to this day that there were. After the murder of Abrams and the death of Phares at the Dixie Arms, there was to be a pause in the rioting as the paratroopers and glider troops of the 82nd were quarantined in readiness for D-Day. All but the still under-strength 504th Parachute Infantry Regiment, who remained in the village of Stoughton, left for Normandy. Following the rioting in May, there was a movement of African American units away from Gaddesby, the 1514th Headquarters Unit was moved to Brigg in Lincolnshire on 10 May, followed a day later by the 2056th, and the 2057th on 16 May.[66] The overlap of Black QM groups certainly gave GIs an opportunity to talk about the 82nd Airborne in Leicester and their supremacist attitudes to their fellow Americans. Indeed, the mobile nature of these units constantly reinforced rumours about, and actual fighting between, Black and white GIs in Leicester.

The heroism of the 82nd Airborne in battle was again evident from 6 June when the division fought for thirty-three continuous days in Normandy without relief and without replacement, returning to Leicester in July, minus a huge number of killed and wounded, to prepare for a second airborne assault in Holland on 17 September in Operation Market Garden.[67] They are rightly still lauded in Leicester for the bravery they showed in these actions and a small remembrance service is still held each year in Braunstone Park in the city.[68] However, before they left Leicester for the last time in September, there was more racial violence involving paratroopers from the 82nd Airborne and African American soldiers. War Correspondent Roi Ottley on a tour of Britain to investigate and report on the experiences of Black soldiers for the African American press, noted racial deaths in Leicester in his diary of 21 September 1944:

> Two weeks of sporadic fighting took place between white and Negro American soldiers in Leicester in the Midlands. Four white soldiers and one MP were killed. Many whites were hospitalised. Numbers of Negroes were hurt and wounded. Following these incidents, signs appeared in a number of public places with variations on the following theme: 'FOR BRITISH CIVILIANS AND U.S.A NEGRO FORCES ONLY'.[69]

The veracity of this incident recorded by Ottley is difficult to prove. However, there are further mentions of rioting by Lieutenant James Myers, who had arrived in Quorn in late July as a replacement soldier for the 505th at Camp Quorn, just north of Leicester. He was not in the city for the rioting in February and May and the racial conflict was new to him, as was the soft segregation of the city:

> At Camp Quorn I learned of the racial tension between American white and black troops ... Violent conflicts often broke out between soldiers of the two races ... Negro troops represented a very small percentage of the overall troop population in England. To avoid trouble, separate pass areas were set aside for blacks. Negroes probably received the least desirable areas.[70]

Myers reports a disturbing level of violence involving the lynching of Black soldiers who had strayed into the white area of the city – or refused to accept the segregation: 'Several of our troops returning from an overnight pass in Leicester, a white pass area, reported they saw several black soldiers hanging by the neck outside the upper windows of the Bell Hotel.'[71]

It has not been possible to find proof of this reported incident, and like the earlier suggestion of lynching, it may be simply a repetition of rumours that began earlier in the summer. Certainly, the Bell Hotel right in the centre of the city was used by American soldiers for meeting 'their girls' but no official reports of lynching have been located, nor are there any memories of such an incident in local oral history interviews recorded since the war. However, the archives of the *Leicester Mercury* do reveal two relevant stories. On 8 September there was news of an American court martial involving a 'Coloured Soldier' about a stabbing incident in Leicestershire during which he 'committed an assault on another American soldier by cutting him with a knife on the back and had attempted to strike two technicians on the body with a knife'.[72] The *Leicester Evening Mail* went further, listing the name of the accused and noting he was from South Carolina, and the names of the four white GIs he was charged with attacking. The *Mail* story also gives the identities of the court martial members and the defence counsel, but the trail then goes cold as 'the witnesses in this case have gone to France' and the trial was therefore adjourned.[73] The fact that this is reported, and is the only story to reflect a racial angle, is unusual and shows a nervous American military perhaps wanting to show the people of the city that they were indeed trying to get to grips with the fighting between its soldiers. Then, on 11 September, during the two weeks Ottley wrote about racial fighting in the city, the *Leicester Mercury* reported that an American soldier had drowned in the canal, giving his unit as a 'glider battalion', something that censors would normally have tried to conceal.[74] Again, the *Leicester Evening Mail* goes further and on its front page identifies the dead soldier 'recovered from the canal near North Bridge' as 'Private Fred Jones attached to a glider infantry battalion', and observes that 'as yet there is no information as to how he got into the water'.[75] Fred Jones was part of the 325th Glider Regiment based at Stoughton and until these news reports surfaced, it had been assumed by historians of the 82nd Airborne that he had died in a training accident. No parachute training occurred in the city and North Bridge is on a major trunk road into the city from the north, the other end of the town from the Stoughton base of the 325th. Quite why Jones would be this far out of the city centre is not clear – was he abducted by Black soldiers in revenge for other events in the city? We just do not know, but it seems likely that this death may have been part of the rioting that Ottley wrote about, with the high-profile death and recovery from the canal being reported to allay local fears. The racial trouble in Leicester was highlighted by Jason Ward in his book *Defending White Democracy*: 'white and black troops in Leicester clashed in two weeks of sporadic rioting, leaving five dead and dozens wounded'. Ward argues it occurred in the two weeks before Ottley filed his report on 21 September 1944, which would fit with the launch of Operation Market Garden on 17 September when the 82nd Airborne left Leicester for the last time.[76]

With rioting in February, May and September of 1944, the citizens of Leicester witnessed the worst aspects of American racism on the streets of their city. Over time, it has faded from local memory with the popular recollections being of the heroism of the 82nd Airborne in Europe, especially in Normandy and the Netherlands, mixed with lasting relationships of wartime romances and GI brides. The contribution of the African American soldiers in logistics and engineering, building local bases and airfields is still missing from the story of the 'Home Front' in the city.

The lack of public records of court martials or military tribunals in the American archives is troubling. In Launceston, Cornwall, a public court martial was held over a single altercation between Black GIs and white MPs in which the following charges were brought:

> attempted murder, unlawfully taking up arms and discharging firearms in a reckless and unlawful manner while making inflammatory statements, rioting and assembling in a violent and tumultuous manner specifically to disturb the peace, and finally mutinying to usurp, subvert and override military authority, to take up arms and fire on military policemen.[77]

Any and all of these charges could have been applied to the incidents in Leicester and yet no evidence of them being brought could be found. Was this due to the proximity of D-Day and the likelihood of death for many of the participants, or the need to keep any court martials involving racial incidents out of the public gaze? However, the lack of local reporting of racial violence and the positive memory of the Americans in Leicester in the local press is a tribute to the public relations work of the American military during and after the rioting of 1944 – and the official censor.

American Military Public Relations in Leicester

Unlike most cities in America, there were no local radio stations in Britain during the Second World War – an innovation that would have to wait until the 1960s. This meant the only source of local news for Leicester was the written press, comprising the *Leicester Mercury*, and the competing *Leicester Evening Mail*, which were both published daily and the *Illustrated Leicester Chronicle* – a weekly paper from the owners of the *Leicester Mercury* that focused on photojournalism. Evidence from the archives of these local papers suggests that the American military had a proactive public relations' strategy in Leicester where positive stories about American GIs, often shown in mixed groups, were used to suggest cordial relations between them. The impact of the racial nature of much of the tension and fighting between African American and white GIs was visible on the streets of Leicester and therefore needed sensitive press management. Like the rest of the British press, the three local papers in the city were forbidden from reporting on the racial nature of incidents, but through their news reports and printed letters from readers they tried as best they could within the rules to give an accurate portrayal of the American presence in the city. The favourite weapon in this PR war was photography, and in the first half of 1944, the local press in the city were invited to events staged for the camera to show what, on the surface, could be portrayed as harmonious relations between the GIs. As a weekly newspaper that concentrated on its photojournalism and lighter features, the *Illustrated Leicester Chronicle* was a perfect vehicle for American PR officers to place pictures for maximum local impact. On 12 February a picture made the front page showing African American GIs taking tea with some of the locals, including the Lord Mayor and Lady Mayoress of Leicester, at the Midland Railway station on London Road. The warmth and spontaneity of the smiles captures the genial local reaction to the African Americans.[78]

In response to the growing tension between Black and white American soldiers and airmen, a photographer and journalist from the *Illustrated Leicester Chronicle* was given access to the American Red Cross (ARC) Service Club in the city. The *Chronicle* carried a full-page montage of eight pictures from inside the club, the exterior of which would have been well known to local people. Opened in November 1943 in Burdett House on Granby Street, the ARC Club employed 267 local workers and volunteers for its twenty-four-hour operation that provided up to 500 meals and 2,400 snacks every day and could sleep 270 soldiers in its dormitories overnight.[79] It was a rare unsegregated club, with many other towns in Britain having both a white and a Black ARC Club. The NAACP highlighted this to its American readers in March 1943 when it carried a photo feature on an ARC centre in London under the title 'This American Red Cross Centre in London is Strictly Jim Crow'.[80] However, the unsegregated nature of the club in Leicester did look to be under strain in the front-page feature carried by the *Chronicle*. Three of the eight photographs show African Americans at the club, but only one of them portrays any 'mixing' with white GIs and is strategically taken at a 'meal counter'. Two other Black GIs are shown in 'inset' blocks on the page rather than in mixed groups and captioned 'Coloured visitors to the club', suggesting this was a 'white space' that tolerated Black visitors rather than a truly mixed club. Also pictured are the club's ARC director and his assistants – all of whom are white.[81] The item appeared on 5 February three weeks before the club was wrecked in the rioting when paratroopers from the 82nd Airborne took exception at having to share the club with Black GIs and took violent action to secure it for themselves.

The reaction of the American Red Cross to the violence and destruction at the club in Leicester was to provide a smaller facility for African American soldiers at another less prominent location in the city, a practice that it had used in other towns such as Ipswich and Kettering – where in both places the 'Negro Club' opened much later than the 'white' one.[82] By the beginning of April, just four weeks after the riot that wrecked the inside of the Granby Street Club, the second ARC Service Club on Yeoman Street was opened specifically for African American soldiers. The *Chronicle* was invited to record the visit of Cyril Osborne of the English-Speaking Union to 'an American Services Club' in the city. No mention was made of it being for Black soldiers, but the published photograph shows the new African American director, the programme director, Miss A. Scott – one of the first African American women to be based in Leicester – and a visiting Black chaplain in this new club.[83] The ARC and the American PR operation acted rapidly after the February rioting to assuage public opinion in the city, which showed some sympathy to Black troops, while at the same time the charity was introducing Jim Crow to its two clubs in Leicester.

In late April 1944, a week before the riot that saw the murders at the Dixie Arms, an edition of the *Chronicle* featured African American GIs on the front page and white GIs on the back. Unwittingly or not, this edition reveals the reality of American segregation. Under the headline 'American Coloured Troops Go Sightseeing', the African Americans are shown on the front page in several photographs taking a tour of Leicester, including Abbey Park and De Montfort Hall Gardens. On the back page under the headline 'Lord Mayor's Big Party for U.S. Soldiers and ATS Girls', white paratroopers from the 82nd Airborne and ATS girls (the Auxiliary Territorial Service for women in the British Army) are shown draped around the staircase of the Palais de Danse.[84] However, perhaps the most interesting of the *Chronicle* picture stories appeared in the edition of 6 May 1944, just five days after the deaths at the Dixie Arms and rioting across the city. It shows a joint group of 'convalescing' African American Air Force troops from QM units and white soldiers on a visit to Mount Saint Bernard Abbey in the Charnwood Forest. The soldiers 'represented almost every State in the U.S.A.', and were described by the paper as being under the charge of a Hollywood film cameraman.[85] The most likely explanation is that this was a fortuitous visit that the PR officers could use to imply to the readers in Leicester that African American and white GIs were getting on just fine. The motto of the 82nd Airborne was 'All American', as they were one of the few units that recruited across the US, which fits the caption. If they were soldiers injured in the fighting in Leicester and brought together for this picture with African American service troops, that would suggest a level of PR control of a very high standard and forethought.

Major rioting in the city could be kept from the press and sympathetic images placed to create a peaceful image, retained by locals over the years as a collective memory. Almost every week in the *Chronicle* there were photographs of local women and their GI husbands on their wedding day, usually pictured outside a church. A typical image from 1944 shows Corporal Lawrence W. Herschberger in his uniform and parachute 'jump boots' of the 82nd Airborne with his new wife, Miss Jessie Elsworthy in her wedding dress at Wesley Hall in Leicester.[86] These and other images in the press in

Leicester were portraying the reality that the Americans wanted to display, while on the ground, there was violence and racism between American troops – with those in the military police trying to keep the sides apart. As African American journalist Roi Ottley noted in a dispatch to the *Pittsburgh Courier* in 1944:

> In frankness I must report that the American race problem is being transplanted to British soil – sometimes with a venom unknown in the United States. For certain white Americans cannot reconcile themselves to the warm reception the British people have accorded the Negro troops.[87]

Conclusion

The 'warm reception' given by Leicester people to African American GIs was a contributory factor to the violence and racism displayed by Americans in Leicester between 1943 and 1944. However, the welcome given by some local women to African Americans and their willingness to accept their company would also prove to be a crucial factor, especially to white paratroopers from the Southern States of America. The evidence is now incontrovertible that the worst race riots in modern Leicester were imported by the American military. There was some minor racial trouble between GIs in 1943, but it was the arrival of the 82nd Airborne Division fresh from combat in Italy that saw rioting break out with a new and fevered ferocity. When they arrived in Leicester, the actions of some 82nd paratroopers make clear that they sought to re-impose American racial order, but it should be recognised that at the same time, their activities would have disempowered those local women who had relationships with African American soldiers.

Research in American and British archives shows that at least fifty American paratroopers and soldiers, both white and African Americans, faced some type of military justice, though no court martial details are available. At least three Americans were arrested and handed over to MPs by the City of Leicester police. American records show that twenty 'colored soldiers were disarmed' after breaking into a weapons store and driving to Leicester to fight, and a further four were arrested for carrying concealed weapons. The fighting across the city saw dozens of soldiers stabbed, a number were shot and at least two were murdered. Rumours of disappearances, lynchings and unexplained deaths were rife and probably added to the toxic nature of American race relations in the city. The number of deaths in Leicester due to racial violence is difficult to verify without further information, but thanks to the *Leicester Mercury* reports of May 1944, we do know that at least one white MP (Abrams) and one white GI (Phares) were killed in fighting in the Dixie Arms on 1 May 1944.[88] Other unexplained deaths include three white American GIs from the same unit who are buried in the American cemeteries in Cambridge, UK, and Boston, Massachusetts. These deaths happened in the same week of May 1944 during the fighting in Leicester and include Roy Jones, Nicholas Pietro and David Rossier of the 3035th QM Bakery Company, who died on 6 May 1944, five days after the Dixie Arms killings. They were based at Boughton in Nottinghamshire, from where it would be straightforward to catch a direct train to Leicester from the neighbouring Ollerton Station, or jump into a jeep and drive, as the city would have been an attractive leave destination with so many other Americans based there. Their deaths are registered as 'DNB' (Died Not in Battle), but while it is impossible to prove they died in Leicester, it does add to the story of rioting in the city. It has only been possible to locate one death in February that may have been because of the rioting, that of Private First Class Oliver Saville, who was serving in the 1120th Military Police Company. Saville's unit was based at Langar in Nottinghamshire, and it is conceivable he came to Leicester as General Matthew Ridgway recalled in his memoirs that MP units from across the region were called in to assist in dealing with the February rioting.

There are only three court martial records for soldiers arrested in Leicester: one is for theft, another for being drunk and a further for sodomy. None are available for the soldiers arrested and noted in the 'Weekly Report' by Superintendent May in February, nor for the events at the Dixie Arms in May. The minutes of the Leicester Police

Committee No. 12 from 24 June 1944 held in the County Rooms in Leicester record that 'Nineteen members of the USA forces were dealt with by their own Courts of Inquiry', though none of these records are available – or can be traced in American archives.[89] After the killings at the Dixie Arms, the grandson of the landlady Elsie May Turner recalled:

> She had a visit from the US Secret Service, and an American Colonel asked her to keep the incident 'hush-hush', as they didn't want any adverse publicity or that US paratroopers were based in the county preparing for D-Day.[90]

British documents from the period remain closed to researchers and new information from the American archives is only slowly coming to light. Two critical documents remain to be examined that may cast further light on events in Leicester. The annual reports to the Home Office of the City of Leicester police for 1943 and 1944 are held in the National Archives in Kew but have been given eighty-five-year closures. The record for 1944 is missing at present but hopefully both will be opened – subject to approval – in 2029 and may show just how difficult the situation in Leicester was for the chief constable and his small staff to handle. In 2004, some sixty years after the riots in Leicester, one veteran paratrooper remained unrepentant about the fighting in the city, telling the *Leicester Mercury* in a retrospective article about D-Day: 'Everybody knew the 82nd Airborne were the boys who ran the niggers out of that town. We sure did, son. And you know what, I reckon they probably had it coming. It was a hell of a mess, though, a hell of a mess.'[91]

This is an epitaph for the violence in Leicester that remains largely hidden, though not from those who had the misfortune to witness it.

CHAPTER FIVE

Life on an 'Army Plantation': Chaplain Edward Carroll

The role of any military chaplain in war is a testing one, but the role of an African American chaplain serving in a segregated unit in the US Army in the Second World War had added complications. Chaplain Captain Edward Gonzales Carroll of the 95th Engineer General Service Regiment (Colored) was expected to act as both a conduit and a confidant between white senior officers and the Black GIs in his unit. Chaplains were in the unique position of having an overview of morale, discipline and the efficiency of both the men and their own fellow officers. In the segregated US Army, both African American chaplains and their Black GIs also had to come to terms with the contradictory wartime aims of fighting fascism as a struggle against Nazi racism and their own lived experiences in uniform. It is therefore perhaps not surprising that Carroll and his fellow Black chaplains got into trouble when they used the 'freedom of the pulpit' to stray into what the US Army considered to be the controversial subjects of injustice and racial problems, especially when interpreting the gospel.[1] Before joining the army, Chaplain Carroll had a backstory in his work in the Methodist clergy and academia of challenging organisations – including his own United Methodist Church (UMC) – about social justice and equality. There was perhaps an inevitability that at some point in his time in the US Army, a confrontation would come. This was especially so as he suffered some of the same petty injustices as the African American

GIs he served. The story of Chaplain Carroll in this chapter portrays an important moment when the US military in Britain was in the public spotlight over its segregation policies and the treatment of Black GIs by some of their white compatriots.

A disciplinary hearing in 1943 against Reverend Carroll by his commanding officer in Britain came and went without the chaplain knowing anything about it. The secret process of the case against Carroll only came to light in the paperwork lodged and forgotten about in the American national archives in Maryland. These show that Carroll was subject to a secret hearing instigated by his fellow white officers in the 95th Engineers, during which he could neither contest the evidence against him nor defend himself. The hearing and investigation were kept from him by Lieutenant Colonel Thompson, his commanding officer, and included the gathering of evidence against him through the interception of his private family mail and reports of his activities recorded by his officer colleagues. Despite the hearing failing to find Carroll guilty of any charge, his officer rating was downgraded by Thompson and he was effectively removed from his post in the 95th Engineers and transferred to the 502nd Port Company – another all-Black unit – based in Scotland. This was a critical event in his life as his transfer to Glasgow led directly to him being one of the many African American soldiers present on Omaha Beach as part of the D-Day landings in June 1944.

Reverend Carroll was one of many strong characters in the US military who served in the European Theatre in the Second World War – both Black and white – who were not afraid to stand up against inherent racism, Jim Crow rules and white supremacy. Indeed, Carroll himself would witness the white commanding officer of the all-Black 502nd Port Company risk his commission by standing up against a more senior officer denigrating Black GIs on Omaha beach in Normandy. Carroll held a firm belief that America could be a better society if social justice and equality were present in daily life, a belief that was evident throughout his life. Before the war, Carroll had travelled to British India in early 1936 with his friend and colleague Howard Thurman, where, along with their wives, they became the first African Americans to meet Gandhi on the subcontinent.[2] They learned about the principles of Gandhi's ultimately successful campaign of 'non-violence' against British rule in India. Thurman's later work on redefining 'non-violence' for the American situation of racism and Jim Crow would later become a significant influence on the work of Martin Luther King Junior.[3] Carroll would also use his experience in India to lobby against segregation in the United Methodist Church, later becoming one of the first African American Bishops in the subsequently desegregated UMC in the 1970s.

This chapter will examine the US Army career of Captain Carroll as he endured the freezing wilderness of Alaska while working on the Alcan Highway, only to be moved out of the 95th Engineers in Great Britain and his eventual army redemption on Omaha beach on D-Day. It will do so in the context of both his pre- and post-war religious life through the family archive held by his son Edward Junior. However tempting it might be to view Chaplain Carroll as a civil rights activist, his son suggests that is too simplistic:

> My father, as far as I can recall, was not a civil rights activist. He believed in a God who loved his creation without fear or favor or preference. He was an integrationist who believed that differences were God's spices to enrich the flavor of the stew of individual ingredients. He was operating in the spiritual realm rather than the legal or political realms.[4]

Nevertheless, examining articles, letters and material in the Carroll family archive, there is plenty of evidence that his father held strong views about the racism faced by African Americans in society. As early as 1937, he wrote about what he termed 'the evils of the black Ghetto, labor discrimination, the Jim Crow system':

> Racial prejudice has both psychological and cultural foundations. Negroes discover that the cultural patterns of the white race furnish names or stereotyped labels for them ... We are looked upon simply as cooks or servants ('Marys' and 'Georges'); and of course we are called by

> that insulting stereotyped label, 'Nigger.' Whether the most saintly or the most wicked, the most learned or the most ignorant, the lightest or the darkest, the Negro is designated according to some stereotyped label.[5]

Reverend Carroll would become personally acquainted with this stereotyping when he joined the US Army in October 1941, two months before the Japanese attacked Pearl Harbor. In the post-war years, as well as having senior roles in the Young Men's Christian Association (YMCA), the United Methodist Church and academia, he was active in the NAACP and the Urban League. If he was not a civil rights activist, then through his fiercely held Christian beliefs he was most certainly a champion of equality and social justice. In examining Carroll's military life, this chapter will develop four themes; first, his early life and the direct links to slavery that influenced his career choice of the ministry; second, the unique view he held of comparing the unequal life of African Americans in the US Army to life on a Southern plantation; third, his battle against the racist practices he witnessed in the army and its secret case against him; and fourth, his return to America and his role in promoting equality in the testing circumstances of the post-war civil rights era.

Early Life: Building a Belief in Equality

In choosing a life in the ministry of the Methodist Church, Reverend Edward Gonzales Carroll was following in a family tradition that stretched back to 1857. Through his male family line, Edward had a direct line back to slavery, his grandfather Henry being born in 1835 as a slave. Henry Carroll was the property of George Dowell at Prince Frederick in Calvert County, Maryland, on the eastern shore of Chesapeake Bay. Crucially, Edward's grandmother was 'free born', meaning that the children of the marriage between his great-grandparents were able to be 'bound out' by their mother to the service of owner George Dowell to 'purchase' their father's freedom.[6] Through the 'relatively liberal' Dowell, the boys were educated, learned to read the Bible and attended the segregated Asbury Methodist

Episcopal Church.[7] In 1857, the freed slave, Edward's grandfather Henry Addison Carroll, became a Methodist minister. Henry's son, Chaplain Carroll's father, the Reverend Julius Carroll, also became a minister in the Methodist Church in 1903, leading the way for his son Edward to become the third generation to serve the church. The family links to Methodism went further as his younger brother Julius also became a Methodist minister and achieved some celebrity in the 1950s and 1960s as 'The Flying Preacher', conducting services via his own private plane across a wide area of Maryland and Delaware.[8]

Reverend Edward Carroll graduated from Morgan State College in Baltimore in 1930, attended Yale School of Divinity and was ordained to the Methodist ministry in 1933. He also graduated with Master of Education degrees from Union Theological College and Columbia University in New York in 1941.[9] Perhaps the most influential of his pre-war experiences was a six-month visit he made to the Indian subcontinent to meet Indian Christians and while there, he took the opportunity to meet Mahatma Gandhi. Edward and his wife Phenola, together with Howard and Sue Thurman, travelled to the Indian subcontinent in early 1936 and were instructed by Gandhi on the power of 'non-violence' in his political battle against British rule in India: 'Gandhi tried to make clear to them that "non-violence", even spelled out as the negation of violence in English was a positive force.'[10]

The Carroll family archive holds a photograph of Mahatma Gandhi meeting Sue Thurman outside his place of sanctuary, where he was in hiding from the British. The photograph was taken by Edward Carroll, who noted that the meeting took place while the British were actively searching for Gandhi and his lieutenants. Despite the work of Carroll and Thurman, the teachings of Gandhi on 'non-violence' were not universally well received in the United States. Newspaper columnists such as George Shuyler in the *Pittsburgh Courier* argued that 'force should be met with force' and that non-violence was unlikely to be successful in overturning the long-held racist views of white Americans.[11] However, Thurman's influence on Martin Luther King and the non-violence he learned from Gandhi did go on to play an important part in the civil rights movement. Actions across the South, such as bus boycotts, lunch counter sit-ins and freedom marches, were part of conscious policy developed in the 1950s.[12] It was the American mix of the gospel and Gandhi that Martin Luther King recognised as having boosted the civil rights movement after the events in Montgomery, Alabama in the 1950s: 'Nonviolent resistance had emerged as the technique of the movement, while love stood out as the regulating ideal. In other words, Christ furnished the spirit and motivation, while Gandhi furnished the method.'[13]

After returning from India in 1937, Edward was appointed to the role of professor of religion at Morgan College in Baltimore. As an academic and clergyman, he was ready to take on the coming fight for the direction of the Methodist Church in America. Carroll expressed his concerns about the potential outcome of a forthcoming 'Uniting Conference' of the Methodist Church that was to be held in Kansas City in 1939. The three American branches of Methodism were to meet to try to form a new United Methodist Church, although Carroll was apprehensive about the direction of travel in terms of equality. The United Methodist Church that emerged from the conference has since been described as 'racially segregated to its core'.[14] The outcome was to place all the Black Methodist churches in a single national 'Central Jurisdiction', while white churches were grouped in a number of 'regional conferences'.[15] Reverend Carroll lobbied against these changes as plans for the Uniting Conference emerged, arguing instead for one united church that would cross racial divides. Writing in the *Zion Herald*, an influential weekly Methodist newspaper, Carroll strongly contended:

> Too long have I listened to the relative values which says the Negro will be better off than he is now, even if the situation is far from ideal; and that the Negro has been and is now segregated generally so why make such a protest in this case and hinder the building of great [*sic*] Methodist society? … When we proclaim such an argument … we have failed to see the 'eternal archetype' of the kingdom which absolutely has no racial, caste, or national barriers.[16]

His article warned against the proposed segregation of the new United Methodist Church, suggesting that some may see his ideal of a truly united church without segregation as 'too much of a unification … a breach of the American cultural pattern'.[17] However, this was a battle that he and others lost and the United Methodist Church remained largely segregated into the 1960s. During his time at Yale, there had been much discussion about the pacifist position promoted by liberal Christianity, and notwithstanding his later pre-war meeting with Gandhi that informed his non-violent approach to civil rights in America, Carroll realised that pacifism alone may not be tenable in the face of Hitler and Nazism. In a reflective note to a researcher at the Student Christian Movement after the war, he accepted what he called 'an evil alternative of armed resistance' that had prompted him to join the US Army as a chaplain.[18]

Joining the US Army as a Chaplain – a Minority Within a Minority

The Reverend Edward Gonzales Carroll joined the US Army Chaplain Corps on 21 October 1941 as a first lieutenant. His discharge papers in July 1945 show his education as eight years in grammar school, four years in high school and four years in college, which hardly does justice to his educational achievements. As noted earlier, these included a Bachelor of Arts from Morgan College in 1930 and a Bachelor of Divinity from the Divinity School at Yale University three years later in 1933 at the age of 23.[19] We can assume that on joining the US Army, Reverend Carroll would have scored highly on the army General Classification Test (AGCT), which every new recruit took. His high score would have been unusual as the AGCT scores in 1941 and 1942 placed fewer than 1 per cent of African American recruits in Category One compared to more than 6 per cent of white recruits. Category One scores marked out potential officers and the AGCT scores ensured it was extremely unlikely that many Black soldiers could go on to become officers. More than eight out of ten Black GIs (84.3 per cent) fell into the two lowest categories and were placed in unskilled and manual jobs as 'service troops'.[20]

Historian George White argues that the army effectively used the AGCT scores to construct its ideal recruit – a white soldier who was therefore a 'real American'.[21] The educational requirements of the AGCT excluded countless Black pastors and ministers without formal further education qualifications from joining the army as chaplains, leaving many African American units without an effective chaplaincy service. The US Navy only appointed two African American chaplains during the entirety of the war and the US Army only increased the number of Black chaplains after pressure from the NAACP.[22]

To put the difficulties for African Americans into further perspective, research for the Wilson Center established just how under-represented African Americans were in the US Army. It found that at the outbreak of the war in December 1941, there were just five Black officers in the US Army, of whom three were chaplains.[23] As he joined in October 1941, it is quite possible that Reverend Carroll was one of those five Black officers in the US Army listed by the Wilson Center researchers. He joined an army in which African Americans were under-represented, undervalued and almost all were serving in non-combat service roles in areas such as construction, trucking and laundry. As an African American officer and a chaplain, Reverend Carroll was now in every sense a minority within a minority. Like any other African American in the US Army during the Second World War, Reverend Carroll was effectively seen as a 'second-class American'.

Carroll was assigned to the 95th Engineer General Service Regiment (Colored), but even as a first lieutenant, he was not able to share the benefits of the officers' mess, sleeping quarters or offices. Instead, he was allocated his own small tent in which he lived, slept and carried out his pastoral duties. Equal treatment, opportunities and respect did not come with the equal pay that African Americans received. For a Black chaplain who had spent his adult life lobbying for equality in both his daily and religious life, the situation was not only unequal but must have been dispiriting. At the age of 31, Reverend Carroll was firmly committed to social change, and yet reading his correspondence, the daily grind of the unequal nature of army life for African American soldiers astonished even him. Carroll served with distinction in Canada and was promoted to captain before his unit was sent to the United Kingdom and US bases in Wales and Scotland, before he participated in the Normandy landings.

Plantation Life – Carroll's alternative view of Army Life

After the attack on Pearl Harbor by the Japanese in December 1941, it was felt imperative for the United States to build a highway to link with Alaska through the Canadian wilderness. This would ensure that military forces and equipment could be sent to Alaska in case of a further Japanese attack. Known as the Alcan Highway, the road runs from Dawson Creek in British Columbia through 1,500 miles of remote and wild terrain via Whitehorse in the Yukon to Delta Junction in Alaska. Today, it is known as the Alaska Highway and much of the original route is still open to traffic.[24] One third of the 10,000 US Army engineers who built the road were African American and segregated not only by regiment but by being given their own sections of highway to complete.[25] The 95th Engineers was one of three Black units engaged in construction, but they received little recognition for their work, as Reverend Carroll observed in a letter home to his wife Phenola in Washington DC:

> I have school teachers, artists, entrepreneurs, farmers, country boys and city slickers – all considered inferior to whites and lacking the bravery to serve in combat but subject to be drafted to serve as ditch diggers, cooks, truck drivers, stevedores [dockworker] and servants, and it's my job to convince them to be happy and compliant with this second class status and abuse of self-ness embedded in custom, doctrine, policy and status quo.[26]

Carroll was chafing at the restrictive conditions imposed on his fellow African Americans, in which he complains about the abusive nature of the status quo of segregation in the army. The role of the Black

95th Engineers in the construction of the Alcan Highway remained hidden for half a century. It was not until the 50th anniversary of the construction of the Alcan in 1992 that a range of events and articles to mark the involvement of African Americans on the project were produced.[27] A travelling exhibition was launched for the anniversary by the University of Alaska, which described the 'finding' of work by Black engineers as a new 'discovery in the history of African Americans'.[28] The 95th Engineers had received some coverage in the August 1942 edition of *Time Magazine*, which included a photograph of the 300-foot-long Sikanni Chief River Bridge in British Columbia, captioned 'Bridged in two days by U.S. Negro Engineers'.[29] But it was not until 2005 that the United States Congress passed a resolution to honour their work on the Alcan Highway. It read: 'Despite enduring indignities and double standards, the soldiers of the Black Corps of Engineers contributed unselfishly to the western defense in World War II and these contributions helped lead to the subsequent integration of the military.'[30]

In further letters to Phenola, Edward set out the many disappointments of his treatment in the army, and particularly that of the Black GIs in the 95th Engineer General Service Regiment. As a Black officer, he not only felt he was an outsider but that his fellow white officers in charge of the 95th Engineers, whom he described as 'Southern Gentlemen', ran the unit like a 'plantation', as he explained to Phenola in March 1942:

> I'm the only Black officer here, because there is no such thing as a Black officer in the command structure. The other officers are decent well-meaning men, but custom and upbringing makes them think what's proper is to run the outfit like a plantation … I'm sure there isn't one of my fellow officers that wouldn't jump at the chance of a transfer to a white unit, including Colonel Schilling [the commanding officer at the time].[31]

Carroll went further by suggesting that the army saw his role as maintaining the men's spirits on the 'plantation', as he wrote in the same letter: 'The Army and Colonel Schilling are most interested in my maintaining morale and serenity on the plantation.'[32] He also lamented to Phenola how his men were treated – by both the army in general and their own senior officers in particular – especially in terms of the work to which they were assigned and the tools and equipment they were allocated: 'Still, the army's made sure our boys are in the remotest area with the poorest, least mechanised equipment: God forbid our Negro troops be given complicated machinery the army believes they don't have the intelligence to operate.'[33]

This comment is rooted in his own pre-war experiences and the many social and cultural stereotypes attributed to African Americans that had their origins in slavery and slave resistance. In their classic article on 'Day to Day Resistance to Slavery' in the United States, Bauer and Bauer argue that white plantation owners believed their slaves to be feckless, lazy and were 'so careless with tools that they were equipped with special tools', including an unbreakable and heavy-duty tool known as a 'nigger hoe'.[34] What slave owners failed to recognise was that their slaves were neither feckless nor lazy but were taking part in an active campaign of resistance. The slaves knew the value of their labour and that it would not be they who would benefit personally from their work, so they set about reducing its worth to their owners by breaking their tools and working slowly.[35] This misreading of slaves by white Americans was charted into the twentieth century by Robin Kelly in his article 'We Are Not What We Seem', which contended that resistance to Jim Crow rules was a continuing feature of Black working life in the 1930s and 1940s.[36] More importantly, the US Army embraced this stereotypical view of African Americans in its own 1925 memorandum on the 'Employment of Negro Man Power in War'. Its conclusions strongly relied on hearsay and reveal a lack of any formal evidence. They included such views as:

> It is generally recognised that the pure blood American negro is inferior to our white population in mental capacity ... All officers, without exception, agree that the Negro lacks initiative, displays little or no leadership, and cannot accept responsibility. Some point out that these

> defects are greater in the Southern Negro … In the past wars the negro has made a fair laborer, but an inferior technician. As a fighter he has been inferior to the white man even when led by white officers.[37]

If the views expressed in this official US Army document were held by the senior officers of the 95th Engineers, it is perhaps not surprising that Reverend Carroll formed his narrative of the US Army being run like a Southern plantation.

Edward's long and pained letters to Phenola also touched on the delicate matter of a constant fear of miscegenation by the US Army, writing that the army ensured his men had no 'access to native women whom they will surely rape, filling this vast wilderness with mongrel children'.[38] This over-sexualised stereotype of Black GIs was not an invention out of thin air by Reverend Carroll, it had its roots in the racial prejudice of senior officers, many of whom believed that 'every Negro was a potential rapist'.[39] It was a racial prejudice that had built up over hundreds of years – during the Second World War, some thirty-eight states had some form of anti-miscegenation laws in place.[40] This characterisation of the Black GIs by their white officers would continue after the unit reached the United Kingdom and was the cause of much of the poor discipline in the regiment.

As the only Black officer on the Alcan Highway project, Reverend Carroll was segregated from his fellow officers and was expected to eat his meals, sleep and counsel the men in his small tent. However, Commanding Officer Colonel Schilling recognised the difficulties this caused in the Canadian wilderness and in one positive note for Reverend Carroll, he was at least allowed to become partly integrated with his fellow officers:

> Colonel Schilling came to my tent and told me he was going to ignore army policy and 'integrate' the unit by having me eat with the rest of the officers instead of alone in my tent. It was written all over him how proud he was of that. He is a Southern boy that made it through West Point to the official status of Officer and Gentleman.[41]

This 'integration' continued when the 95th returned to its base in the Southern States, even after Schilling left to join an engineer regiment in England and Carroll built up a good working rapport with his replacement, Lieutenant Colonel Thompson. However, this relationship would become strained when the 95th Engineers were posted to Britain in the summer of 1943.

Undermining Army Segregation? Carroll Versus the US Army in Britain

The 95th Engineers embarked on the Atlantic crossing to Britain on 16 July 1943. With their ship constantly changing course in a zigzag pattern to avoid German U-boats, the crossing took twelve days to complete.[42] While waiting to sail from New York, racial tension and Carroll's self-proclaimed status of his men as 'second-class Americans' again came to the fore. The men in the regiment had been told they would have twenty-four hours' leave before the ship sailed, so many paid for their wives and families to come to New York to spend time with them before they left. At the last minute, their leave was cancelled by the army as 'white soldiers on leave in New York City might object to having black soldiers on leave, and fights might break out'.[43] It is difficult to imagine the blow to morale that this would have had on the African Americans denied the chance to meet their loved ones before departing for the European Theatre of Operations. It was another example of the military putting the welfare of its 'fighting' white troops above those of African American 'service' troops. This incident would also set the scene for later problems with discipline in the 95th Engineers when they arrived in Wales and accentuated the nervous manner in which the men were viewed by their white officers. Things got no better as the regiment neared Liverpool. Reverend Carroll recalled that his relationship with Lieutenant Colonel Thompson was damaged after a regimental meeting before disembarkation in England:

> Lt. Col. Thompson and I became good friends and remained so until we reached England. As we steamed

> into Liverpool, the Colonel called a Regimental meeting and announced to his soldiers, who were all Black, that since there were only White girls in England, they would not be allowed to associate with them. You can imagine the reaction.[44]

The trouble caused by Thompson in trying to ban his men from associating with local women drove dissatisfaction with his leadership, a fall in morale and the beginning of a lack of discipline within the regiment. As soon as they met other African Americans stationed in England, they would have found out about how British civilians – including local women – had been welcoming to them. By trying to stop his men meeting British women, Thompson was storing up the seeds of his eventual downfall and a personal conflict with Captain Carroll.

When the 95th Engineers arrived in a bomb-scarred Liverpool on 27 July 1943, Reverend Carroll and his fellow engineers got their first taste of the war in England through the extensive bomb damage left from the heavy Luftwaffe air raids on the city and its docks in what became known as the 'Liverpool Blitz'.[45] The 95th Engineers were moved to their base in Newport, South Wales, where the work they undertook included building bases to house incoming troops for the invasion of Normandy, and the repair and maintenance of American military infrastructure across South Wales. During his time in Wales, Reverend Carroll spoke 'about 100 times in September, October and November to groups outside of my military group', which he said was 'a grand opportunity … to interpret the Negro Race to people in the United Kingdom'.[46] Discipline in the 95th remained poor through into the autumn, with Reverend Carroll as chaplain feeling both a personal responsibility towards the conduct of his men and a recognition that they were being led poorly by their white officers, as he wrote in a letter to Phenola at home in Washington DC. Her reply, sent in early October 1943, suggests that Carroll had even considered resignation – something she discouraged him from. 'I don't think resignation or a transfer is the solution to your problem,' she wrote.[47]

In his letters to Phenola, he expressed his concern about the poor record of problems between the African American GIs and white officers in the 95th. In her reply of 10 October, she suggested he stay the course and continue to fight for justice for the men:

> Your analysis of the Negro soldier's reaction to army life is extremely good. I hope you hammer it home often to your colonel and the other officers. If you haven't already given them the picture that you gave me of the criteria for effective functioning in accordance with human values, I hope you will do so. They deserve to know the men with whom they must work as well as they can.[48]

The poor discipline in the unit was also a major cause of concern for the officers of the 95th and by December 1943, they had convinced themselves that a major factor was not their leadership of the regiment but the role of the chaplain in spreading dissent. As a result, they began to build up a case against their fellow officer and chaplain – a case that would be held in secret and in which Carroll would not be given any opportunity to represent or defend himself.

The Jersey Beach Hotel was an austere, imposing, three-storey Victorian brick and stone building in Port Talbot, Wales. It has since been demolished, but during the Second World War it stood prominently overlooking the seafront.[49] At 'about 10am' on the cold, misty morning of 12 December 1943, the men of the US Army's 95th Engineer Regiment (Colored) were standing in 'reveille formation' on the forecourt of the hotel next to the beach.[50] Standing at ease, the men were being addressed by Reverend Carroll, who told them:

> I have gotten permission from our Commanding Officer to talk to you all and instruct you on the history of our race so that when you talk to the civilians here about us you will be able to refute the terrible stories that our white brothers are spreading around here about us.[51]

After attending the 'Reveille' at the Jersey Beach Hotel, his fellow officer Captain John H. Walsh reported back to his commanding officer, Lieutenant Colonel Thompson, with quotes from Carroll to his men. This became 'Exhibit "A"' in the case against Carroll, in which Thompson was keen to make a number of points in his submission. First, that Carroll was highlighting the matter of race and inequality in the US Army, as he quoted Walsh's report in which Carroll told the men:

> I was surprised when I was in Carmarthen and asked some of our men questions about our race, such as 'How many Congress men do we have in the States' they didn't know. I am in a position to devote most of my time to our great problem and since I have been in this country have made about 90 talks to civilian groups acquainting them with our problem.[52]

Second, that he was trying to ready the men for life in the United States after the war and the need for great equality and social justice: 'You can help and I will pass on all the information I can to help you for when we leave over here our problems are just beginning.'[53]

And third, that he was attempting to drive a wedge between Black and white GIs by getting his men to fight any cases of racism and inequality that were affecting them:

> If any of you are in any affairs with white soldiers I would appreciate it if you would come in and tell me. For then we can get all the facts together and some punitive action can be taken and I will go all the way to the war department and jeprodize [*sic*] my job if necessary to secure that action.[54]

'Exhibit "B"' was a mail intercept of a V-mail letter from Reverend Carroll to his father in which he refers to his meetings in churches and civilian groups up and down the United Kingdom:

> The response has been wonderful … I've spoken to several university colleges … In January I hope to visit

> Cambridge University where I will address a group of Congregational students. What I'm trying to do in my small way is to help in the effecting of better relations between this country and ours.[55]

A disciplinary case conference was held on 12 December 1943, in which the two exhibits above were entered as evidence against Carroll by Thompson and his executive officer Colonel Gavin. They argued that Carroll was exceeding his role by his 'tendency to fan the "Race Consciousness" of his men' and talk about 'Racial Discrimination', 'Equality', and 'the aspirations of his Race, with regards to conditions after the War'.[56] Thompson was determined to lay the blame for the poor discipline in the 95th on to Reverend Carroll, citing the above points and incidents of racial violence involving the men.

The presiding officer, Captain Allison, the port intelligence officer, made some important points about the case in his summing up on 21 December 1943, noting:

> There had been some minor racial trouble involving clashes between members of the 95th Engr. Regt., and white troops, the most serious incident involving white troops and members of the regiment at a dance in Llanelly on 1 December ... the white troops in this instance had been the agressors [*sic*].[57]

Crucially though, Allison did not lay the blame on Reverend Carroll, pointing out: 'It is not believed that SUBJECT'S activities constitute an offense under the Articles of War.' While finding in Carroll's favour, Allison did accept Colonel Thompson's request to transfer Carroll out of the 95th without letting the reason for the transfer be known: 'It was felt that an open command transfer at this time, or any indication that SUBJECT'S Racial Activities were the underlying cause, would be resented among the men as being 'Racial Persecution', with resultant unfavorable reaction.'[58]

However, Allison did suggest that Carroll might be 'Transferred to a Chaplain's School, or to some similar duty, and from that assignment be sent back to the U.S. The reason assigned for the transfer being some other than his present activities'.[59]

Even though Reverend Carroll was found to be operating within his brief, it was still felt reasonable by senior officers to try and send him back to the United States without any suggestion that his work on equality was the reason. But before any decisions could be taken to make any such transfer, Allison concludes his summing up by stating that Colonel Thompson had been 'relieved of his Command of the 95th Engr. Regt.' and an 'investigation is currently being carried out by an Inspector General, from W.B.S. [Western Base Section], into the question of White-Negro problems in that organisation'.[60] Thompson's attempt to lay some of the blame for the problems with his unit on the chaplain failed, and he eventually was held to account for his poor leadership.

Rev Carroll, knowing nothing about the case against him, was therefore surprised that the departing Lieutenant Colonel Thompson dropped his officer rating from excellent to poor. Carroll was clearly upset by this downgrading and again considered resignation from the army. He wrote about this period in his memoir, which clearly shows he had no knowledge about the case his fellow officers took out against him:

> The soldiers got so much out of hand that Col. Thompson was transferred out. As an officer transfers he must rate his officers. Col. Thompson dropped me from excellent to poor. When that happens in the army, one has to fight to avoid being busted out. My regional Chaplain came to see me, sized up the situation and recommended that I be transferred to a Port Battalion in Scotland rather than thrown out of the army. Hence, I reported to the 502d Port Battalion in Glasgow Scotland.[61]

Carroll remained with the 95th through until February 1944 and continued his preaching in local churches. For example, on 2 February he gave a sermon at the Methodist church in the Welsh coastal town of Mumbles.[62] Reverend Carroll took up his post of chaplain in the 502nd Port Battalion in Glasgow, Scotland, in March 1944. His transfer to Scotland was resented by the Black GIs in the 95th Engineers, as revealed in a letter to him from one of them expressing praise for his work in the regiment and their sorrow that he had been transferred. It also lays bare the low level of morale in the regiment:

> Morale is still very low and Court Martials have jumped above '95th Normalcy' (Smile). Just this week we must have had about fifteen, plus men being sent to W.B.S. [Western Base Section] for a General Court-Martial. These four were from the Court Martial Famous 'A' Company charged with stealing and over turning four GM Trucks … Although the boys were wrong I hope they won't be dealt with too severely because I think that if there were more recreational devices and other morale building projects in the Outfit it would help.[63]

The letter also includes details of a move to a new camp for the 95th, who were to be relocated in North Wales, and makes implicit that leadership was still poor: 'We are still here expected to move to North Wales next week. It is some tented camp I understand near Builth Wells. Col. Finnell is still here and so far has said 'nary' a word to his men. Some C.O.!!'[64]

Reverend Carroll clearly made an impression in local Methodist circles around the 95th Engineers base in South Wales. One letter in the family archive to Edward from 'Betty and Wyndham' in Morriston, Swansea refers to him as 'our little ray of sunshine' and they go on to ask about his family: 'How is your family? We trust young Edward is restored to his former health. Please give them our regards when you write to them.'[65] The reception he received from local civilians was appreciated and valued by Reverend Carroll, who on his return to America named his daughter (born in 1946) Nansi, using the Welsh spelling, as his son Edward Junior noted:

> While in Wales … my father made deep friendships with the church connected civilians who established

> correspondence with my mother that allowed us a means of correspondence that skirted army censorship. My sister was named Nansi after one of the Welsh women in one of the families closest to my father.[66]

D-Day and beyond

Moving to the 502nd Port Battalion brought Reverend Carroll closer to wartime action as his new unit was one of many African American service and support units that would take part in the Normandy landings. There is a familiarity to the story of D-Day and especially the fierce fighting on Omaha and Utah Beaches, where the Americans came ashore. The experience has been etched into our collective memory by the testimony of GIs who were on the beaches. The visceral, violent fighting shown in contemporary newsreel footage and movies such as Th*e Longest Day* and *Saving Private Ryan* is an uncomfortable watch. Movie recreations of the beach landings are not only a gut-wrenching experience but view the combat through a Hollywood filter that features only white GIs on the beaches. More recent research places African Americans on the Normandy beaches on D-Day as medics, stretcher bearers, port workers and operators of barrage balloons to disrupt enemy warplanes.[67] Chaplain Captain Edward Carroll and the men of the 502nd Port Battalion (Colored) are some of the many Black presences on Omaha beach on D-Day. As a chaplain, Carroll – like all the other chaplains carrying out their duties on the beach that day – was unarmed, which must have taken extreme bravery, as indeed was shown by the thirteen chaplains who had parachuted into Normandy six hours before the invasion.[68] The 502nd Port Battalion arrived on Omaha Beach under fire from German snipers, as Carroll's personal memoir of the Normandy invasion describes:

> The minute D-Day struck our convoy left Southampton … I slept on my air mattress under a half-track vehicle … The water was rough because of storm and we had to go down ladders on to landing craft to get to shore … On the

> way bodies were floating past and the ship I was on had a huge shell hole right by my side.[69]

The sight of bodies floating in the water is also a memory shared by white GIs in the first waves ashore. Once on the beach, Reverend Carroll and his men were welcomed by the white GIs already in action:

> When we got on shore the marines seemed happy we were there. We bunched up greeting each other until the Colonel reminded us that snipers were aiming at us. My first assignment was to go up and down the beach urging groups to break up … When I came to a boat my men were unloading a soldier toppled off the top. He had been shot by a sniper.[70]

In such an action, it was important to have a strong commanding officer and Reverend Carroll was delighted to have the kind of leadership that had been lacking in Wales: 'Col. Pierce was our Commanding Officer. He was a hardy old line soldier who swore every other word. We were good friends and it was a joy to serve with him on the invasion of Normandy.'[71]

The reminiscences of Captain Carroll on Omaha Beach are somewhat sanitised as they were written as a memoir for the family and much of what must have been a gruesome experience is toned down. Nevertheless, he does recall one of his men being shot by a sniper and falling from the deck of a ship, and he goes on to tell of the injury that was to rob the unit of its commanding officer:

> Rommel had planted anti-personnel mines as thick as daisies and we had to be careful where we walked. Col. Pierce drifted among the soldiers and showed them how to examine tufts of grass, discover mines and unscrew the caps. He went back to his foxhole and was joking with his administrative officer when he stepped on a mine which blew off his right foot. As I went to his side to comfort

> him until the medics got to him, he swore and said, 'all this time I have a corn on my left foot and I had to blow my G.D. right foot off'.[72]

A *Detroit News* story commemorating the 75th anniversary of D-Day features an interview with J. Bernard Taylor, an African American GI who was also in the 502nd Port Battalion and recalled the same incident when Colonel Pierce stepped on a landmine.

> He lost his leg, not his life. He was saved in a field hospital built and stocked with materials and supplies offloaded by a port company operating under fire and without anything purporting to be a dock. 'We loved that man,' says Taylor, and in a slow-paced afternoon of reminiscing, a white officer is the only subject that brings tears.[73]

The replacement for Pierce was Major Martin Hayden, who was a reporter for *The Detroit News* in civilian life before the war. In a contemporary letter to the Mayor of Detroit in July 1944, Hayden was effusive about his men: 'If I ever needed it, I got complete proof of the fallacy of the theory that Negroes scare easier than other people.'[74] Reverend Carroll concurs in his memoir, and reveals the high regard that Major Hayden was held in by the Black GIs of the 502nd:

> One thing brought me closer to Major Hayden. Our men were unloading ships steadily and could not be relieved because of the storm. A superior officer in charge of the unloading noticed our men were resting and some were sleeping. He ordered Major Hayden to get the men on their feet and to continue unloading. He unfortunately remarked that 'Niggers can sleep standing up.' Major Hayden responded to that remark in a fashion that got him removed from his command. He appealed and got a hearing that exonerated him and restored his command.[75]

Hayden would later go on to become the news editor of *The Detroit News*. Here was a battalion chaplain doing an exceptional job in difficult circumstances while maintaining the respect of his white fellow officers in the 502nd Port Battalion and high regard for a unit of Black GIs under his command. A unit that was welcomed onto Omaha Beach by white US Marines showing that not all white GIs regarded their African American compatriots with disdain. Indeed, the horrific circumstances of the Normandy invasion show how African American and white GIs could combine and work together with mutual respect while under withering enemy sniper fire. Reverend Carroll wrote some less sanitised notes of his time in Normandy for a colleague at Morgan College, who was researching a book about the Student Christian Movement. In this extract, he talks about an episode while guarding German prisoners: 'German prisoners were assigned to our unit to guard and the brutality of war came home to me. This was not just the killing through guns but the bad treatment of prisoners … I had to stop one of our soldiers urinating on a prisoner.'[76]

However, more remarkable was his recollection of how he met a fellow Yale student among the prisoners.

> I turned to see a prisoner I recognised. Would you believe it? It was a classmate I had at Yale who was a German Padre. We violated the rules by communicating with each other. This particular person I had met at Dwight Hall on Yale's campus on the occasion of an international student fellowship.[77]

Quite how chaplains on either side of the conflict viewed each other is not set out in Carroll's notes, but it is not a stretch to think that he might have had both moral and ethical questions to ask of a padre serving in the Wehrmacht.[78] From Normandy, Carroll pushed on through France to serve the troops running the Red Ball Express – a vital communication supply link between the Normandy beaches and the constantly moving front lines – he even took the 502nd Port Battalion Jazz Band to entertain the

GIs along the route. The reason for Carroll's roving role was a shortage of African American chaplains in the European Theatre of Operations. A post-war report on the future of the chaplaincy suggested the maximum ratio of chaplains to troops should be 1 to 850, yet in February 1945 'the ratio of colored chaplains to colored troops in the Advance Section was 1 to 3,750'. The report went on to note that 'there were only thirty-one colored chaplains' in the European Theatre, outlining why chaplains like Carroll felt under so much pressure.[79]

For Carroll, his wartime experience was mixed. The positive reflections of senior officers in Normandy were not indicative of his overall experience in the US Army, and when an offer came to take up the post as associate secretary to the general secretary of the National Student YMCA in the United States, he accepted. Captain Reverend Edward Gonzales Carroll resigned his commission as a chaplain in the US Army on 21 April 1945. He arrived back in the United States on 5 May just two days before the German surrender and left the US Army from Fort Dix, New Jersey, on 23 July 1945, having completed two years and eight months in the European Theatre of Operations.[80]

Post War: Pushing for Social Justice

Reverend Carroll arrived in New York in the summer of 1945 to take up the role of associate secretary of the National Student YMCA. He returned to a city where 'segregation was widespread and lawful' and where the early skirmishes in the post-war fight for 'Negro Rights' would set some of the themes and targets for the developing civil rights movement in the 1960s and 1970s.[81] Given his pre-war experiences, his time in the US Army and the state of racial injustice in New York in the 1940s, it is perhaps natural that as well as his ecclesiastical associations Reverend Carroll was also active in the NAACP and the Urban League.[82] In 1950, the Carroll family moved back to the South and Baltimore, where, as well as church ministry, Reverend Carroll was an advocate for local neighbourhoods. Having attended Morgan College in the city, Reverend Carroll was well aware of the problems with civil rights locally, a city which saw some of the first sit-ins at segregated lunch counters by college students from Morgan.[83] In addition to his advocacy for local Black people throughout the 1950s, Reverend Carroll continued his efforts to bring equality and justice within the United Methodist Church, assisting in organising conferences in the city.[84] Black ministers in Baltimore, including Carroll at Sharp Street Memorial Methodist Church, backed an NAACP campaign to recruit up to 100,000 new Black voters in the city – breaking the target in 1958.[85] Ensuring his own family was part of breaking down barriers, in 1952 he enrolled his son, Edward Junior, then aged 14 to Friends, a Quaker School in the city. He was the first Black student to enrol at the school for more than half a century. Edward Junior recalled that a group of parents had raised the money to pay for a scholarship for a Black pupil and forced 'the stone-cold racist' principal to accept the policy. This was two years before *Brown v Board of Education* and Edward Junior remained the only Black pupil at the school throughout his four years of study.[86]

With the ending of segregation in the United Methodist Church (UMC) in the late 1960s, Reverend Carroll left Baltimore to become the first African American minister at Marvin Memorial Methodist Church on the outskirts of Washington DC in 1968. By 1972, he had been appointed as a bishop to serve in the UMC in Boston, covering a wide area including parts of Maine and New Hampshire. As a bishop in the UMC in Boston, Carroll had an influential voice in the city, which he used in responding to racial violence. Boston was to all intents and purposes still a segregated city in the 1970s, with areas that whites and Blacks avoided, and Carroll played a significant part in calming racial tension. The late 1970s saw an increase in racial attacks across the city, with beatings and murders on the streets gaining prominence in the media. According to Th*e New York Times*, Black people represented one fifth of the population of Boston but they 'accounted for 71 per cent of the victims of racially motivated crimes in the first half of 1979'.[87] In response, senior clergy from across the denominations led by Cardinal Medeiros, the Catholic Archbishop of Boston, and Bishop

Carroll held a press conference calling for restraint and peace. Bishop Carroll told the reporters:

> The recurring episodes of violence and hatred cannot be tolerated any longer in our city. It is the task of all citizens of this city to act affirmatively to allow, but more to foster and celebrate in the spirit of love the unity and the diversity that is our human community … All of us as religious leaders have a sacred trust to preach the word in season and out of season. That word is the love of God and the love we ought to have for one another. Let us join together and renew our covenant. A covenant of justice, equity and harmony.[88]

After he retired as a bishop, Carroll continued to advocate for social justice. He was a visiting professor at the Boston School of Theology and an interim director of the Morgan Christian Centre at his old university in Baltimore. He also reached out beyond academic circles. In 1980 for example, he met the chairman of the Boston Schools Committee at an NAACP 'Banquet' and lobbied him about bussing and segregation in Boston schools.[89]

Conclusion

Reverend Carroll's wartime experience in Britain gave him renewed vigour to push the American racial boundaries in both daily and ecclesiastical life. He experienced the British through two completely different lenses. In India, Ceylon and Burma, he witnessed the inequality between the British colonisers of the Raj and the indigenous people of the Indian subcontinent. He met Gandhi in the mid-1930s while he was in hiding from the British and their relentless search for him during his campaign of civil disobedience against British rule. The non-violence expounded by Gandhi matched Carroll's Christian values and along with Howard Thurman, who became a mentor to Martin Luther King, he followed these ideas in his search for social justice in the United States. In stark contrast to India, in the United Kingdom Reverend Carroll witnessed at first hand the warmth and generosity of ordinary British civilians to himself and his men, and their unease at the imported Jim Crow restrictions and strict segregation of the US military forces.

His view of the US Army managing African American GIs as though they were slaves on a plantation was a unique take on segregation in the American military – it is also a pertinent one. Reverend Carroll's own personal links to slavery gave him the knowledge and understanding to take this view. In the 95th Engineers and the 502nd Port Company, he operated as a bridge between the white officers and Black GIs and saw how morale could be hit or uplifted by the actions and policy decisions of senior officers. As a highly educated African American officer and chaplain, he was invited to local churches and student groups to preach, and was seen as a threat by his fellow officers in the 95th Engineers who tried and failed to remove him from the European Theatre of Operations.

The hidden or untold stories of African Americans like Chaplain Carroll on D-Day are also important because they give a wider picture of their place in the history of the Second World War – a place that has been either devalued or forgotten. It may be that Carroll was the only Black officer on the invasion beaches on D-Day. Historian Linda Hervieux, who rediscovered the history of the 320th Barrage Balloon Battalion and their role on D-Day, confirmed this undervaluing of the African American contribution:

> they returned home, there were no parades. They slipped back into the lives they had left behind, which meant Jim Crow and all that it entailed: separate restrooms and restaurants, seats at the back of the bus. No matter if the restaurant patron or passenger was wearing a crisp army uniform decorated with a medal or two. If America was grateful to these men for their service, they weren't aware of it.[90]

Reverend Carroll was not searching for recognition on his return to the United States but the values of justice and equality that he continued to champion throughout his life. His experiences in the US Army brought these values into sharper focus and his time in Britain, particularly travelling across the country to preach and talk to white congregations and organisations, gave him new insights into how post-war America might look different.

Bishop Edward Gozales Carroll died on 1 January 2000 in Florida, just six days short of his 90th birthday.

CHAPTER SIX

Crossing an American 'Color Line': The African American GI Who Married His English Sweetheart

When Louis Edmead, formerly of the US Army Air Force, and Patricia Venn, a young English woman, got married in Bristol, England, in 1947, they formalised a relationship that not only seemed unlikely but in many American states would have been illegal. During the time between their first meeting in England in 1943 and standing together before the altar at the local church in Bristol, their wartime relationship overcame American and British social, cultural and bureaucratic obstacles. Theirs was one of comparatively few marriages between African American GIs and British women, despite an estimated 100,000 American military personnel marrying the partners they met during overseas service.[1] The largest proportion of these so-called 'GI Brides', around 70,000, came from the United Kingdom.[2] The weddings of these British GI Brides were covered in photographs in local papers across Britain from 1943 to 1945, and what they all had in common was that they and their husbands were white, so Louis and Patricia's 'mixed' wedding was extremely rare. Thanks to this coverage, it is the story of white brides that has persisted in popular memory in Britain of American GIs and their new wives. It is also what makes the story of the love affair and marriage of Patricia Venn and Louis Edmead quite different.

Patricia Venn, from the port city of Bristol in the South West of England, was 18 years old when she met Private Louis Edmead, a 25-year-old African American GI from New York, while he was serving in the city. In a grainy black and white image that survives from 1943, the couple are shown lying on their fronts on a rug in the sunshine near to the security fence of 'Muller's Orphanage', a segregated American base for Black GIs located in the Bristol suburbs. Patricia is facing the camera, her face in full sun as she smiles at the photographer, and Louis, looking smart in his army uniform, with his cap casually pulled back above his forehead, is smiling at Patricia. It's a tranquil picture presumably taken by a friend in the summer sunshine that portrays a young couple very much at ease with each other in public. Given the social mores of the time, it is a rarity to see a photograph of a Black GI and an English girl together and certainly not one posing like this, lying on an army blanket in the grass. It was not easy in Bristol in 1943 for Patricia and Louis to be together. Louis was part of the 1944th QM Truck Company (Colored) and just being with each other was a cause of friction with some white American GIs and local people.

This chapter features the wartime love story of Patricia and Louis, their separation after the war and their post-war reunion in Bristol, where they married in 1947. Placing their relationship in the context of daily life in wartime Bristol and post-war New York and Bristol, it will deal with the difficulties they faced as a mixed-race couple. Their story endures in the documentary evidence they left behind, including a collection of around 300 letters posted between them from 1943 to 1947. The letters are beautifully written and phrased, many are typed by Louis on his US Army typewriter, and they provide a glimpse into the ups, downs and many difficulties they faced every day in their relationship. Patricia also wrote a private family memoir recording her reflections of falling in love with Louis in wartime Bristol and his struggle to get back to her from New York after the war. Having become linked to the wider community of 'Brown Babies' born to African American GIs and British women, the Edmead family are keen that the story of their parents' relationship reaches more people as they believe it adds another, more positive strand to the history of Black GIs in Britain. Patricia wrote a moving and poignant personal memoir in which she recalls her wartime experiences in Bristol, when she met and fell in love with Louis, 'the love of her life'. The memoir is titled *Time on My Hands*, after the wartime tune that Louis and Patricia danced to, and the section featuring her wartime experiences has been added as an appendix at the end of this book.

Patricia, Louis and Wartime Bristol

Patricia was the eldest daughter of Bob and Charlotte Venn, who had married in Bristol in 1925. Her father Bob was an 'old soldier' who had fought in the First World War. While serving in the British Army in France, he been caught in a gas attack and also suffered injuries to his legs, and as a consequence he constantly struggled with his health. As Patricia recalls in her memoir, it was because of his previous army service that her father welcomed Louis as an Allied soldier into the family home: 'I overheard my father tell him he would always be welcome in our house,' she wrote.[3] The Venn's were a typical English working-class family of the time, living in a terraced house in the suburb of Horfield in Bristol, where Patricia's father worked as a bricklayer.[4] Coincidentally, Horfield was also the birthplace of Archie Leach – aka Cary Grant, the Hollywood film star. When war broke out in Europe in September 1939, Patricia was 14, had just left school and was looking for a job:

> When we left school, some boys served apprenticeships, which meant they learned a trade, ran errands etc, and were paid very low wages. Some girls went into domestic service. They 'lived in', worked long hours and had very little time off. I was grateful to escape that drudgery … Even bright, clever girls, didn't have much choice, as it was assumed they would marry, and that further education would be wasted.[5]

The jobs – not careers – available to working-class girls on leaving school were indeed, as Patricia states in her memoir, of low status. Historian Selina Todd argues that class and social status were a clear marker of what young women were able to do when leaving school at the age of 14.[6] Patricia found work with a bookbinder in Bristol city centre, located among the many small business and factories in the tightknit central area where she was able to walk and discover her way around the city by delivering printed goods to other business. The war, despite 'rationing, blackouts' and life becoming 'drab', was not an entirely dour existence for Patricia, as it included regular dances in a local community hall:

> My sister, Midge and I and our friends, Rose, Renee and Joan, all ran around together ... Dances were held in a wooden hut three times a week. We all learned to dance and the old hut would shake with our exuberance ... We met many types of men too, but it was all innocent fun. Being in a gang protected us. We were young, free and having the time of our lives.[7]

On the other side of the Atlantic, Louis, her future 'wartime sweetheart', grew up as a twin, born in New York City in 1917 to Herbert and Louise Edmead. His father had arrived in New York from the Caribbean island of St Kitts in 1906 at the age of 14 and lived the working-class life of many immigrants to the city at the turn of the century. The Edmead family had an apartment in a four-storey brick-built block on Manhattan Avenue, on the edge of Central Park and Harlem. Herbert Edmead was not alone in migrating to New York from the Caribbean – by 1920 it was estimated that one quarter of the Black population in the city were immigrants from Caribbean islands seeking out a better life in America.[8] Working-class life in the Black community in New York, where Herbert Edmead worked as an 'interior decorator', was tough and became more so after his wife Louise died in 1927 when the twins were just 10 years old.[9]

After Louis graduated from high school, he worked at a shipping business in the city while completing a four-year part-time commercial course at the New York Evening College, graduating in 1940.[10] He joined the US Army in September 1941, some three months before the Japanese attack on Pearl Harbor, as the American military ramped up its readiness for its defence. He enlisted at Camp Upton in New

York before moving to his first training base at Moody Field in Georgia – where he would become personally acquainted with the Jim Crow laws operating in the South. Moody Field was 10 miles north of Valdosta City, and the violence during the war that he witnessed around the base continued in the post-war era as local police brutality and the killing of returning Black GIs brought the town to national attention.[11] The violence and casual racism from white GIs and local people around his training base followed Louis across the Atlantic to Britain, where he arrived in late 1942 as part of the segregated US Army.[12] His proficiency in the shorthand and typing he had learned at night school in New York was put to good use in his unit, the 1944th QM Truck Company (Aviation). The 1944th was an all-Black unit working in the local docks at Avonmouth and later further afield in Wiltshire, responsible for distributing military supplies across the country.

Britain may have been a non-combat zone in terms of direct fighting between enemy forces on the ground but bombing by the Luftwaffe caused much destruction and thousands of casualties in Bristol. According to figures retrieved from the German Luftwaffe archives, between November 1940 and June 1941, only London, Liverpool and Birmingham received more bombing raids than Bristol.[13] In 1945, as hostilities ceased, Bristol City Council accounted for the physical damage caused in the air raids on the city: '89,080 properties had been destroyed or damaged by enemy action, and this included 81,430 dwelling-houses and shop flats, of which number 3092 were either totally destroyed or subsequently demolished.'[14]

In addition to property damage, some 1,229 people were killed and 3,205 injured in the 548 air raids suffered by the city.[15] The 'blitz' left parts of central Bristol devastated, leaving only memories of a vibrant city centre, as Patricia recalled in her memoir:

> Before the November 1941 Blitz, Castle Street, in the centre of town, was alive on Saturday nights with families buying week-end supplies … All along the street were shops selling hot pies, faggots [a kind of meatball], peas, gravy, pease pudding and bangers [sausages] … In those

> days the Centre and Horsefair was a maze of interesting lanes and alleyways. I was to discover these when I went to look for a job to help the family budget.[16]

It was into this bomb-ravaged Bristol and its surrounding areas that more than 300,000 American military personnel would either pass through or be stationed in during the Second World War. The American arrivals brought new experiences for Patricia and her friends: 'Yanks brought gaiety and novelty to our bleak existence.'[17] Among the first African Americans to arrive in Bristol was Louis Edmead and his 1944th QM Truck Company. They began their crossing to the city on 5 August 1942 on the ship *West Point*, which docked in Liverpool on 17 August after taking an irregular route to avoid German U-boats. The 1944th first spent time in Wortley, South Yorkshire, and Melchbourne Park in Bedfordshire before they moved to Bristol on 6 October 1942.[18] This was barely ten months after Pearl Harbor and shows how rapidly the American military machine was mobilised.

When Patricia was growing up in the 1930s, there was only a small number of people of colour living in Bristol.[19] This is despite the heritage of the city being one of the leading British ports in the transatlantic slave trade and therefore having a complicated legacy of its relationship with Black people. Between 1698 and abolition in 1807, it is estimated that over 500,000 slaves were transported from the African coast to the Caribbean and the United States on ships sailing out of Bristol.[20] Historian David Olusoga points out that in the Georgian period, Bristol was home to many former slaves who were under a constant threat of deportation back to the Caribbean.[21] Even by the 2001 census, fewer than 8 per cent of the population of Bristol – some 30,400 – classed themselves as 'non-White ethnic minorities', many with roots in the Caribbean, a number that is far less than in other British cities.[22] So when an estimated 25–28,000 Black GIs were based in Bristol and the neighbouring counties during the Second World War, it had a major impact as the largest community of colour the city had ever witnessed. Some of the African American GIs worked in the docks at Avonmouth and, like Louis, stayed for months, while others would be based in the city for just a few weeks before moving on to new bases.[23] Given the large number of GIs in the city, it would have been quite natural for local girls and off-duty Black GIs to pass each other in the street or local parks in the course of their daily lives.[24] Patricia Edmead and her girlfriends, Rose, Renee and Joan, met their first African Americans in Bristol on what she described as a quiet and boring summer Sunday:

> One summer Sunday in the early Forties, my friends and I were walking round looking for something to do. We observed some negro [*sic*] servicemen. The uniforms were unfamiliar, so we were probably staring at them – we had rarely seen negroes before that. They spoke politely to us. We were intrigued and ended up in a circle in the park, discussing pre-conceived notions of others' lives and cultures. Being young, naïve and honest, we told them we had always imagined that negroes walked barefoot, and all lived in hot countries. They told us that they had imagined the English all rode horses, wore top hats or bowlers, and spoke with 'plummy' accents.[25]

In a later contribution to the BBC's WW2 People's War project in 2005, Patricia recounted how the small world of her friendship group was expanded by their relationship with the African Americans and how they were received by the locals:

> From '42–'45 we made lots of friendships. Our narrow world opened up with picnics, ice-cream, Christmas parties … My sister and I went to the local dances. We met more soldiers who taught us to jive and jitterbug … The Bristol adults liked our new friends. They were polite and cheerful and brought gaiety to our drab lives.[26]

Here, Patricia is probably referring to African American GIs as the jitterbug was their speciality dance and its exuberant form was a key to attracting young British women.[27]

The innocence of youth that comes across in this memory contrasts with the experience of a Black corporal based in Bristol who complained that American officers did all they could to keep them apart from local girls: 'The MPs lock us up for anything and especially if they see us talking to white women.'[28] The attitude of white GIs is evident in a typical 'Morale Report' for March 1944 from the Western Base censor based in Bristol, who disclosed that more than 600 intercepted letters featured negative comments about African American GIs:

> The majority of the letters mentioning Negro Troops comment with amazement and indignation that the English do not recognise the color bar, and that English girls associate with negro troops. Writers express the belief that this will cause trouble when the Negroes return to the US. The Negro Troops themselves express pleasure with the opportunities thus provided for entertainment and companionship. Some Officers in charge of Negro Troops state they are well pleased with the conduct of their men and appreciate the lack of discrimination against the Negro among the English.[29]

A number of excerpts from intercepted letters are highlighted, including this from a white officer in the all-Black 999th QM Salvage Collection Company, based in Bristol, in a letter to his family:

> One thing is particularly annoying me over here. The English people have no conception whatsoever of colored people and as a result one sees many colored boys dating the white English girls. To us Americans it is very revolting but the English think nothing of it. When this war is over the relationship enjoyed over here by the colored boys is going to cause many hardships on us in the States. Believe me it is really going to be quite some problem and I hate to think about it.[30]

With violence between Americans in Bristol spiralling, local people noted that the white and Black GIs tended to segregate themselves by choosing their own 'public houses': 'If a negro goes into a pub that has been adopted by the whites he runs the risk of being beaten up, but there are other pubs where no white American will go. The Bristol people leave certain pubs to the Americans.'[31]

The Secretary of the NAACP Walter White toured Britain in 1943 to find out both how Black GIs were getting on with British people and examine their place in the segregated military. White was also a columnist for the NAACP monthly magazine *The Crisis* and *The Chicago Defender*, which described him as 'one of the nation's best-informed men on the entire race problem'.[32] In Britain, he reported that African American GIs had 'their first experience of being treated as normal human beings and friends by white people', but he also reported that many Black soldiers told him about the racism and biased justice that they suffered from in the US Army.[33] Another American journalist writing about Gloucestershire, which included parts of Bristol, said that 'Negroes were welcomed with open arms on a footing of complete equality'.[34] This would have been helped by the lengths the GIs went to build bridges with local people. *The Western Daily Press* carried a story in late 1943 of local children being given a party at Bristol Zoo by the soldiers from Louis Edmead's unit based in Muller's Orphanage. Under the small headline 'Children Entertained', the readers were told:

> Yesterday the coloured troops of an American unit gave some 300 or 350 children … a treat at the zoo … The party was suggested by the soldiers themselves, and they had to give up a fortnight's sweet rations to cater for the children. They also spent a lot of money on food.[35]

Nevertheless, from the time the Americans arrived in Bristol in 1942, there were reports of racial antipathy between Black and white GIs. This ended up in fights that occurred so often that the Black GIs reportedly introduced a system of lookouts to warn of the presence of white GIs.[36] Attempts by the US Army to control things in May 1944 led to Black units being banned from Bristol to lessen the friction, which was something that kept Louis and Patricia apart, as Louis wrote in a letter to Patricia on 17 May 1944:

> Well, mate, it looks as though that one night of restrictions I told you about is being stretched into one whole week … The C.O. might change his mind in a few days. I'm annoyed and angry, so I'll close until next time. Yours, with constant affection, Louis.[37]

This anger felt by Louis was also felt by his fellow Black GIs and within weeks in July 1944 the tense situation in Bristol erupted into a riot on Park Street, where an estimated 400 African Americans fought with 120 MPs, resulting in the death of one Black GI, with dozens of others receiving knife wounds.[38] Historian Neil Wynn suggests that local people sided with the Black GIs and were even said to have fought with them.[39] The riot in Park Street made a big enough impact in US Army circles to warrant coverage in the Black press in the United States. By August, the *Jackson Advocate* in Jackson, Mississippi, was reporting: 'Army Not Yet Content With Bristol Probe'. The report in the paper suggests early enquiries for the War Department had 'not found satisfactory evidence for the riot' and gives more detail on the fracas:

> It appears that two Negro soldiers were beaten by two white soldiers, newly arrived in the area, without provocation. The next evening there was a general clash between Negro and white soldiers, apparently as a result of the previous incident … One Negro soldier is said to have been fatally stabbed and was then shot to death by another MP … As a result of the general disorder all American troops were barred from Bristol for three nights.[40]

The observation that 'newly arrived' white soldiers were to blame for starting the riot is important. New recruits arriving in Britain had to come to terms with the lack of a colour bar and the mixing of Black GIs and white women, which for many was well outside of their normal 'Jim Crow' experience. Therefore, with a constant feed of new GIs – both Black and white – arriving in Britain, there was never a plateau to the violence, it was a constant threat to the US Army. In Bristol, the relationship between white and Black GIs was visibly toxic, while that between local people with the Black GIs was more complex. Many of the Black GIs worked at the docks at Avonmouth and despite early issues with the Dockworkers Union, were accepted and appreciated. One dock official told a Mass Observation survey: 'these Negroes have done their best and been a great help', while other dock workers suggested: 'they are not like we've seen them on the films … not stupid and dull … they are educated, some of them'.[41] One of the GIs working at the docks was Louis Edmead, as Patricia recalled:

> His army unit was based at Ashley Down, in Mullers Orphanage (the children had been evacuated). It was a collection of huge, grey, stone buildings and the Americans occupied it for three years. They organised supplies and the running of the docks and the transporting of goods all over the country.[42]

When Patricia and Louis met and fell in love, it was an unexpected emotion for Patricia: 'How can you describe the turmoil inside you when you are young, inexperienced and falling in love? (Hits you for six.) You go from carefree to confused. I know, because it happened to me, too, that summer, when I met Louis Edmead.'[43]

There is only one oblique reference in Patricia's memoir that some of the locals were not content to see African American GIs and local women getting together. The couple had a secret meeting place where they would wait for each other, and where they first became aware of this local sentiment:

> When I arrived, Louis was talking to a runny-nosed urchin. He told me later that the boy had asked him if he

> was 'waiting for his tart'. We assumed this was a short word for 'sweetheart'. We found out later, that some people judged all girls who went out with Americans to be immoral.[44]

Reading through the letters that Louis sent to Patricia in the early days, there is a passing reference to the reaction of the locals and other white American GIs, which he calls the 'usual unpleasantries':

> Since we began seeing other we have had less to happen to keep us apart than most people I know. The little places we have been, the little times we've had a good laugh for, and the way we have escaped the usual unpleasantries all help me feel less like grumbling … Yours, With undying affection, Louie.[45]

Though Black GIs were generally welcomed by local citizens, there was still a nervousness and even some hostility shown to them when they mixed with local women, and questions were asked of the morals of white women who associated with them. According to historian Sonya Rose, this moral outrage extended to all American soldiers but was especially seen as problematic when the soldiers and any potential illegitimate babies might be Black.[46] Letters to the then Lord Mayor of Bristol from British soldiers serving abroad and retained in the Bristol Archives show the strength of feeling about the issue. One Royal Navy sailor wrote: 'We are absolutely disgusted that the young ladies of Bristol should lower their degree of dignity and womanhood in front of the remainder of the respectable citizens.'[47]

An officer serving in the RAF wrote: 'Firstly, incredulity that women of our own race, up to now regarded as the finest in the world, could be capable of such a thing. Secondly, utter revulsion.'[48]

These letters were received at a time when there was a prevalence of scurrilous rumours about local women and Black GIs circulating in the city. One suggested that the local Southmead Hospital 'was virtually a lying-in house for local girls who had been seduced by Negroes'.[49] This rumour places the blame for the pregnancies on the Black GIs not the girls themselves and is another example of the African Americans being seen as 'over-sexualised'. It took the intervention of the Medical Officer of Health for Bristol to quell this rumour by announcing in the local press on 10 March 1943 that 'no black babies had been born in Bristol up to that time'.[50] As lewd stories of local girls and Black GIs continued to circulate, the wife of the vicar in Worle near Weston-Super-Mare, a small seaside town on the coast near Bristol, drew up a six-point code for local women to help them 'deal with' Black GIs. She went as far as to hold a public meeting to inform them about how to avoid talking with, or socialising with, what she termed 'American coloured troops'. Mrs May's six-point code found its way into the national *Sunday Pictorial* newspaper, which shared such 'rules' as crossing the street to avoid 'passing coloured soldiers' and moving seats in the cinema should 'a coloured soldier sit in the next seat'. The code rather backfired as the article also included a plea from an impassioned local woman who was opposed to Mrs May's ideas:

> Any coloured soldier who reads this may rest assured that there is no colour bar in this country and that he is as welcome as any other Allied soldier. He will find that the vast majority of people here have nothing but repugnance for the narrow-minded, uninformed prejudices expressed by the vicar's wife ... There is – and will be – no persecution of coloured people in Britain.[51]

The last sentiment expressed about 'persecution of coloured people in Britain' may have persisted during the war, but as soon as people from the Caribbean began to settle permanently in Britain in the 1950s, racism became endemic on British streets. Something that would prove problematic for Patricia and Louis in later years.

Louis and Patricia found their relationship tested in late 1944 as Louis and the 1944th QM Truck Company were moved to a new camp at Baverstock near Salisbury in Wiltshire, some 50 miles from Bristol. In wartime, this distance was difficult enough for civilians to travel and the couple faced long periods apart until Louis could find occasional transport to and from Bristol in US Army trucks and even by hitch-hiking. At Baverstock, the men slept in tents, which they 'winterised': 'The sides have been boarded and doors are being hung in an effort to keep out as much of the cold and damp as possible.'[52] Given these conditions in camp, it is perhaps not surprising that Louis would do his best to try to spend as many of his free weekends with Patricia in the Venn family home in Bristol. He was welcomed by Patricia's mum and dad, who let him stay in one of the bedrooms. The weekends that he could get to Bristol were clearly enjoyed, as his letters to Patricia show:

> Tuesday Morning … How's your Mum? She seemed much better. It's swell of her to put up with our shameless love-making right before her like Sunday after-noon! How did Mum ever get used to it? Ha! – I'll bet she'd never believe her future son-in-law-to-be was a guy that intensely disliked any display of affection … and even physical contact beyond a kiss or so … As ever yours, Louis.[53]

By 1944, the couple had made plans to marry despite US Army restrictions and were working out how to make it happen. In another of his letters to Patricia, Louis talks of how troubled he felt about the concerns of local people about mixed relationships when Rose, a friend of theirs, had become pregnant by her African American boyfriend:

> Mum [Patricia's mum] mentioned that soon the neighbors would expect 'the Venns' to be as unfortunate as Rose is. That is all she <u>said</u>. For almost a year I did not have the opportunity to cause the house to be 'talked about'. During that time I was <u>learning</u> to love you as fiercely as I do now … if it means that the talk Mum spoke about will lessen Pat, <u>I will not come to the house when I hear that its members are affected unpleasantly</u>.[54] [Underlining by Louis]

As his underlining of this sentence in his letter shows, he was clearly concerned about the effect his weekend visits might have on the perception of his relationship with Patricia and how it might be seen by the Venns' neighbours. Rose, who had become pregnant, was one of the girlfriends that Patricia had known since childhood and whom she described as 'a natural wit and comedienne', but she also 'sensed a sadness and reticence underneath the comic façade', as she described in her memoir:

> Rose fell in love. It was the first and only romantic love in her short life. She became pregnant, but marriage was out the question. After her son was born she was ill and seemed to give up. When she died, the doctors attributed her death to tuberculosis. I believe her heart was broken.[55]

Later, Patricia gave an interview to the film-maker Jonathan Beamish during his research for the feature documentary *Terry's GI Dad*, in which she was more forthcoming about Rose's boyfriend, whose nickname was 'Red'. Patricia described going out for a walk with Rose, who by now was heavily pregnant with 'Red's' child:

> She said she wanted to go to the Cabot Cinema … and he came out with a girl on his arm. She was my friend … well she just gave up, stopped taking her medicine [For TB], she just gave up. It was a disgrace to be pregnant then.[56]

This episode throws more light on the story of relationships between African American GIs and British women, of Black GIs living for the moment, of young girls enjoying their newfound freedom in wartime and for Rose, the shame of pregnancy outside marriage. Heartbroken at seeing the man she loved with another woman, coupled with the element of shame and judgement that she endured, it was clearly too much for Rose and, as Patricia observed, she just 'gave up' on life. Rose died shortly after the birth of her son Robert but as a family, the Edmead's have kept in touch with Robert since the war and still meet today.

Interracial relationships between young white women and Black GIs in Britain raised much comment in the national press. In her regular column as a wartime 'Agony Aunt' in *Woman's Own* magazine, Leonora Eyles questioned the advisability of having a relationship with an African American soldier and gave this advice to her readers:

> Although coloured people are just as good as white ones, you must see that a marriage between you would have little chance of happiness for either of you. The truth is that the white woman who marries a coloured man is an outcast; his race does not like her and her friends do not like him, and if they have children they are often unhappy. I think you would be very wise to end the friendship.[57]

In her memoir, Patricia Edmead talks about the relationships her friends enjoyed with American GIs and how they could be easily 'overwhelmed' by the generosity of the soldiers:

> Many girls then were inexperienced in life and had received little warmth and affection. It was inevitable that they would be overwhelmed by the attention and generosity of the easy-going strangers amongst us. These men were away from their own country and were lonely … Relationships blossomed. Some led to babies being born.[58]

Despite the debunking of the rumour about Southmead Hospital, there were to be many children born to local women and African American GIs. Holnicote House in nearby Somerset became a nursery for the mixed-race children who were born locally and given up for adoption. These young children were labelled 'Brown Babies' by the American press, a name that has stuck to the present day. Today, the 'Brown Babies' and their descendants see this as a proud marker of their African American ancestry and even have their own social media group.[59] The 'Brown Babies' born in Bristol were often removed from their mothers within two weeks of birth and by 1948, there were forty-five such children living in Holnicote House, then a run-down country mansion.[60]

Having a liaison with an African American soldier may have been difficult but consideration of marriage was impossible, as a US Army file compiled to assess the problem of marriages between Americans and British women set out:

> Perhaps the most distressing of all the marriage problems in the ETO were the miscegenous [*sic*] unions, which threatened to cause the most serious situations, should the American husband attempt to move his British wife or any children born of the union to the United States. Officers felt prompted to issue the warning that several states do not recognise the validity of miscegenous [*sic*] unions between certain races; hence the liability of the wives and the children of those concerned that might become a public charge.[61]

As a guide – or warning – to local women about the difficulties of GIs getting permission to marry local women, the *Western Daily Press* carried an information item titled 'Anglo-U.S. Marriages'. Without referring to colour, the report says that soldiers needed to give two months' notice to get permission from their commanding officer 'to insure [*sic*]that the applicant will enter into the marriage without violating any of the laws of the United States'.[62] This is in effect pointing to the many states where mixed marriages were against the law and therefore requests by African American GIs were routinely turned down by the US Army officers in Britain. For Louis and Patricia, there was no chance of marrying while he was still in the army. There are no official statistics from the period on interracial marriages in the United States, but after the war, American journalist Ormus Davenport, writing about the 'Brown Babies' born in Britain during the war, argued in a column in *Reynolds News* in 1947 that no brides 'going back to the US under the US government scheme is the wife of a Negro'.[63] More recent research in 2003 suggests that among the 300,000 marriages between American soldiers and European women between 1944 and 1950, 'some black soldiers did succeed in marrying the white women they met abroad'.[64] Historian Neil Wynn also notes that a number of British women did go to the United States after the war to marry their African American GI boyfriends.[65] The marriage in Chicago of Hazel Byrne from Manchester, England, and Buford Simpkins, a Black GI based in her home city during the Second World War, is featured by Romano as an example of the increasing number of interracial marriages in the post-war United States.[66]

Interdepartmental memos between the British Air Ministry and the Foreign Office set out the British position on mixed marriages, which it noted were 'regarded as odious' in parts of the United States. The correspondence suggested 'a marriage which is against the law of any state of domicile of either party will be invalid everywhere'.[67] It is why Englishwoman Margaret Goosey, who became engaged to an African American GI in England and followed him to Virginia to marry him, received little sympathy from British government ministers. Virginia had perhaps the strictest laws on miscegenation and Goosey found herself in jail and then deported back to England, while her partner was incarcerated in the state farm.[68] The case reached the Westminster Parliament but Goosey received little sympathy from the British Foreign Secretary Ernest Bevin, who told the House of Commons:

> I have ascertained that the action taken in this case was in accordance with Virginia State Law, and that Miss Goosey was warned by the State Authorities beforehand. I therefore see no ground for action other than the inquiries we have already made. At her own request Miss Goosey is being repatriated to the United Kingdom by the United States Authorities.[69]

The question of dating Americans found its way into popular culture through music hall jokes and songs. The hugely successful music hall and British movie star George Formby recorded the song 'Our Fanny's gone all Yankee'. It neatly captures the moral questions about associating with GIs through its mix of suggestive lyrics and implied sexual impropriety – needless to say, it was not broadcast by the BBC:

> Our Fanny isn't the girl she used to be,
> The Yanks have surely carried her away,
> Although she comes from Wigan by the Sea,
> You'd think she was born in the U.S.A.
>
> …
>
> Hot dogs she loves to eat and have a cuddle in the street,
> Our Fanny's gone all Yankee
> She don't wait for the dark when she wants to have a lark,
> In a bus or a train she does her hanky panky,
> And when she argues with her mum she shouts,
> 'Ha, ha you've had it chum.'
> Our Fanny's gone all Yankee[70]

There was a serious undertone in Britain that while mixed marriages were not – and never have been – illegal, they were not generally welcomed either. For women like Patricia in Bristol as the war came to a close, the seeming impossibility of marrying an African American GI was brought into sharp focus as rumours circulated of the GIs impending departure for the United States. The fact that Louis had been accepted by her parents must have made a difference for Patricia, making it easier to cope with any resistance in the wider community. Nevertheless, for Louis and Patricia, a long separation was about to begin.

And suddenly … Louis and the Black GIs were gone

As the war came to a close, the GIs based in the West Country were repatriated to the United States. For Louis Edmead, this meant boarding a troopship leaving Avonmouth Docks on 25 August 1945 after two years, seven months and seventeen days based in Bristol and nearby Wiltshire.[71] It also meant the separation of Louis and Patricia for eighteen months until he could wade through the bureaucracy of getting a passport, a visa to return to Britain and sail back to Bristol. For Patricia, this was a heartbreaking moment:

> Louis came to the house to say good-bye. The family had got used to him being around and my dad and the children were going to miss him. Just before he left the house, I overheard my father tell him he would always be welcome in our house. 'Thank you,' replied Louis. 'Will I be welcome as a son-in-law?'[72]

This departure was also a wretched moment for many other young women in Bristol as they saw their African American 'boyfriends' ship out to the United States. Graham Smith cites a report of hundreds of young women 'aged 17 to 25' surrounding the barracks of Black soldiers who were getting ready to leave the city. Barriers were broken and the gates at Temple Meads Station in the city were rushed in desperate attempts by the girls to get to their departing American boyfriends.[73] Louis had recognised that this might be the case and persuaded Patricia not to come to see him away as she recalled in her memoir:

> Temple Meads station that night was a sad place, as many girls went there to say their goodbye's. The barracks also had girls waiting outside, even though it was supposed to be a secret departure. I was in bed as Louis didn't want me to go to the camp or the station. I believed and hoped he would return when the war ended. I had no inkling of the difficulties and the time it would take.[74]

Louis wrote the first of many letters to Patricia during their separation from onboard his ship at Avonmouth Docks. It captured his desolation at having to leave her behind:

> Dearest Pat, With 'sailing time' so near, the first feeling despair … has been replaced by a feeling of quiet

> determination to find my way back to you – where I belong – as soon as possible. And to prevent the intense love I feel for you from causing me to do something that would eventually only harm 'us' ... like getting off this wretched ship right now. I was glad you did not stay around that wall Friday evening for I would have been tempted to take you away in the darkness.[75]

While Patricia was not tempted to try to follow Louis to New York, some young women did take extreme measures to follow their GI boyfriends. An Alaskan newspaper, *The Home Nugget*, carried a report on a 'twenty year old British girl', identified as coming from Bristol, who said she 'was engaged to an army man' and had stowed away on a ship from Southampton to try to marry him.[76] The story was different for the hundreds of local women engaged or married to white American GIs and who were allowed to settle in the United States. After the end of the war in Europe, the American Red Cross in Bristol held a regular 'Brides' Hour' for young women from the region. The *Western Daily Press* reported that the first such information evenings about life in the United States attracted 'some 350 British girls, the wives or wives-to-be of American soldiers' who 'stormed the Services' Club at the Royal West of England Academy, Bristol'.[77] For Patricia, who could not attend the events as the partner of a Black GI this must have seemed a dispiriting sight.

By September 1945, Louis had left the army and returned to the family apartment in Harlem, which only increased his sense of desperation to get back to England. On 9 September, he wrote via Air Mail to Patricia:

> the weather is good and the water is fine, but there is no you ... You are so much a part of me that it is like only half living to be without you. Can you imagine my feeling growing without the stimulation of your caress, your nearness, your mouth. It has been more than a month – it seems – since the last time I knew the indefinable fineness of your body close to me in the familiar way,

> and yet your warmth and sweetness are ever hauntingly fresh inside me. Y'know, Red, this daze of being away from you permits me the knack of recapturing our last embraces as though they were yesterday.
>
> Until – I am yours completely – Louis.[78]

In many of the letters from Louis, he signed off with the intensely personal and heartfelt message to Patricia 'All of my love, all of my life. Louis'. The thought of returning to Patricia and Bristol sustained Louis as he plotted how he could part-fund his return to Britain through an education and subsistence grant using the GI Bill. When he returned to New York on 31 August 1945, he immediately began to plan a route back to Bristol, hoping that the GI Bill of 1944 would indeed provide the financial support he needed to get a British visa.

The 'Serviceman's Readjustment Act 1944' (The GI Bill)

During his time in England, Louis's unit held familiarisation lectures on the Servicemen's Readjustment Act of 1944, more commonly known as the GI Bill. The Unit History of the 1944th notes that one session was held in Baverstock on 22 September 1944 and 'Fifty (50) men were in attendance and showed great interest in the discussion'.[79] Louis Edmead was comparatively lucky that he had been born and raised in New York City and was therefore relatively well educated. His home state had a more enlightened view than those in the South, where contemporary studies showed that spending in the 1930s on the education of Black children was up to ten times lower than that spent on white children.[80] After the war, a New York State Commission set up by Governor Dewey in 1946 led to the setting up of the State University of New York and the passing of additional legislation to ban discrimination in the admission processes of private colleges. In addition, in 1947, New York paid a $250 'veteran bonus' to GIs from the state who had served in the American armed forces during the Second World War.[81]

Louis technically had access to education and home-loan funding through the GI Bill, which was enacted to provide all returning Second World War veterans with funds for college education, unemployment insurance and housing. By 1956, more than $14.5 billion had been distributed for education and training and 4.3 million home loans totalling $33 billion had been granted to veterans.[82] The result of this investment by the Federal Government was to build a new educated middle class in America, but the effect was not universal and many Black GIs were to miss out on this funding. Academics and commentators point out that because many African American GIs, particularly in Southern States, missed out on the benefits of the Bill, it intensified a persisting inequality of wealth and income between white and Black Americans. Bound and Turner argue that even though the Bill did have a positive effect on the educational attainment of both white and Black men born outside the South, it 'exacerbated rather than narrowed the economic and educational differences between blacks and whites from Southern States'.[83] Bryan Greene, a contributing writer to *Smithsonian Magazine* among other publications, goes further by suggesting:

> The benefits that white Americans received from the GI Bill versus the exclusion of African Americans is probably one of the greatest single factors for present day economic inequality in the United States. Just a couple of generations since then the benefits that home ownership has provided in terms of wealth creation have turbo boosted white economic advantage versus Black wealth.[84]

Because of segregation and Jim Crow, the inequality of access to the GI Bill in the South was 'baked-in' from the beginning. Despite the majority of Southern veterans being African American, a 1947 survey by Howard Johnson found that in one Southern State, the Veterans Administration charged with distributing the benefits of the Bill comprised 1,700 veterans, of whom 'only seven were Negroes'.[85] Hilary Herbold contends that while some Black veterans did manage to benefit from the Bill, and that a Black middle class did emerge, many Black colleges in the South were underfunded and had to turn veterans away – all part of a persistent disadvantage.[86] It was a similar story in housing, as the U.S. National Archives outlined in its commentary of the GI Bill:

> Unfortunately, not all veterans were able to take advantage of the benefits of the G.I. Bill. Black vets were often unable to get bank loans for mortgages in Black neighborhoods, and they faced prejudice and discrimination that overwhelming excluded them from buying homes in 'white' suburban neighborhoods.[87]

For Patricia Edmead in Bristol, the impact of the GI Bill was to be very real. If Louis could get his education funded in Britain, it would help him obtain a visa to return, so she began sending Louis information on local colleges:

> Eighteen months after Louis's departure for New York, I was waiting anxiously to hear when he would return. During our separation I had visited schools and colleges, collecting information about Adult Education … All U.S. Serving Forces were to receive an educational grant. Louis decided to transfer his to England. He would attend Clarks College and we would live on any money left over.[88]

Given the difficulties many African Americans experienced in gaining access to support from the GI Bill, Louis began his quest for funding early, especially as there was the added difficulty in trying to get his college grant transferred to England. In his possessions in the family archive is a copy of a guidance booklet on the GI Bill prepared for veterans by the Yanks Service Bureau of the *Chicago Sun* newspaper. It sets out the benefits of the Bill: each veteran could apply for funds to cover tuition fees for a full school year and additional money each month for subsistence if a claimant had dependants. Importantly for Louis, the guide also points out that 'foreign schools may be approved'.[89] His first thought had been to study at the University of Bristol, as he told Patricia in a letter:

> I've been reading a good deal lately ... things that should refresh my mind in case I am required to take an examination before preparing for entrance to Bristol University as I may have to create the impression that I intend entering some British school in order to get Official permission to enter England.[90]

However, it was highly unlikely that he would have been successful in a university application as fewer than 5 per cent of the British population achieved suitable A levels to attend university in the late 1940s, and a priority was also given to returning servicemen who had missed enrolment because of their war service.[91] Patricia wrote to Louis from Bristol in November 1946 with information about Clarks College in Bristol and its more accessible 'Extensive Secretarial Courses'. She underlined the start of the new term in January 1947: 'I noticed this cutting in the paper today about the start of the next term. Wasn't it last term that started in April, I guess it won't make much difference though Louis they won't give you the visa until you decide.'[92]

Louis did manage to get his US Passport and visa to Britain in 1947 and his GI Bill funding followed later in 1949. He was successful in obtaining a grant under the GI Bill of $120 a month to cover the fees at Clarks College and his subsistence allowance for him and Patricia. This was paid from April 1949 for a period of two years and one month via the American Embassy in London – he received a total of $3,000 during his course.[93]

Because he left the United States in 1947, we do not know if Louis Edmead joined the fight for civil rights, but one unforeseen effect of the GI Bill was to give a boost to the movement. It is powerfully contended by Suzanne Mettler that even when Black GIs, especially in the South, made use of the Bill to gain a college education, they merely returned to the same discriminatory job market that continued to offer them low-paid, low-skilled, menial employment. Frustrated, many used their new educational qualifications and transferrable skills to become organisers and officials in the civil rights movement. Mettler cites Medgar Evers, who completed a college degree in business administration in Mississippi, William Henry who studied pharmacy science in New Orleans, and W.W. Law, who obtained a biology degree in Georgia, as examples of African American veterans who became leading figures in the NAACP.[94]

The fight for the benefits of the original GI Bill still continues. In 2023, an NBC News television report highlighted the still relevant effect of the Bill on Black Second World War veterans and their dependants through the story of 112-year-old Lawrence Brooks of New Orleans. As an example of the inequality suffered by Black GIs after the Second World War, it was reported that Brooks had for decades only received a $91 a month pension, but after an appeal in 2015, it was increased to the $1,931 a month he should have been receiving for some years. Before his death in 2023, Brooks was also given an honorary degree from his local Delgano College, a degree that his daughter Vanessa said broke her heart – 'He didn't achieve this. He always wanted to go to school. He never got the opportunity to go to school.' The report also highlighted the unsuccessful efforts of Members of Congress to compensate the descendants of Second World War veterans through a GI Bill Restoration Act.[95] But for Louis Edmead, the GI Bill did work as intended and funded his further education at Clarks College in Bristol.

Returning to England and marriage

Life in New York was difficult for Louis as the immediate post-war years saw a rise in crime and a new militant mood for civil rights and equality in the local Black communities. For Louis, this highlighted his wartime experience in Bristol, as he expressed to Patricia in a letter just before Christmas in 1945.

> Whenever I think of Dad and Mum [Bob and Charlotte Venn] I get homesick for England!!! Can you imagine

> that? – and I was never homesick for this place. You gave me happiness I had never known … I can wait a lifetime for that happiness … that warmth … that lift.[96]

Apart from his fiancée, the increase in crime and racism immediately after the end of the war was another strong reason for Louis to leave New York. He was concerned enough to warn Patricia to be careful of crime in Bristol:

> You might have read of the 'Crime Wave' that New York is undergoing. Well I have been warned by the police to be careful of prowlers, hold-up men and the like. I've been rather lucky I suppose, but I'll not push that luck too far as I might because now I must always think in terms of 'you and me'… I want you to be careful, too, darling. I understand that 'crime' increases after each war … all over.[97]

In America, newspapers ran lurid headlines about murder and other serious crimes in New York. In late 1945, the *Chicago Daily Tribune* ran a series of stories culminating in this headline from 20 November: 'CRIME RIDDEN N.Y. SENDS OUT "ARSENAL" CARS: Citizens Are Aroused by Lawlessness'. The copy set out the scale of the problem:

> Murders and manslaughters have averaged more than one a day for more than two months. Sixty-two lives have been taken in 70 days. Five policemen have been slain this year. Holdups by armed bandits are increasing almost daily … Police sent out 19 'rolling arsenal cars' to patrol the city streets 24 hours a day. The machines are equipped with tear gas grenades, machine guns, rifles and search lights.[98]

There was no Jim Crow in post-war New York but racism still existed in more subtle forms. Historian Chin Jou cites a *New York Times* article on 'Negro segregation in the North', which suggested that in New York, 'segregation is as much a fact of life as it is in the South' and argues that for African Americans 'almost invariably the color of skin determines where he goes to school and how he makes his living'.[99] In the immediate post-war period of the late 1940s, Biondi argues that the lives of African Americans in New York City were blighted by discrimination, unofficial and official segregation and police brutality.[100] This was the violent and ugly New York that by early 1947 Louis was almost ready to leave for Britain. He wrote to Patricia about his desire to leave the city behind:

> Now that people realise that I am more determined to be leaving here as soon as I can, they are asking about you … they know that you must be quite a bit of alright … Gee, I'm always bragging to myself 'I'm going to marry that ginger tart (as those little urchins once called you!!) Pat Venn – and won't I be the lucky one.'[101]

Having managed to get his passport and a visa to enter Britain, with Patricia's mother guaranteeing him accommodation a key factor, Louis was ready to leave New York for Bristol. His last letter to Patricia before he left expresses both his excitement and last-minute self-doubt – would she still want him, would he settle in England:

> Gee, darling, do you ever think that sometime next month all this (??) will be behind us at long last??!!! I often wonder if you ever regret this … this waiting for a guy who has so little to offer – when you could have done better. I wonder if you will ever forgive me for not sending for you instead of taking a chance by leaving this place I am fairly familiar with for the comparative uncertainties of another place … So you're getting married to a quite daft lad! And it's too late to get out of it.[102]

There the letter trail goes cold as Louis worked his passage back to Bristol from New York. He arrived in a country gripped by the freezing temperatures of the winter of 1947, one of the coldest of the century. Patricia's memoir picks up the story of his sudden arrival at her Bristol home:

> Cold, tired and fed-up, I retired to my lonely back bedroom, where, eventually, I fell asleep … I was awakened by a sharp cracking noise and went to the window. Looking out, my heart leapt to see Louis standing there, smiling. He had thrown a stone up to my window to wake me. In my surprise and excitement, I said, foolishly, 'Oh, don't go away, I'll come down and let you in.' Louis replied, 'I have come three thousand miles. I am not about to go anywhere.'[103]

For Louis and Patricia, this was the beginning of another chapter in their lives. They overcame the social and cultural difficulties of being in a mixed-race wartime romance and had fought bureaucracy to get GI Bill funding and a British visa. Louis and Patricia were married on Saturday, 12 April 1947, at the stone-built, rather austere-looking Eden Grove Methodist Church in Bristol. This was the local Methodist church near to the home they shared with Patricia's family on Cropthorne Road in the Bristol suburb of Horfield. When they married, Louis was 29 and Patricia was 22 years old and working as a seamstress. The couple lived in the city for the next forty-three years, during which Louis worked for the NHS as a medical secretary for three decades. Described as having a 'happy marriage', Louis and Patricia were together until his death at the age of 72 in 1990.

This book has highlighted a hidden history of the experience of African American GIs in Britain and juxtaposes this with the welcome they received from many British civilians and the racism they faced in the US military. The story of the love affair between Louis and Patricia Edmead provides a contrast to this narrative as they surmounted these same wartime issues and were together for almost fifty years – as part of what would become a new mixed-race Britain. Theirs was one of the few successful and happy outcomes of the hundreds of relationships between African American GIs in Britain during the Second World War.

CHAPTER SEVEN

Lost Then Found: The Memory of African American GIs in Britain

On the evening of Sunday, 18 April 2010, around 7 million people in the UK sat down to watch the latest instalment of *Foyles War*, a popular television police drama set in the English seaside town of Hastings during the Second World War.[1] During that night's episode, titled 'Killing Time', the full range of problems between American GIs and British civilians came tumbling out in the plot.[2] These included segregation and racism in the US Army, mixed relationships between Black GIs and English women, the birth of a 'Brown Baby' and the complicated reaction of civilians towards African American GIs. For viewers from the post-war generations in Britain brought up on a steady diet of constantly repeated war movies from the 1950s and 1960s, the programme was a new twist on a story they thought they knew well. This was popular television drama as part of a twenty-first-century phenomenon in Britain to revisit the war years in ways that challenged the accepted collective memory of the war – including the presence of African American troops in Britain.

The memory of African American GIs has been lost in the British mythologies about the war that partly grew out of the retelling of familiar stories through movies such as *The Dam Busters* (1955), *Reach for The Sky* (1956), *Dunkirk* (1958), *The Longest Day* (1962) and *Battle of Britain* (1969). These 'blockbuster' movies and popular culture in general helped build and reinforce a memory that sees the

British underdog always winning through against the odds. Over the years, these wartime myths of national moods, such as 'the Blitz spirit' or 'Britain alone', have been set against current events to such an extent that historian Geoff Eley argues '"Remembering" World War II requires no immediate experience of those years'.[3] Indeed, the British myths of the Second World War are constantly in the public discourse. Historian Andrew Roberts conducted a two-week survey of references to the war that were connected to current events in 2003. He found that over half a century later, the Second World War was continuing to make headlines, almost on a daily basis.[4] This phenomenon persists a further two decades on. Writing about his book on war and British identity on the 80th anniversary of the outbreak of the Second World War, historian Thomas Colley examined how the war shaped the reportage around Brexit:

> EU leaders have been bemused at right-wing British politicians suggesting that it is 1940 once more and the EU are the Nazis Britain should stand alone against rather than longstanding allies. This would not have been surprising for the interviewee who, sat in his living room in Birmingham, explained to me that he saw the EU as representing the final conquest of Europe Germany has always wanted.[5]

The Second World War, and a particular view of it, has therefore never been far from the mindset of the British and continues to shape coverage of contemporary events from huge political issues such as Brexit right through to international football matches between England and Germany.

In all of this cultural 'noise', the memory of African American GIs serving in Britain during the Second World War has been largely lost from view, hidden away in academia, local histories and personal memories. Memories that include American race riots in Leicester, Bristol, Launceston and Bamber Bridge; the estimated 2,000 'Brown Babies' left behind by Black GIs; and individual stories of the warm reception by British civilians have been lost to wider public view.

While academics have featured the African American experience, few books have broken out of academia, with notable exceptions, including Graham Smith's *When Jim Crow met John Bull: Black Soldiers in World War II Britain*, published in 1987 and David Reynold's *Rich Relations:* The *American Occupation of Britain 1942–45* from 1995, which features an excellent chapter on African Americans in Britain.[6]

However, the 2020s have seen a resurgence in interest in this hidden British and American history, and a number of new books have been published focusing on different aspects of African American GIs in Britain, from following individual units to examining the rough justice they suffered. In *An American Uprising*, historian Kate Werran tells the story of the mutiny that took place in the Cornish town of Launceston and its important impact on British–American relations in the run-up to D-Day.[7] Historian Anya Page's book *We Prepare the Way* takes just one unit, the 923rd Engineer Aviation Regiment (Colored), and pulls together their story – including their friction with white American units – during the three years from 1942 to 1945 that they spent in Suffolk on the east coast of England, building and repairing bomber airfields of the United States Army Air Force.[8] One of the more troubling recent books has been Simon Webb's *Fighting for* the *United States: Executed in Britain*, in which the story of every American soldier executed in Britain is examined, including a disproportionate number of Black GIs.[9] Webb's analysis reveals soldiers guilty of heinous crimes including child rape and murder, while others were hanged for rape, which was not a capital offence in Britain. The story of how pressure from the British public and press helped to free African American GI Leroy Henry, who was accused and tried for rape, from the gallows in 1944 is explored in *Black Yanks*, a story that revealed the extent of racial bias in the American military justice system.[10] A number of other pamphlets and books by local history societies across the UK are also bringing the experiences of Black GIs to life, for example, *1944 We Were Here: African American GIs in Dorset*, by poet Louisa Adjoa Parker was written as part of a community outreach project funded by the National Lottery.[11]

These books are part of a renaissance in Britain of portraying the experiences of African American GIs to preserve this important history before it disappears. In the wider public media, new documentaries, films, television programmes and podcasts are also bringing this history to the fore. Several factors driving this renewed interest include the regular anniversary events around the Second World War celebrating 'the last of the heroes' and a desire in the media to find new angles to cover – getting away from the 'accepted' version of the war. It also reflects the changing ethnicity of the British population and a desire by some strands in the media to be more reflective of this new demographic reality.

The legacy of the so-called 'Brown Babies', the early post-war steps towards an ethnically diverse Britain, is now much better understood. The families of 'Brown Babies' are now able to actively search for their American roots in a way they were unable to in the past thanks to the exponential growth of DNA databases – especially in America. Accessible digital connections through social media have also made it easier for interested parties to come together in new collaborative ways that were also not possible in the past. The 'Brown Babies' Facebook page, with over 750 members, through which they organise conferences, offer advice on family tracing and a safe space to share their experiences, is one example.[12] Another is the online exhibition of the Mixed Museum, which has developed into a really useful space for stories of 'Brown Babies' and their GI fathers.[13] More archival material is also being digitised and made available to British researchers via American military establishments such as the Air Force Historical Research Agency based at Maxwell, Alabama and by many American universities.

British Television and Film

Speaking to the Royal Television Society in 2015 on the 70th anniversary of the end of the war in Europe, Catherine Oldfield, the script editor of *Foyle's War*, put her finger on why the war is featured on British screens so often: 'There were 48.5 million people living in Britain during the Second World War and nobody's experience of the war was the same as anyone else's. That immediately gives you a gateway into fascinating stories and they keep coming to light.'[14]

More than that, since the 60th anniversary events around D-Day and VE day in 2005/6, British television programmes have begun to feature the experiences of African Americans in Britain in some detail. In drama, *Foyles War* stands out, as has been mentioned above. It was conceived by screenwriter Anthony Horwitz in 2000 to 2001 to feature a wartime detective 'whodunnit' story and blend the fictional narratives with historically significant events. The opening scenes of the episode entitled 'Killing Time', first broadcast in 2010, are set in a dowdy wood-panelled committee room in Hastings on the south coast of England in May 1945, as the war in Europe is coming to an end. Around the boardroom table are local councillors, town officials and a Major Westcott, an American officer who is asking the Town Council to introduce a colour bar in the town:

> Unfortunately, we've had a number of incidents between our colored and white troops, fighting has broken out in public, and it seems to be getting worse now everyone is itching to get Stateside. My commanding officer feels a color bar could help to prevent trouble flaring up between the troops like it did at Bamber Bridge a while back … a brawl between white and colored soldiers escalated into a full-blown mutiny.[15]

The response to Major Westcott from the local police, led by Chief Superintendent Christopher Foyle, is not one the American officer wants to hear: 'Well, that's fine but this is Great Britain not America and we don't practise segregation … it's important to remember what we have been fighting for, freedom from oppression wasn't it?'[16]

Chief Superintendent Foyle captures the perhaps smug British attitudes to American racism, but the episode also neatly encapsulates the contradictions of the relationship experienced by African American GIs. In featuring the birth of a baby to young local girl and a Black GI who wants to marry her, the drama portrays local antipathy towards women who associated with them. *Foyles War* brought the experiences of African American GIs, albeit in a dramatised form, right into millions of British homes.

In the summer of 2022, many of the same issues drove the narrative of *The Railway Children Return*, a film that followed the experiences of British children evacuated to the countryside to escape the bombing of major cities. While discovering their new rural home, the children find an under-age African American GI who has deserted from his unit and is hiding in a railway carriage parked in a rail siding. The plot of the movie follows their successful attempts to help him to find justice and a release from the US Army. As with *Foyle's War*, there are scenes in which local villagers witness aggressive treatment of Black GIs by US MPs, who also try to split up mixed couples in a pub. This is a movie aimed at children but the production does not shy away from highlighting the racism endured by Black GIs across Britain by their white American compatriots.[17]

Television documentaries have also brought the story to mass audiences in a manner that academia struggles to do. In 2024, the Channel 4 programme *Churchill: Britain's Secret Apartheid* tells its history through a series of interviews and films from across Britain. It features the Bamber Bridge mutiny, the American rioting in Leicester and the shooting of John Hendricks in Cardiff. In a striking finale, the producers brought Nancy Crossland, the niece of Private William Crossland, who was shot dead by an MP in June 1943, to England for the first time. They took her back to the scene of the shooting at the Hob Inn, where she was surprised to meet locals who still keep the memory of her uncle alive.[18]

The BBC documentary series *Black and British* places the African American presence in a wider context of Britain's Black history in an episode titled 'The Homecoming'. Historian David Olusoga visits Pontypool in Wales to record the story of the all-Black 320th Barrage Balloon Battalion that served on the D-Day beaches protecting the invading soldiers from enemy aircraft and providing medical assistance. The programme outlines the warmth of the welcome they received in the town through a surviving letter from a local white mother to the mother of Wilson Monk, a 19-year-old African American GI from New Jersey:

> Mrs Monk, you have a son to treasure and feel very proud of. We love him very dearly and will do anything in the world for him. We have told him he can look upon our home as his home while in our country and I will try to fill your place if only in a small way. We will look upon him now as our own. Mother to mother, very sincerely with loving thoughts, Jessie Prior. Xxxx.[19]

Black and British also includes interviews and memories of the children of Black GIs born in Pontypool during the war. Brian Lawrenson, whose father was an African American GI, was born in Liverpool in May 1944 and has been successful in tracing his American family. He says he and his fellow 'Brown Babies' have noticed this increased interest in this story: 'Oh yes. There is. There is a lot of interest, and I think the media have gone a long way to doing that, to get interest. I was in a film made by Channel Four, which was an hour-long programme about my quest to find my father.'[20]

'Brown Babies', a Revived British–American Heritage

After the war, the 'Brown Babies' remained as a visible reminder that African American GIs had been stationed in Britain. For many, especially those in care or who were adopted, their American heritage was never fully explained to them. Now, after decades of living in the shadows as a result of the shame many of their mothers were made to feel, they are positively 'owning' their American heritage. Television documentaries have played a large part in highlighting this formally hidden and complicated history.

In *Britain's Secret War Babies* on Channel 4, two of the 'Brown Babies' trace their GI fathers through DNA and travel to Chicago and San Diego to meet brothers and sisters they had never known about.[21] Similarly, in the BBC programme *DNA Family Secrets*, another of the 'Brown Babies' finds out about his American family through the DNA techniques developed at the University of Leicester.[22] A common theme throughout is the desire expressed by the participants to know who they are, why were they not told about their fathers and to pass on the details of their American heritage to their own families. Most grew up knowing they were not connected to the Windrush generation from the Caribbean, and that they were different, but not being able to prove their African American heritage was a personal burden for them. A feature documentary team followed Terry Harrison as he searched for his father in a film titled *Terry's GI Dad*. Terry was born in Leicestershire after a relationship between his mother and a Black GI in the 1938th QM Truck Company (Aviation). In the film, Terry's emotion cuts through his tears as he sees a picture of his father for the first time in over eighty years of searching:

> Amazing. Amazing. You know what, all these years … my dad! … I so wanted to see this. Well, I never thought I'd see a photograph of my father, I'd have travelled around the world to see this picture. It's an amazing, amazing feeling, because I never thought this day would come.[23]

A 2024, podcast for the National Trust, *WWII 'Brown Babies': A Hidden History*, was recorded in Holnicote House, one of the trust's properties. Set in the Exmoor National Park, Holnicote House was a children's home after the war for 'Brown Babies', given up for adoption by their mothers. Interviewees include Professor Lucy Bland:

> The women who went on and had children with Black GIs were treated often very, very badly. Often they're quite young, they're living at home, their families often reject them and certainly say, 'Get rid of this child.' They're sent to mother and baby homes. There, they're really pressurised to give the child up and if they were married and the man comes back, he might pressurise her to give up the child. So, it was incredibly hard, and I think just

> over half of the mothers, or possibly the grandmothers, did keep the child despite all this.[24]

Director of the Mixed Museum Chamion Caballero is also interviewed, in her case about the role of DNA in tracing the American families of these children:

> What is possible now is through the science of DNA testing, answers can be found that were much more difficult to find before. When we receive the enquiries [from people wanting to find their Black GI relatives], some of those come from what we call 'the original Brown Babies', but increasingly we are getting enquiries from their children and their grandchildren … We really had to let people tell their stories because so many people grew up isolated, not meeting anybody else who looked like them. And so … they felt themselves outsiders even where they knew that they had Black heritage.[25]

In 1946, the American *Ebony* magazine ran a picture feature on the 'Brown Babies' in Britain. The report was based in the African Churches Mission in Liverpool and shows a number of children and their adult carers in a variety of settings.[26] One of the babies pictured in the article is Brian Lawrenson:

> I was in a cot with – I think it was Mrs Roberts – hovering over me, over the bed. It wasn't the ideal place because it would be better to be with your biological parents, you know. But they did all they could for us with the little amount of money that they had coming in.[27]

When the childcare facility at the African Churches Mission was closed, Brian was moved to a local authority children's home in Fazakerley in Liverpool until he left school, moving to foster parents until adulthood. He met his mother when he was 20 after seeking her out through Liverpool Social Services. From her, he found out that his father, who had been based in Maghull on Merseyside during the war, had continued to send money over from America for his upkeep. For Brian, as for other 'Brown Babies', finding his American roots was a critical factor in discovering his true identity:

> Oh yes, very important, especially knowing them because they are a really nice family. If my father was anything like his sister, then I really did miss out on knowing him. I think roots are very important. It was to me anyway. My foster parents did a lot for me, you know, but I had a deep-rooted feeling I wanted to find my roots. It meant so much to me that I asked the American Government for my citizenship and I got an American passport.[28]

The 'Brown Babies' and their families are now a growing living link to the Black presence in Britain during the Second World War. With their history no longer hidden, they are rightly proud of their American heritage and their identity.

American Memorials in Britain

As anniversary celebrations and commemorations of the Second World War came round from the 1960s, they were often accompanied by the unveiling of memorials and plaques to the American presence in Britain. For example, from the mid-1960s, local people in Leicester began a campaign to build a memorial to the 82nd Airborne Division in the city. It was a campaign covered and supported by the local newspaper the *Leicester Mercury*. A typical story appeared in 1967 titled 'What about another war memorial?' in which the journalist William Kidd, who worked on the paper during the war, lays out the now-recognised story of the 82nd Airborne. Kidd argues that the 82nd 'enjoyed the hospitality and found romance in our city', and at the end of the war 'took with them their brides and left behind their memories'.[29] It took until 1986 for the memorial to be erected in the form of a piece of local granite with a modest plaque in Victoria Park in Leicester. There are now nine local memorials that mark the presence of the 82nd Airborne in Leicestershire but there are no memorials to the African American GIs who were based in the city and county, and who were here for longer – from 1942 to 1945. It is a similar picture across the country, where memorials to Black GIs are few and far between, but this is slowly changing partly driven by the greater exposure to their story in the British media. Local history groups have raised interest in the subject and several new memorials and plaques have been unveiled, four of which are highlighted below.

In Bamber Bridge, where Private William Crossland was shot by a white American military policeman, a plaque telling the story has been placed outside the Hob Inn in the centre of the village. The Preston Black History Group were behind the initiative, which also includes a memorial garden in the village with a large slate base bearing the legend, 'The Battle of Bamber Bridge, 24th June 1943'.[30]

A number of local history groups from across South Wales came together at the Carew Cheriton Control Tower museum in Pembrokeshire at a ceremony to honour the contribution of the 30,000 African American GIs who served in Wales during the war. Among those present at the unveiling of a plaque in their honour was April Hill Jackson, the granddaughter of a Black GI and a Welsh woman, who told those present at the ceremony:

> Theirs are incredible stories of their experience of war and love and the journeys they made. It's so important that this ceremony recognises the efforts of the Afro-American soldiers – they were exposed to hatred and hostility in the US. They made such a huge sacrifice, laying down their lives for a country which didn't recognise their rights as human beings.[31]

Another memorial in Wales can be found in Pontypool, at the home base of the African American 320th Barrage Balloon Battalion for serving on the beaches of Normandy. The BBC programme *Black and British* placed a number of plaques on buildings associated with British Black history and included Trinity Methodist Church in

Abersychan near Pontypool to remember the men of the 320th and other Black GIs stationed in the town.[32]

One of the more remarkable stories of African Americans in Britain is of the 6888th Central Postal Directory Battalion. A movie titled *The Six Triple Eight*, released by Netflix in 2024, revealed the history of the battalion in England.[33] The 6888th were based at the King Edward School in Birmingham, England, while they turned around the failing postal service of the US Army, boosting the morale of GIs on the front lines as they finally received mail from home. The then American Ambassador to Britain 'Woody' Johnson presented a plaque to the school in a ceremony in May 2019 to mark and celebrate the work of these pioneering African American women.[34]

The number of memorials to African American GIs who served in Britain is small considering up to 240,000 were stationed here or passed through on their way to Europe. However, more are appearing thanks to the diligent work of local community and history groups uncovering their local past.

Everything Changes ... and Nothing Changes?

The experiences of African American men and women in Britain during the Second World War had an important influence in both the US military and post-war American society. The GIs returned home to their families without fanfare or even acceptance of their contribution to the war effort. The title of a book about the African American 320th Barrage Balloon Battalion who were on Omaha Beach on D-Day is perhaps apposite for all of the returning Black GIs – it is titled: *Forgotten: The Untold Story of D-Day's Heroes, At Home and At War*.[35] Historians now regard the experience of African Americans in Britain and their reception on returning home as 'crucial in the development of the early civil rights movement'.[36] Many Black veterans returned to America determined to fight for equality and voting rights but were met with defiance by white supremacists. An African American veteran related a typical story:

> In Salina Texas one group of black soldiers were refused service at lunch counters and entrance to a movie theatre. What took them aback most was the sight of German prisoners of war being served at a lunch counter from which they had been excluded because they were black. As one of the soldiers noted 'the people of Salina would serve these enemy soldiers and turn away American G.I.'s'.[37]

Between 1945 and 1947, more than twenty-five veterans were killed in racially motivated incidents, one of the most infamous being the attack by police on Isaac Woodward in South Carolina in February 1946. Still in his army uniform, Woodward was beaten so severely that he was blinded, yet no action was taken against the police officer involved. Woodward was held in custody for five weeks after his arrest following an argument with the driver of a Greyhound bus. His case was fought by the NAACP, which used *The Crisis* magazine to publicise the details. Despite still being in uniform, the War Department refused to help Woodward, classing him as a 'civilian', even though he had only been discharged three hours before his arrest.[38]

This and other cases led President Truman to establish the President's Committee on Civil Rights.[39] Many returning veterans, such as Medgar Evers in Alabama and Reverend Edward Carroll in Baltimore, became prominent local members in civil rights movements and ran campaigns for voter registration. Historian Leon Litwack argues that the returning veterans made 1946 'the true birth of the Civil Rights Movement'.[40] In a supreme irony, African-American veterans fighting for civil rights found themselves on the opposite side of the social and political arguments to white veterans in many Southern States.[41] Congress passed the GI Bill to fund housing loans and college education for returning veterans but far from enabling African Americans, the bill was written to favour the segregated Southern States, leaving Black veterans who did get funding to struggle at poorly resourced Black colleges.[42] As late as the 1960s, only 5.8 per cent of African Americans were enrolling in higher education compared to 93.7 per cent of white Americans, highlighting both the glacial pace of equality and take-up of the benefits of the GI Bill.[43]

However, there were some early glimmers of change for African Americans in the military. The 82nd Airborne, partly responsible for some of the worst racial disturbances in England (see Chapter Four), became the first integrated division in the US military. Their commanding officer, General James Gavin, became a strong supporter of equality and some of his Second World War paratroopers changed their views about the role of African Americans. The Black 555th Parachute Infantry Battalion, stationed in California during the war, was invited by Gavin – against the will of more senior officers – to join with the 82nd in the victory parade in New York in 1945.[44] The 555th, known as the Triple Nickles, were then allocated by the army to a segregated area of Fort Bragg, home of the 82nd. Gavin sensed the injustice of their poor segregated accommodation and integrated the whole division in 1947, bringing the 555th into the 82nd. Despite the segregation and racial problems in the local North Carolina towns, Gavin ensured that within Fort Bragg there was equal treatment between his men.[45] It was another year later in July 1948 that President Truman issued Executive Order 9981, beginning the racial integration of the American military.

Gavin was one of two senior officers serving in the 82nd Airborne during the Second World War who made a mark with radically different political books in the 1968 presidential election in America. The other was Strom Thurmond, who became a senator for North Carolina and was a prominent segregationist; in 1954 he attempted to filibuster the Civil Rights Act by speaking for over twenty-four hours.[46] By the mid-1960s, he had switched from the Democrats to the Republicans and his book *The Faith We Have Not Kept*, written for the 1968 election, made clear where he thought the problems of American Society lay:

> Since 1957, the succession of civil rights proposals that tended to expand the power of the Federal Government provide the best examples of legislation that exceeds the

> bounds of the Constitution. The Voting Rights Act of 1965 arrogated certain criteria for voting, and specifically authorised illiterates to vote, in violation of state laws and constitutions.[47]

His use of the word 'illiterates' is code for African Americans, some of whom by 1968 had taken a peaceful role in the search for civil rights while others were involved in riots in several American cities. Gavin, who had worked closely with the Kennedy brothers and was running a management consultancy, made the opposite argument to Thurmond about civil rights. In his book *Crisis Now, Crisis in the Cities, Crisis in Vietnam, A Commitment To Change*, he laid bare what he saw as the problems facing African Americans:

> Riots are wrong, but I can understand what the rioters want. They want the opportunity to become everything they can be. So did I. I had that chance. The ghetto dweller does not. The Negro who finishes school has less chance to obtain a job than the white dropout. I could live where I wanted. They cannot. I was judged, most of the time, on my ability. They are not. I was paid the same as other men for what I did and promoted as fast. They are not. We cannot enforce order on all and deny opportunity to some. We all require both.[48]

The argument Gavin made in 1968 is still relevant in the American military of the twenty-first century, where African Americans are under-represented in the higher officer levels. For the white veterans of the 82nd, there was some regret expressed in their memoirs. John D. McKenzie, who served in the 376th Parachute Field Artillery Battalion of the 82nd based in Leicestershire, concludes his book written five decades after the war with this poignant observation: 'I cannot help but wonder how much improved race relations would be if blacks had been allowed to serve in combat on an equal basis with whites in World War Two. I believe the country would now be better off.'[49]

The Second World War did provide new impetus in a changing social and political climate to begin vigorous moves towards equality, especially in the military. It unfortunately also fired the starting gun on the resistance to change in Southern States.[50]

The African Americans featured in this book played their part in shaping the post-war world in their own less public and personal ways. Quartermaster GI Louis Edmead came back to England from New York after the war to marry his sweetheart Patricia in Bristol (See Chapter Six). The Edmeads and their children were one of only a small number of mixed households in England in the 1940s, but more than that, they were pioneers of a new mixed-race Britain. From the 2021 census, the Office for National Statistics (ONS) reported that one in ten (10.4 per cent) households in England were made up of multiple ethnic groups, rising to more than a fifth (22.3) in London.[51] According to some projections, Britain will be 30 per cent mixed race by the end of this century, rising to 75 per cent by 2150.[52]

For Reverend Captain Edward Carroll of the 95th Engineers, his many positive interactions with churches and religious groups in Britain during the war must have confirmed his view that a socially equitable society was the way forward for the United States (see Chapter Five). His work in the United Methodist Church (UMC) and wider society after the war was part of a movement that led to the end of segregation in the church in the 1960s. As a bishop in Boston in the 1970s, he worked to calm racial tensions in the city and continued to lobby through the NAACP after he retired. However, the battles he fought in the UMC still continue into the present. A 2023 survey of 650 Black clergy and lay people in the church found that discrimination and racism were top of their concerns about the future direction of the church.[53] The warm welcome Carroll received in British churches has been replaced with similar concerns of Black clergy in the Church of England about institutional racism.[54]

The shooting by white MPs of John Hendricks of the 1938th Truck Company (Aviation) at what was essentially a traffic stop in Cardiff, Wales, in 1944 was captured in the court martial papers of the trial of MPs, who were found not guilty of his murder (see Chapter Three). As shocking as it may have been at the time, it is still not an unusual occurrence in the United States. Figures analysed by the University of Illinois, Chicago, show that though Black males represent 6.1 per cent of the population of the United States, they represent a quarter (24.9 per cent) of people killed by law enforcement.[55] Following the May 2020 death of George Floyd in police custody, the issue of Black males killed by law enforcement officers was brought to the wider attention of the media, and in turn to a worldwide audience.[56] A subsequent Harvard University report published in *The Lancet* found that the killing of Black men by the police had a demonstrably detrimental effect on the mental health of the wider African American population.[57] Speaking to the family of Lewis Carter of the 1938th Truck Company, who was in the US Army truck when John Hendricks was shot by white MPs, they told me he never drove again in America and did not tell them about the incident in Wales. They were shocked when, as part of the research for this book, they were shown his testimony in the transcripts of the court martial of the Shore Patrol officers who shot John Hendricks. As Britain has changed with immigration of people of colour since the 1950s, so the country now faces similar challenges around the relationship of Black people and the police – with Black people in Britain up to seven times more likely to die following restraint by the police.[58]

Conclusion

This book has shown that the experience of African Americans in Britain during the Second World War was an important factor in the post-war changes towards civil rights in America. Indeed, the desegregation of the US military in 1948 by President Truman, in part as a result of the treatment of returning Black veterans, has been described as 'the first victory of what we know call the civil rights movement'.[59] During their time in Britain, they faced the contradictory situations of racism from many of their fellow white Americans that contrasted sharply with the generally good reception they received from British civilians. For Black GIs, their time in Britain was part of a physically and socially liberating journey that showed that relationships with white people did not have to be as they were in pre-war America. The genuine warmth they received in Britain masked a latent racism that came to the fore where their relationships with white women were concerned. As the largest group of people of colour yet experienced in Britain, the welcome the Black GIs received was part of a complicated relationship that Britain has with questions of race. The children of Black GIs and British women faced a difficult childhood in Britain. Often rejected by their British mothers and given up for adoption, 'Brown Babies' were in the vanguard of a new, less forgiving social order. Much to their credit, they now take pride in the name given to them after the war by the American press. As they and their families continue to search for their American roots, they remain a living link to a unique American social experiment in Britain during the Second World War when 240,000 Black GIs came to Britain. A unique mixed-race bridge between Britain and America.

Appendix: A Wartime Love Story

Chapter Six was based on the remarkable Edmead family archive about the marriage of American GI Louis Edmead, a Black soldier from New York and Patricia, a young girl from Bristol. The archive contains their personal letters, photographs, press cuttings and a beautiful memoir written by Patricia. In this appendix we can hear the voice of Patricia in an abridged extract from her memoir *Time on My Hands*. It allows us to sample the experience of just one of the many thousands of English women who fell in love with African American soldiers in Britain during the Second World War. It is a remarkable story worthy of reproducing below in a fuller version than in the extracts that have been quoted above. … Pat takes up the story:

> One summer Sunday in the early Forties, my friends and I were walking round looking for something to do. We observed some negro servicemen. The uniforms were unfamiliar, so we were probably staring at them – we had rarely seen negroes before that. They spoke politely to us. We were intrigued and ended up in a circle in the park, discussing pre-conceived notions of others' lives and cultures. Being young, naïve and honest, we told them we had always imagined that negroes walked barefoot, and all lived in hot countries. They told us that they had imagined the English all rode horses, wore top hats or bowlers, and spoke with 'plummy' accents.

Many girls then were inexperienced in life and had received little warmth and affection. It was inevitable that they would be overwhelmed by the attention and generosity of the easy-going strangers among us. These men were away from their own country and were lonely … Relationships blossomed. Some led to babies being born.

But how can you describe the turmoil inside you when you are young, inexperienced and falling in love? (Hits you for six.) You go from carefree to confused. I know, because it happened to me, too, that summer, when I met Louis Edmead.

At first I found it hard to very difficult to adjust to being in a relationship, which I later realised I was more than lucky to be in. Louis, the optimist (everything is possible). Patricia, the pessimist (a product of her Nordic ancestry).

In those early days Louis and I often ran into each other. Louis was keen to find out about this English city he found himself in. In my wanderings I would see him flash by in a jeep with his fellow servicemen. On leaving them he asked if he could join me. We would walk to Blaise Castle or Snuff Mills – Almondsbury. All the childhood haunts the Sunday School teachers had introduced me to. Later, we borrowed bicycles to go to beaches. Louis was an excellent swimmer and taught many children here to swim.

His Army Unit was based at Ashley Down, in Mullers Orphanage (the children had been evacuated). It was a collection of huge, grey, stone buildings and the Americans occupied it for three years. They organised supplies and the running of the docks and the transporting of goods all over the country.

Louis didn't always know when he could get away, so we had a secret meeting place. At weekends I would go there and wait for him. More often than not he would come bouncing along, usually followed by children and the inevitable war-time cry of 'Got any gum, chum?' I remember one little boy saying, 'Have you kissed your sweetheart, Mister?' Louis replied 'No, but I'm working on it'. Another time I was late. When I arrived, Louis was talking to a runny-nosed urchin. He told me later that the boy had asked him if he was 'waiting for his tart'. We assumed this was a short word for 'sweetheart'. We found out later, that some people judged all girls who went out with Americans to be immoral.

Then things started to change. Men couldn't leave the barracks so often. One night they were moved to Salisbury Plain, where they slept under canvas in the woods. Everything was hush-hush. As we know now, they were preparing for the Normandy Landings. Louis sometimes borrowed transport to get away or hitched to Bristol and stayed overnight. We were unaware our idyll was coming to an end. It was a glorious summer, weatherwise, when it somehow leaked out that the men were leaving. They were back in Bristol but unaware of the sadness the girls would feel when they left.

Louis came to the house to say good-bye. The family had got used to him being around and my dad and the children were going to miss him. Just before he left the house, I overheard my father tell him he would always be welcome in our house. 'Thank you,' replied Louis. 'Will I be welcome as a son-in-law?'

Temple Meads station that night was a sad place, as many girls went there to say their goodbye's. The barracks also had girls waiting outside, even though it was supposed to be a secret departure. I was in bed as Louis didn't want me to go to the camp or the station. I believed and hoped he would return when the war ended. I had no inkling of the difficulties and the time it would take.

I believed Louis would return, but everything would be different in peacetime. Was I ready for responsibility? Maybe I should be finding out what he wanted from a committed relationship. What about his dreams? What would he be giving up for me? How would his father feel about losing his son to England?

Eighteen months after Louis's departure for New York, I was waiting anxiously to hear when he would return. During our separation I had visited schools and colleges, collecting information about Adult Education. Having finally obtained a Landing Visa; Louis was informed he would not be able to work here straight away. My mother guaranteed him a home. He was working hard and saving for a simple wedding.

During our separation, my dad had died, aged 49 years. Mum was at an all-time low.

All U.S. Serving Forces were to receive an educational grant. Louis decided to transfer his to England. He would attend Clarks College and we would live on any money left over. February 1947 was one of the coldest winters on record. Snow lay everywhere, frozen pipes, coal hard to come by. The farmers couldn't dig the fields. We couldn't buy vegetables. Some foods were scarce and many were still rationed.

Cold, tired and fed-up, I retired to my lonely back bedroom, where, eventually, I fell asleep … I was awakened by a sharp cracking noise and went to the window. Looking out, my heart leapt to see Louis standing there, smiling. He had thrown a stone up to my window to wake me. In my surprise and excitement, I said, foolishly, 'Oh, don't go away, I'll come down and let you in.' Louis replied, 'I have come three thousand miles. I am not about to go anywhere.'

Louis and I were eventually married in 1947. We were together for 43 years, until his death in 1990.

Pat Edmead

Produced with thanks to Kerry Edmead, the son of Pat and Louis, who manages the family archive.

Endnotes

Preface

1. Hegseth, P., *The War on Warriors: Behind the Betrayal of the Men Who Keep Us Free* (Fox Books, 2024), p.12.
2. See: Chivvis, C.S., and Lauji, S., 'Diversity in the High Brass: Why there are relatively few African Americans in the senior ranks of the U.S. military and what can be done about it', Carnegie Endowment for International Peace, 6 September 2022, https://carnegieendowment.org/research/2022/09/diversity-in-the-high-brass?lang=en (accessed 24 April 2025).
3. See: Bryson, D., 'Two Black Cadets and the struggle for diversity at an elite US military institution', Reuters, 30 March 2024, https://www.reuters.com/investigates/special-report/usa-race-academy/ (accessed 24 April 2025).
4. Walsh, S., 'Why Does The Navy Have So Few Black Admirals? Some Blame A Culture Of Discrimination', NPR, 6 November 2020, https://www.npr.org/2020/11/05/931808280/why-does-the-navy-have-so-few-black-admirals-some-blame-a-culture-of-discriminat (accessed 24 April 2025).

Chapter One

1. Cambridge American Cemetery, Cambridge, England, https://www.abmc.gov/video/cambridge-american-cemetery/ (accessed 20 March 2025).

2. See: Sanders, T., *The Last Good War: The Faces and Voices of World War II* (Welcome, 2010).
3. See: Greene, B., 'After Victory in World War II, Black Veterans Continued the Fight for Freedom at Home', *Smithsonian Magazine*, 30 August 2021, https://www.smithsonianmag.com/history/summer-1946-saw-black-wwii-vets-fight-freedom-home-180978538/ (accessed 20 March 2025).
4. There is no official number of African American GIs who passed through Britain during the Second World War. The Imperial War Museum puts the number at 150,000, but National Museums Liverpool suggest 240,000, as does the Black History Month organisation in Britain and the online Mixed Museum. The 240,000 figure is also becoming more widely quoted by historians such as Professor Lucy Bland in her book *Britain's 'Brown Babies'*.
5. Rowe, M., 'Sex, 'race' and riot in Liverpool, 1919', *Immigrants & Minorities: Historical Studies in Ethnicity, Migration and Diaspora* (v19, 2000), p.55.
6. Olusoga, D., *Black and British: A Forgotten History* (Pan, 2016), p.459.
7. Quoted in Olusoga, *Black and British*, p.459.
8. See: Simpson, K., 'Aliens' in *Unreliable Sources: How the 20th century was reported* (Macmillan, 2010), pp.47–63.
9. Sherwood, M., 'Walter White and the British: A Lost Opportunity', *Contributions in Black Studies*, vol 9, (1992), Article 14, p.1.
10. Wynn, N., *The African American Experience during World War II* (Rowman & Littlefield, 2010), p.xiii.
11. Barksdale, S., 'Prelude to a Revolution: African American World War II Veterans, Double Consciousness, and Civil Rights, 1940-1955', PhD Thesis, University of North Carolina, 2014, https://core.ac.uk/download/pdf/210604882.pdf (accessed 20 March 2025).
12. Schaffer, G., 'Fighting Racism: Black Soldiers and Workers in Britain during the Second World War', *Immigrants and Minorites*, 28.2–3, pp.246–265, p.260
13. Leicester Corporation Annual Health Reports, 1940–1946 (ROLLR, File LG 14), and Leicester Diocesan Moral Welfare Association, Annual Reports, 1942–1945 (ROLLR, File DE6058/11).

14. Newman, M., *The Civil Rights Movement* (Edinburgh University Press, 2004); Fairclough, A., *Better Day Coming: Blacks and Equality, 1890–2000* (Penguin, 2001); Litwack, L.F., *How Free is Free: The Long Death of Jim Crow* (Harvard University Press, 2009); Ward, J.M., *Defending White Democracy: The Making of a Segregationist Movement and the Remaking of Racial Politics, 1936-1965* (The University of North Carolina Press, 2011).
15. Morehouse, M.M., *Fighting in the Jim Crow Army: Black Men and Women Remember World War II*, (Rowman & Littlefield, 2000); MacGregor, M., *Integration of the Armed Forces: 1940–1965* (US Defense Committee, 1979); Motley, M.P., *The Invisible Soldier: The Experience of the Black Soldier, World War II* (Wayne State University Press, 1987); Mershon, S and Schlossman, S., *Foxholes and Color Lines: Desegregating the U.S. Armed Forces* (John Hopkins University Press, 1988).
16. Latty, Y., *We Were There: Voices of African American Veterans, from World War II to the War in Iraq* (Amistad, 2005); McGuire, P., *Taps for a Jim Crow Army: Letters from Black Soldiers in World War II* (ABC-CLIO, 1983).
17. Lilly, R.J., *Taken by Force: Rape and American GIs in Europe during World War II* (Palgrave Macmillan, 2007), p.50
18. See Webb, S., *Fighting for the United States, Executed in Britain: US Soldiers Court-Martialled in WWII* (Pen & Sword, 2021).
19. See Werran, K., *Black Yanks: Defending Leroy Henry in D-Day Britain* (The History Press, 2024).
20. Reynolds, D., *Rich Relations: The American Occupation of Britain 1942–45* (Phoenix Press, 2000); Gardiner, J. *'Over Here': The GIs in Wartime Britain* (Collins & Brown, 1992); Longmate, N., *The G.I.'s: The Americans in Britain, 1942–45* (Hutchinson of London, 1975).
21. Smith, G., *When Jim Crow Met John Bull: Black Soldiers in World War II Britain* (Tauris, 1987).
22. For examples see Reynolds, D., *Rich Relations: The American Occupation of Britain, 1942–45* (Phoenix Press, 2000); Smith, G., *When Jim Crow Met John Bull: Black Soldiers*

in World War II Britain (Tauris, 1987); and Werran, K., *An American Uprising in Second World War England: Mutiny in the Duchy* (Pen & Sword, 2020).

23. Bland, L., *Britain's 'Brown Babies': The stories of children born to Black GIs and white women in the Second World War* (Manchester University Press, 2019).
24. See Kruse, K.M. and Tuck, S., (eds), *Fog of War: The Second World War and the Civil Rights Movement* (Oxford University Press, 2012).

Chapter Two

1. British Foreign Office papers, FO 954/29, Note A8190/6535/G, Mr Eden to Viscount Halifax (Washington), 1 September 1942.
2. FO papers, Eden to Halifax.
3. FO papers, Eden to Halifax.
4. Reynolds, D., *Rich Relations: The American Occupation of Britain 1942–1945* (Phoenix Press, 2000), p.218.
5. National Archives, British Government Cabinet papers, Memorandum by the Secretary of State for War, 'United States Coloured Troops in the United Kingdom', 3 October 1942, p.83, https://webarchive.nationalarchives.gov.uk/ukgwa/20231023132625mp_/http://filestore.nationalarchives.gov.uk/pdfs/large/cab-66-29.pdf (accessed 22 March 2024).
6. Cabinet papers, October 1942, p.84.
7. Cabinet papers, October 1942, p.84.
8. See: US Archives, *Census of the British Empire, 1901* (Census Office, London: 1906), https://ia801309.us.archive.org/15/items/cu31924030396067/cu31924030396067.pdf (accessed 23 March 2024).
9. Charles, E., 'Black Americans in Britain in World War Two', Imperial War Museum, London, (accessed 26 February 2024).
10. Estimates of the exact number of African American troops that passed through Britain ranges from 120,000 to 240,000 in a range of sources. The higher figure is used by Professor Lucy Bland in her book *Britain's 'Brown Babies'* published in 2019, and a number of subsequent newspaper and internet sources.

11. Reynolds, D., 'The Churchill Government and the Black American Troops in Britain during World War II', *Transactions of the Royal Historical Society*, vol 35 (1985), pp.113–133, p.113.
12. Fairclough, A., *Better Day Coming: Blacks and Equality, 1890–2000* (Penguin, 2001), pp.161–162.
13. Fairclough, A., *Better Day Coming*, p.162.
14. Mershon S. and Schlossman, S., *Foxholes and Color Lines: Desegregating the U.S. Armed Forces* (John Hopkins University Press, 1988), p.8.
15. Equal Justice Initiative, *Lynching in America: Confronting the Legacy of Racial Terror, Third Edition* (Montgomery, Alabama, 2017), https://lynchinginamerica.eji.org/report/ (accessed 25 March 2024).
16. Editorial, 'Can the States Stop Lynching?', *The Crisis*, January 1939, p.9, https://archive.org/details/sim_crisis_1939-01_46_1/page/n7/mode/2up (accessed 23 March 2024).
17. See: Wood, A.L., *Lynching and Spectacle: Witnessing Racial Violence in America, 1890–1940* (University of North Carolina Press, 2009), p.263.
18. Greenberg, C.L. (author), Moore, J.M. and Mjagkij, N. (eds), *To Ask for an Equal Chance: African Americans in the Great Depression* (Rowman & Littlefield, 2011), p.43.
19. Greenberg, *To Ask for an Equal Chance*, p.21.
20. Hart, J.F., 'The Changing Distribution of the American Negro', *Annals of the Association of American Geographers*, vol 50, no 3 (September 1960), pp.242–266.
21. MacGregor, M., *Integration of the Armed Forces; 1940–65* (US Defense Committee, 1979), p.14.
22. Moskos, C., 'From Citizens' Army to Social Laboratory', *The Wilson Quarterly*, 17.1 (winter 1993), p.2.
23. Craf, J.R., 'ASTP', *The Journal of Higher Education*, 14.8 (November 1943), p.15.
24. Moskos, 'Citizens' Army', p.3.
25. See: Palmer, R.R., Bell, I.W. and Keast, W.R., *The Army Ground Forces: The Procurement and Training of Ground Combat*

Troops (Center of Military History, 1991), https://history.army.mil/portals/143/Images/Publications/catalog/2-2.pdf.
26. Schiffman, J. 'The Education of Negro Soldiers in World War II', *The Journal of Negro Education*, vol 18, no 1 (winter, 1949), p.24.
27. Fairclough, *Better Day*, p.167.
28. Finkle, L., 'The Conservative Aims of Militant Rhetoric: Black Protest During World War II', *The Journal of American History*, 60.3 (December 1973), pp.. 692–713.
29. See: Tuskegee Airmen, Lee Rayford, Biography, https://tuskegeeairmen.org/wp-content/uploads/2021/09/Rayford_Lee_TA_Bio.pdf (accessed 24 August 2025).
30. 'The Negro in the American Army', Editorial, *The Crisis*, February 1942, p.47.
31. Ibid.
32. Motley, M.P., *The Invisible Soldier: The Experience of the Black Soldier, World War II* (Wayne State University Press, 1987), p.27.
33. 'Treatment of Negro Soldiers', NARA, RG 498, File: 291.2 Race – Negroes and Colored Troops.
34. 'Our History', NAACP website, https://naacp.org/about/our-history (accessed 1 March 2025).
35. Litwack, L.F., *How Free is Free: The Long Death of Jim Crow* (Harvard University Press, 2009), p.73.
36. Ward, J.M., *Defending White Democracy; The Making of a Segregationist Movement and the Remaking of Racial Politics, 1936–1965* (University of North Carolina Press, 2011), p.46.
37. Huddle, MA (ed), Roi *Ottley's World War II: The Lost Diary of an African American Journalist* (University Press of Kansas Press, 2011), pp.37–38.
38. Padmore, G., 'The Second World War and the Darker Races', *The Crisis*, November 1939, p.327, https://archive.org/details/sim_crisis_1939-11_46_11/page/326/mode/2up (accessed 24 March 2024).
39. See: Sherwood, M., 'Walter White and the British: A Lost Opportunity', *Contributions to Black Studies: A Journal of*

African and Afro-American Studies, vol 9 (1992), pp.216–226, p.216.

40. Lee, U., *The Employment of Negro Troops* (U.S. Army Center of Military History, 2001), p.430.
41. 'American Troops in Britain', BBC Written Archive Centre, File R34/189.
42. Virginia Health Bulletin, 'The New Virginia Law To Preserve Racial Integrity, March 1924', *Document Bank of Virginia*, https://www.lva.virginia.gov/collections/educator-resources/dbva/items/show/226 (accessed 26 November 2024).
43. See: National Constitutional Center, *Loving v Virginia* at https://constitutioncenter.org/the-constitution/supreme-court-case-library/loving-v-virginia (accessed 26 November 2024).
44. See: Roberts, M.L., *What Soldiers Do: Sex and the American GI in World War II France* (University of Chicago Press, 2013); and Lilly, R.J., *Taken By Force: Rape and American GIs in Europe during World War II* (Palgrave Macmillan, 2007).
45. Gavin, J. Personal Diary Entry, 22 February 1944, Gavin Papers, Box 10, Folder 4, U.S. Army Heritage and Education Center.
46. Huddle, M.A. (ed), *Roi Ottley's World War II: The Lost Diary of an African American Journalist* (University of Kansas Press, 2011), p.45.
47. Home Intelligence Report No. 98, 21 August 1942, BBC WAC, File R34/189, American Troops in Britain.
48. See, 'Britain's Brown Babies: Illegitimate tots a tough problem for England', *Ebony* magazine, November 1946, pp. 19–23, https://archive.org/details/sim_ebony_1946-11_2_1/page/19/mode/1up?view=theater, (accessed 25 November 2024).
49. Carswell, J. Johnson, R and Kirrane S., *Ours to Defend; Leicestershire People Remember the Home Front* (Leicester Oral History Archive, 1989), p.58.
50. Letter, 'Coloured', *Leicester Mercury*, 15 February 1943, p.4.
51. Letter, 'Allies', *Leicester Mercury*, 17 February 1943, p.4.
52. 'The Black GI and the Runaway Daughter', *Leicester Mercury*, 22 March 1994.

53. Hazel Rayns, b. 17.2.1926, Interview with author at Gaddesby Leicestershire, 12 June 2024.
54. See Bland, L. and Caballero, C., 'Brown Babies', The National Archives, 2021, https://blog.nationalarchives.gov.uk/brown-babies-second-world-war/ and BBC News, 'How the GI influx shaped Britain's view of Americans', 3 November 2012, https://www.bbc.co.uk/news/magazine-20160819 (both accessed 22 June 2025).
55. Chapman,B.,'ANurseinWartimeLeicester',BBCWW2People's War website, http://www.bbc.co.uk/history/ww2peopleswar/stories/63/a7790763.shtml (accessed 18 June 2025).
56. 'Illegitimate baby births have risen to one in fourteen', *Daily Mirror*, 12 October 1944, p.5.
57. Leicester Corporation Health Report, 1945, p.1, ROLLR, File LG14.
58. Cook, H., *The Long Sexual Revolution: English Women, Sex, and Contraception 1800–1975* (Oxford University Press, 2004), p.103.
59. Leicester Diocesan Moral Welfare Association, Annual Report 1945, ROLLR, file DE6058/11.
60. Moral Welfare Association (Ibid).
61. Moral Welfare Association (Ibid).
62. See, 'Britain's Brown Babies', *Ebony* magazine, November 1946, pp.19–23.
63. See: Bland, L., *Britain's 'Brown Babies': The stories of children born to Black GIs and white women in the Second World War* (Manchester University Press, 2019) for an excellent survey of 'Brown Babies' and their experiences.
64. See: Bland, Lucy, *Britain's 'Brown Babies'*.
65. Jennifer (surname withheld), b. 5 December 1944, Interview with author at Leicester UK, 16 December 2015.
66. See, Bland, L., 'Interracial Relationships and the 'Brown Baby Question': Black GIs, White British Women, and Their Mixed-Race Offspring in World War II', *Journal of the History of Sexuality*, 26.3, 2017.
67. See, 'Britain's Brown Babies', *Ebony* magazine, November 1946.

68. City of Leicester Corporation Health Board, Annual Reports, 1943–1946, ROLLR, File LG 14.
69. Lilly, R.J., *Taken By Force: Rape and American GIs in Europe during World War II* (Palgrave Macmillan, 2007), p.12.
70. Clines, F., 'When Black Soldiers Were Hanged: a War's Footnote', *New York Times*, 7 February 1993.
71. Webb, S., *Fighting for the United States, Executed in Britain: US Soldiers Court-Martialled in WWII* (Pen & Sword, 2021), p.62.
72. See: Webb S., *Fighting for the United States* – Webb details each American execution in England.
73. Roberts, M.L., *What Soldiers Do: Sex and the American GI in World War II France* (University of Chicago Press, 2013), p.199.
74. 'US Army Special Reports 1943', BBC WAC, File R61/41/2.
75. NAACP, 'Black and White Rape', *The Crisis* magazine, July 1944, p.217, https://archive.org/details/sim_crisis_1944-07_51_7/page/217/mode/1up?view=theater (accessed 24 November 2024).
76. Joiner, East Midlands Oral History Archive (EMOHA) Interview.
77. Hannah, A, Oral History Interview, EMOHA, LO/132/038.
78. Crime Figures, City of Leicester Police Records, ROLLR, DE 5491/325.
79. Roberts, M.L., *What Soldiers Do: Sex and the American GI in World War II France* (University of Chicago Press, 2013), p.9.
80. PC Bull, Beat Book, City of Leicester City Records, ROLLR, DE 3831/289.
81. DS Lacy, Daily Journal, City of Leicester Police Records, ROLLR, DE 3831/292.
82. PC Bull, Beat Book.
83. Hazel Rayns, b. 17.2.1926, Interview with author at Gaddesby Leicestershire, 23 July 2024.
84. Huddle, *Roi Ottley's World War II*, p.161.
85. In Smith, H.L., *Britain in the Second World War: A Social History* (Manchester University Press, 1996), p.55.
86. Censorship and American Liaison, MOD, 'D' Notice, 1942. BBC WAC, File R61/41/2.

87. Letters, 'Colour Bar', *Daily Mail*, see: 8th Air Force Command History, 1942–45, File ADM 536, Administrative History Collection, Historical Section, ETOUSA.
88. Ibid.
89. *Daily Sketch*, 'Colour Bar Barred at British Dance', 19 February 1944, see: 8th Air Force Command History, 1942–45, File ADM 536, Administrative History Collection, Historical Section, ETOUSA.
90. See: Walck, P., 'Mutiny at Bamber Bridge: How the World War II Press Reported Racial Unrest among US Troops and Why It Remains in British Memory', *American Journalism*, 37.3 (2020), p.350
91. BBC, 'Listener Research Report, LR/2370', (1943), BBC WAC, File, R9/9/7.
92. Public Relations on Negro Personnel; NARA, RG 498, File: 291.2 Race – Negroes and Colored Troops.
93. Ibid.
94. 'Report on certain factors tending to cause friction between U.S. Troops', December 1943; NARA, RG 498, File: 291.2 Race – Negroes and Colored Troops.
95. 'Leadership of Colored Troops', NARA, RG 498, File: 291.2 Race – Negroes and Colored Troops.
96. Gough, Allison, J. 'Messing Up Another Country's Customs: The Exportation of American Racism During World War II', *World History Connected,* October 2007, http://worldhistoryconnected.press.illinois.edu/5.1/gough.html (accessed 17 May 2025).
97. 'Relations between Colored and White Troops', NARA, RG 498, File: 291.2 Race – Negroes and Colored Troops.
98. See: Werran, K., *An American Uprising in Second World War England: Mutiny in the Duchy* (Pen & Sword, 2020), p.216
99. 'Censorship Report on Inter-racial relations', NARA, RG 498, File: 291.2 Race – Negroes and Colored Troops.
100. Ibid.
101. 8th Air Force Command History; 1942–45, File ADM 536, Administrative History Collection, Historical Section, ETOUSA.

102. Williams, MV, *Medgar Evers: Mississippi Martyr* (University of Arkansas Press, 2011), p.275.
103. 'Eastland Takes Up FEPC Fight', *Tuscaloosa News*, 29 June 1945, p.1.
104. 'AMERICAN VETERANS PROTEST EASTLAND SLUR', *Jackson Advocate*, 14 July 1945, p.1.
105. 'SOMEBODY LIED', *Arkansas State Press*, 13 July 1945, p.1
106. Schiffman, J. 'The Education of Negro Soldiers in World War II', *The Journal of Negro Education* (winter 1949), 18.1, p.22–28, p.24.
107. Latty, *We Were There*, p.31.
108. Latty, *We Were There*, p.31.
109. Milner, Lucille, B., 'Jim Crow in the Army', *New Republic*, 13 March 1944, p.339.

Chapter Three

1. Bland, L., *Britain's 'Brown Babies': The Stories of Children Born to Black GIs and White Women in the Second World War* (Manchester University Press, 2019), p.3.
2. Bristol Junior, D., 'What Can We Learn About World War II From Black Quartermasters?', The National WW2 Museum, New Orleans, August 2021, https://www.nationalww2museum.org/war/articles/world-war-ii-black-quartermasters (accessed 19 January 2024).
3. UnitHistory,1938thQMTruckCompany(Avn),1November1944, US Air Force Historical Research Agency, IRIS 00028887, Reel A0385.
4. See: Mormino, G.R., 'Gi Joe Meets Jim Crow: Racial Violence and Reform in World War II Florida', *The Florida Historical Quarterly,* 73.1 (1994), pp.23–42.
5. Mershon, S. and Schlossman, S., *Foxholes and Color Lines: Desegregating the U.S. Armed Forces* (John Hopkins University Press, 1988), p.139.
6. Mormino, p.24.
7. Mershon and Schlossman, p.139

8. Unit History, 1938th QM Truck Company (Avn), 1 March 1944, US Air Force Historical Research Agency, IRIS 00028882, Reel A0385.
9. See: Evans, J., 'The Origins of Tallahassee's Racial Disturbance Plan: Segregation, Racial Tensions, and Violence During World War II', *The Florida Historical Quarterly*, 79.3 (2000), pp.346–364.
10. Evans, 'Tallahassee', p.354.
11. Farrell, S., 'Not Just Farms Anymore: The Effects of World War II on Mississippi's Economy', Mississippi History Now (2001), https://www.mshistorynow.mdah.ms.gov/issue/the-effects-of-world-war-II-on-mississippis-economy (accessed 30 April 2024).
12. Oral History Transcript, Leroy Reese Collection, Institute on World War II and the Human Experience, Accession number 04.0163, Florida State University.
13. Oral History Interview transcript, Leroy Reece Collection, Institute on WW2 and the Human Experience, Accession No 04.0181, Florida State University.
14. Smith, G., *When Jim Crow Met John Bull, Black Soldiers in World War II Britain* (Tauris, 1987), p.31.
15. Information film, *A Welcome to Britain*, U.S. National Archives You Tube channel, https://www.youtube.com/watch?v=SyYSBBE1DFw (accessed 2 March 2016).
16. Unit History, 1938th QM Truck Company (Avn), 1 March 1944.
17. 'WWII–1943, England: US Army Black Soldiers Jive March Thru Kettering', 1943, Footage Farm 221750, https://footagefarm.com/reel-details/civil-rights/generic/wwii---1943-england--us-army-black-soldiers-jive-march-thru-kettering (accessed 30 March 2024).
18. Tony Smith's Kettering on Facebook, the full Movietone Newsreel film can be found 11 minutes 26 seconds into the film: https://www.facebook.com/watch/?v=1256216676219513 (accessed 7 July 2025).
19. Unit History, 1938th QM Truck Company (Avn), 1 March 1944.
20. Rogerson, D., *The Battle of Bamber Bridge: The True Story* (Purple Parrot, 2022), p.47.

21. Werrell, K., 'Mutiny at Army Air Force Station 569: Bamber Bridge, England, June 1943', *Aerospace Historian*, 22.4 (December 1975), pp.202–209.
22. Werrell, 'Mutiny', p.208.
23. Walck, P., 'Mutiny at Bamber Bridge: How the World War II Press Reported Racial Unrest among U.S. Troops and Why It Remains in British Memory', *American Journalism*, 37.3 (2020), p.347.
24. Walck, 'Mutiny', p.347.
25. Reynolds, D., Rich Relations: The American Occupation of Britain 1942–45 (Phoenix Press, 2000), p.320.
26. JAG, Courts Martial Records, vol 3, p.59, http://www.loc.gov/rr/frd/Military_Law/ETO-Board-of-Review-Decisions.html, (accessed 22 February 2024).
27. Miller, D.L., *Masters of the Air: America's Bomber Boys Who Fought The Air War Against Nazi Germany* (Simon & Schuster, 2006), p.229.
28. Exchange of correspondence, Provost Marshall and Western base Section Commander, 2–7 October 1943, NARA, Negroes and Colored Troops, File RG 498, File: 291.2.
29. Reynolds, *Rich Relations*, p.321.
30. 'General Courts Martial Statistics', European Theatre of Operations (ETO) Administrative History Collection, File 218, Negro Troops.
31. Huddle, MA (ed), *Roi Ottley's World War II: The Lost Diary of an African American Journalist* (University Kansas Press, 2011), p.100.
32. Huddle, *Ottley*, p.161.
33. ETO, Court Martial Review of Opinions, Judge Advocate General, ETO, USA v Forester and Bryant, 20 June 1944, pp.11–22, https://tile.loc.gov/storage-services/service/ll/llmlp/ETO-BOR_Vol-6/ETO-BOR_Vol-6.pdf (accessed 20 April 2025).
34. Reynolds, *Rich Relations*, p.110.
35. Freeman, R., *The Friendly Invasion* (Lavenham Press, 1992), p.58.
36. Longmate, N., *The G.I.'s: The Americans in Britain, 1942-1945* (Hutchinson of London, 1975), p.130.

37. Reynolds, *Rich Relations*, p.306.
38. 'American Red Cross', ETO Historical Section, File ADM 20A, p.37.
39. Reynolds, *Rich Relations*, p.310.
40. Cross, G., 'African Americans in Suffolk', The Friendly Invasion: Conflict and Commemoration website, www.8thaf.co.uk, 2024 (accessed 4 November 2024).
41. Millgate, H.D., *Got Any Gum Chum? GIs in Wartime Britain, 1942–1945* (The History Press, 2009), p.70.
42. Longmate, *The G.I.'s*, p.132.
43. Longmate, *The G.I.'s*, p.134.
44. Smith, G., *When Jim Crow Met John Bull: Black American Soldiers in World War II Britain* (Tauris, 1987), p.145.
45. Wakelin, A, 'The black GI and the runaway daughter', *Leicester Mercury,* 22 March 2004.
46. *Melton Times,* 'Hard Labour for Leicester Girls: Escapades with Coloured Soldiers', 25 June 1943.
47. *Melton Times*, 'Girls Found in Fields', 21 April 1944.
48. Letter to Chief of Staff Western Base Section from Deputy Theatre Provost Marshall, 7 December 1943, File 291.2, Race – Negroes and Colored Troops, NARA, RG 498.
49. Byrne, E., *Bristol Post*, 'Love, Jealousy and Riots: How Bristol welcomed the US army during WW2', 23 June 2019, https://www.bristolpost.co.uk/news/bristol-news/love-jealousy-riots-how-bristol-3006514, (accessed 11 March 2024).
50. See: Smith, *When Jim Crow Met John Bull*, pp.145–147.
51. Unit History, 1938th QM Truck Company (Avn), 1 April 1944, US Air Force Historical Research Agency, IRIS 00028883, Reel A0385.
52. Sullivan, C., 'Tiger Bay Blues', *The Chap*, 12 November 2020, https://thechap.co.uk/tiger-bay-blues/ (accessed 19 June 2025).
53. Sullivan, Lt G.A., Finding of Facts, USA v McKenna and Ritchie, John L. Hendricks Personnel File, US Military Personnel Records (Terry Harrison Personal Archive).
54. Walker, W., Court Martial Testimony, USA v McKenna and Ritchie, John L. Hendricks Personnel File, US Military Personnel Records (Terry Harrison Personal Archive).

55. Hill, C., Court Martial Testimony, USA v McKenna and Ritchie, John L. Hendricks Personnel File, US Military Personnel Records (Terry Harrison Personal Archive).
56. Sullivan, Lt G.A., Finding of Facts, USA v McKenna and Ritchie, John L. Hendricks Personnel File, US Military Personnel Records (Terry Harrison Personal Archive).
57. Walker, Testimony.
58. Calloway, R., Court Martial Testimony, USA v McKenna and Ritchie, John L. Hendricks Personnel File, US Military Personnel Records (Terry Harrison Personal Archive).
59. Carter, L., Court Martial Testimony, USA v McKenna and Ritchie, John L. Hendricks Personnel File, US Military Personnel Records (Terry Harrison Personal Archive).
60. Memorandum from Provost Marshall to Commander Services of Supply, ETO, 23 December 1943, NARA, Race – Negroes and Colored Troops, RG 498, File: 291.2.
61. Hill, Testimony.
62. Walker, Testimony.
63. Questions to Stanley N. Ritchie, USA v McKenna and Hardy, John L. Hendricks Personnel File, US Military Personnel Records (Terry Harrison Personal Archive).
64. Finding of Facts, USA v McKenna and Ritchie, John L. Hendricks Personnel File, US Military Personnel Records (Terry Harrison Personal Archive).
65. Terry Harrison Interview in *Terry's GI Dad*, a feature documentary on the search for his father. See https://local-colour.co.uk/Terrysgidad (accessed 7 July 2025).
66. Unit History, 1938th QM Truck Company (Avn), 1 May 1944, US Air Force Historical Research Agency, IRIS 00028884, Reel A0385.
67. Unit History, 1938th QM Truck Company (Avn), 1 May 1944.
68. Unit History, 1938th QM Truck Company (Avn), 1 May 1944.
69. Correspondence to the parents of John Hendricks, John L. Hendricks Personnel File, US Military Personnel Records (Terry Harrison Personal Archive).
70. Ibid.

71. Ibid.
72. Quoted in Smith, *When Jim Crow Met John Bull*, p.130.
73. Unit History, 1938th QM Truck Company (Avn), 1 July 1944, US Air Force Historical Research Agency, IRIS 00028885, Reel A0385.
74. Unit History, 1938th QM Truck Company (Avn), 1 July 1944.
75. Unit History, 1938th QM Truck Company (Avn), 1 September 1944, US Air Force Historical Research Agency, IRIS 00028886, Reel A0385.
76. Unit History, 1938th QM Truck Company (Avn), 1 October 1944, US Air Force Historical Research Agency, IRIS 00028888, Reel A0385.
77. Unit History, 1938th QM Truck Company (Avn), 1 September 1944.
78. Unit History, 1938th QM Truck Company (Avn), 1 January 1945, US Air Force Historical Research Agency, IRIS 00028889, Reel A0385.
79. Court Martial, ETO, 4550, Jones & Moore, ETO Board of Review Opinions, vols 13–15, pp.27–35, https://tile.loc.gov/storage-services/service/ll/llmlp/ETO-BOR_Vol-13/ETO-BOR_Vol-13.pdf (accessed 22 February 2024).
80. Jones & Moore, CM Review, p.33.
81. Jones & Moore, CM Review, p.29.
82. Jones & Moore, CM Review, p.35.
83. Unit History, 1938th QM Truck Company (Avn), 1 April 1945, US Air Force Historical Research Agency, IRIS 00028893, Reel A0385.
84. American Battle Monuments Commission website, https://www.abmc.gov (accessed 19 June 2025).
85. Unit History, 1938th QM Truck Company (Avn), 1 May 1944, US Air Force Historical Research Agency, IRIS 00028894, Reel A0385.
86. Unit History, 1938th QM Truck Company (Avn), 1 October 1945, US Air Force Historical Research Agency, IRIS 00028899, Reel A0385.
87. See: Meier, A and Bracey, J.H., 'The NAACP as a Reform Movement, 1909–1965: 'To Reach the Conscience of America',

The Journal of Southern History, 59.1 (February 1993), pp.3–30.

88. See: Bristol, D.W. and Stur, H.M. (eds), *Integrating the US Military: Race, Gender, and Sexual Orientation Since World War II* (John Hopkins University Press, Baltimore: 2017).
89. Carter Farms website, https://thecarterfarms.com (accessed 5 November 2024).
90. Montalvo, S., 'Carter Farms: A Growing Agent of Change in the state of Virginia', *Vinegar Hill Magazine*, https://vinegarhillmagazine.com/carter-farms-a-growing-agent-of-change-in-the-state-of-virginia/ (accessed 5 November 2024).
91. Osur, Alan M., 'Blacks in the Army Air Forces During World War II: The Problem of Race Relations' (Office of Air Force History, 1977), https://apps.dtic.mil/sti/tr/pdf/ADA036585.pdf (accessed 19 June 2025).

Chapter Four

1. Ruddy, A.J., *To the Last Round: The Leicestershire and Rutland Home Guard 1940–1945* (Breedon Books, 2007), p.70.
2. Reynolds, D., *Rich Relations: The American Occupation of Britain 1942–45* (Phoenix Press, 2000), p.227.
3. Holyoak, V., *But for These Things: Leicester and its people in WWII* (Matador, 2014), p.187.
4. 8th Air Force Command History, 1942–45, File ADM 536, Administrative History Collection, Historical Section, ETOUSA, pp.9–11; 9th Air Force History, NARA, RG 498, File: 291.2 Race – Negroes and Colored Troops, p.7.
5. Reynolds, *Rich Relations*, p.110.
6. Reynolds, *Rich Relations*, p.111.
7. Wills, D., *Put on Your Boots and Parachutes! The United States 82nd Airborne Division* (Deryk Wills, 1992), p.41.
8. Personal Archive, Kevin Madelin, Gaddesby, Leicestershire, viewed 12 June 2024.
9. Longmate, N., *The G.I.'s: The Americans in Britain 1942–45* (Hutchinson of London, 1975), p.117.

10. Nash, D. and Reader, D., *Leicester in the Twentieth Century* (Alan Sutton Publishing, 1993), p.184.
11. Peake, T., Oral History Interview, EMOHA (East Midlands Oral History Archive), 901 LO/080/032.
12. Peake, T., Oral History Interview.
13. Pat Pickering, b. 26 April 1931, Interview with author, Leicester, UK, 3 May 2016.
14. Michael Dally, b. 18 February 1934, Interview with author, Leicester, UK, 3 May 2016.
15. OHI, Dally, M.
16. Reynolds, *Rich Relations*, p.310.
17. Ibid.
18. Ibid.
19. See: Holyoak, V., *But for These Things: Leicester and its people in WWII* (Matador, 2014), p.178.
20. Hurst, Tony, East Midlands Oral History Archive, Accession Number, EMOHA38/121.
21. Police Superintendent May, 'Weekly Report No. 6.', NARA, RG 498, File: 291.2 Race – Negroes and Colored Troops.
22. For example, PC Bull, Beat Book, City of Leicester Police, ROLLR, DE 3831/289.
23. Oral History Interview with Kenneth West Affective Digital Histories: Re-creating Britain's De-industrial Places, 1970s to the Present, Oral History, http://cdm16445.contentdm.oclc.org/cdm/ref/collection/p16445coll8/id/224 (accessed 29 May 2025).
24. Wartime Flashbacks, *Leicester Mercury*, 14 September 1964, *Leicester Mercury* Archives, University of Leicester Special Collections.
25. Wartime Flashbacks, *Leicester Mercury*.
26. Police Committee Minutes, January 1944, City of Leicester Police Records, ROLLR, DE 3831/13.
27. Beazley, B., Peelers to Pandas: An illustrated History of the Leicester City Police (Breedon Books: 2001), p.153.
28. Martin, H.M., *Soldier: The Memoirs of Matthew B. Ridgway* (Harper & Brothers, 1956), pp.99–100.

29. Knotts, K.I., Photograph Collection and White Album, US Army Heritage and Education Center, File RG 886S, p.38.
30. Gavin, J., Personal Diary Entry, 22 February 1944, Gavin Papers, Box 10, Folder 4, US Army Heritage and Education Center.
31. LoFaro, G., *The Sword of St. Michael: The 82nd Airborne Division in World War II* (De Capo, 2011), p.15.
32. LoFaro, *The Sword of St. Michael*, p.27.
33. 'Weekly Report No. 6': NARA, RG 498, File: 291.2 Race – Negroes and Colored Troops.
34. Gavin, J., Personal Diary Entry, 22 February 1944, Gavin Papers.
35. Gavin, Diary Entry.
36. May, 'Weekly Report No. 6' (Ibid).
37. Ibid.
38. Unpublished Interview with Home Guard Ray Elgood by Austin Ruddy, *Leicester Mercury*, 14 December 2003. Copy obtained from Austin Ruddy.
39. Ibid.
40. Shute, N., *The Chequer Board* (Heinemann, 1947), p.191.
41. Library of Congress, ETO Court Martial Records, https://www.loc.gov/collections/military-legal-resources/?q=court+martial+eto (accessed 12 July 2024).
42. May, 'Weekly Report No. 6'.
43. Gavin, J., Personal Diary Entry.
44. Ridgway, *Memoirs*, p.100.
45. Wills, D., *Put on Your Boots*.
46. Guidry, P.F., *Treasures in My Heart: A true WWII love story* (iUniverse, 2004), p.237.
47. Wills, *Put on Your Boots*, p.41.
48. Bennett, G.H., *Destination Normandy; Three American Regiments on D-Day* (Stackpole Books, 2007), p.47.
49. Covais, J.S., *Battery! C. Lenton Sartain and the Airborne G.I.s of the 319th Glider Field Artillery* (Create Space, 2010), p.188.
50. Ibid.
51. Ibid, p.189.
52. Ibid.

53. 8th Air Force Command History, 1942–45, File ADM 536, Administrative History Collection, Historical Section, ETOUSA, pp.9–11
54. Ridgway, *Memoirs*, p.100.
55. 1514th Battalion Quartermaster Headquarters Unit History, Iris 00028294, Reel AO 383, US Army Heritage and Education Center.
56. 1946th Quartermaster Truck Company (Aviation), Iris 00028970, Reel AO 385, US Army Heritage and Education Center.
57. 2034th Quartermaster Truck Company (Aviation), Iris 00029961, Reel AO 390, US Army Heritage and Education Center.
58. Freda Parker, b. 1 August 1926, Interview with author, Leicester, UK, 12 April 2016.
59. 'MIDLANDS FRACAS: TWO U.S. SOLDIERS DIE', *Leicester Evening Mail*, 2 May 1944, p.1.
60. 'U.S. Army Policeman killed in Leicester', *Leicester Mercury*, 3 May, 1944, p.1.
61. Alan Boot, b. 31 January 1928, Interview with author, Leicester, UK, 4 July 2014.
62. Holyoak, V., But for These Things.
63. Berry, A., *And Suddenly They Were Gone: An Oral and Pictorial History of The 82d Airborne Division in England, February – September 1944* (Overlord, 2015), p.24.
64. 9th Air Force History, NARA.
65. Hazel Rayns, b. 17.2.1926, Interview with author at Gaddesby, Leicestershire, 23 July 2024.
66. 2056th QM Truck Company (Aviation) Unit History, Iris 00030216, ReelA0390; 2057th QM Truck Company (Aviation) Unit History, Iris 00030223, ReelA0390.
67. See, LoFaro, *The Sword of St. Michael*, p.263.
68. See, Braunstone History Group Facebook Page, https://www.facebook.com/groups/381469573645481/posts/851378166654617/ (accessed 29 May 2025).
69. Huddle, M.A. (ed), *Roi Ottley's World War II; The Lost Diary of an African American Jou*rnalist (University of Kansas Press, 2011), p.103.

70. Nordyke, P., *All American All the Way: The Combat History of the 82nd Airborne Division in World War II* (Zenith, 2005), p.409.
71. Nordyke, *All American All the Way*, p.411.
72. 'Coloured Soldier on knife charges', *Leicester Mercury*, 8 September 1944, p.5
73. 'U.S. Court-Martial: Coloured Soldier on Knife Charges', *Leicester Evening Mail*, 9 September, p.4.
74. 'US Soldier Drowned at Leicester', *Leicester Mercury*, 11 September 1944, p.6.
75. 'American's Body in Leicester Canal', *Leicester Evening Mail*, 11 September, 1944, p.1.
76. Ward, J.M., *Defending White Democracy: The Making of a Segregationist Movement and the Remaking of Racial Politics, 1936–1965* (University of North Carolina Press, 2011), p.47.
77. Werran, K., *An American Uprising in Second World War England: Mutiny in the Duchy* (Pen & Sword, 2020), p.7.
78. 'COSY SPOT WHILE WAITING FOR TRAINS', *Illustrated Leicester Chronicle*, 12 February 1944, p.1.
79. 'American Red Cross Centres', ETO Historical Section, File ADM 20A, p.37.
80. 'This American Red Cross Centre in London is Strictly Jim Crow', *The Crisis*, March 1943, pp.76–77.
81. 'THIS SURE LOOKS LIKE HOME FROM HOME', *Illustrated Leicester Chronicle*, 5 February 1944, p.1.
82. 'American Red Cross Centres', ETO Historical Section, File ADM 20A., p.37.
83. 'American Forces Chaplain's Visit', *Illustrated Leicester Chronicle*, 1 April 1944, p.4.
84. *Illustrated Leicester Chronicle*, 22 April 1944.
85. 'Americans Tour Charnwood Monastery', *Illustrated Leicester Chronicle*, 6 May 1944, p.4.
86. *Illustrated Leicester Chronicle*.
87. *Roi Ottley's World War II*, p.103.
88. Holyoak, *But for These Things*, p.193.
89. Holyoak, *But for These Things*, p.196.

90. Letter from Adrian Turner, grandson of Elsie May Turner, landlady of the Dixie Arms to the author.
91. Wakelin, A., 'The Secret War on Our Streets', *Leicester Mercury*, 24 March 2004.

Chapter Five

1. See: Piehler, G.K., *A Religious History of the American GI in World War II* (University of Nebraska Press, 2021), pp.18–19.
2. Gordon, LA., 'Mahatma Gandhi's Dialogues with Americans', *Economic and Political Weekly*, 37.4 (26 January – 1 February, 2002), pp.337–352, p.342.
3. See: Heltzel, P.G., 'Building the Beloved City: Howard Thurman and Martin Luther King Jr.', in *Resurrection City: A Theology of Improvisation* (William B Eerdmans Publishing Company, 2012).
4. Correspondence with author from Edward Carroll Junior, October 2024.
5. Carroll, E.G., 'Building a Great Methodist Society: Reflections on Unification', *Zion Herald*, 24 March 1937, p.367.
6. Washington Conference of the Methodist Episcopal Church, Minutes of the 50th Session, 1913, p.52, Carroll Family Archive.
7. Washington Conference of the Methodist Episcopal Church, p.52.
8. *Ebony* magazine, 'The Flying Preacher: Washington Minister has a private plane', February 1961, pp.52–56, https://books.google.co.uk/books?id=9GTDhY-D20UC&pg=PA54&dq=Edward+Carroll&hl=en&sa=X&ved=2ahUKEwiE_vSanLWOAxVvV0EAHZldHqIQuwV6BAgJEAc#v=onepage&q=Edward%20Carroll&f=false (accessed 11 July 2025).
9. Edward Carroll Honorary Degree citation, Barrington College, Rhode Island, 19 May 1979, Carroll Family Archive.
10. Gordon, LA., 'Mahatma Gandhi's Dialogues with Americans', p.341.
11. Gordon, LA., 'Mahatma Gandhi's Dialogues with Americans', p.340.

12. See: Slate, N., 'The drama of nonviolence: Theatre as education in the American civil rights movement', *Ride: The Journal of Applied Theatre and Performance* (2022), 27.1, pp.73–87.
13. King, M.L. Junior, *Stride Toward Freedom: The Montgomery Story* (Harper & Row, 1958), p.67.
14. Davis, M.L., *The Methodist Unification: Christianity and the Politics of Race in the Jim Crow Era* (New York University Press, New York, 2008), p.1.
15. Davis, *The Methodist Unification*, p.1.
16. Carroll, E.G., 'Building a Great Methodist Society: Reflections on Unification', *Zion Herald*, 24 March 1937, p.366.
17. Carrol, *Zion Herald*, p.366.
18. Captain Reverend Edward Carroll, Research notes for Fern Babcock Grant, Carroll Family Archive.
19. Honorary Degree citation, Barrington College, Spencer, Massachusetts, 1979, Carroll Family Archive.
20. White, George Junior, '"I Am Teaching Some of The Boys:" Chaplain Robert Boston Dokes and Army Testing of Black Soldiers in World War II', The Journal of Negro Education, 81.3 (Summer 2012), pp.200–217, p.206.
21. White, 'Army Testing of Black Soldiers', p.214.
22. Piehler, G.K., *A Religious History of the American GI in World War II* (University of Nebraska Press, 2016), pp.12–18.
23. Moskos, C., 'From Citizens' Army to Social Laboratory', *The Wilson Quarterly (1976–),* 17.1 (winter 1993), pp.83–94.
24. See the Alaska Highway website of the Government of Canada, https://www.canada.ca/en/public-services-procurement/services/infrastructure-buildings/bridges-docks-dams/alaska-highway.html (accessed 25 August 2025).
25. 'Alcan Highway: Rendezvous '92', *Florida Constructor*, May/June 1990, p.22, Carroll Family Archive.
26. Letter, Carroll to his wife, 24 March 1942.
27. For example, see: 'A Nation's 'Call To The Wild'', *Teaching Equity*, 4.5, February 1992, Carroll Family Archive.
28. 'A Nation's 'Call To The Wild''.

29. Dean, C., 'In Road-Building, Black Soldiers Defied Prejudice', *New York Times*, 23 July 2012.
30. US Congress, Congressional Record – House, 17 February 2005, H757 https://www.congress.gov/109/crec/2005/02/17/CREC-2005-02-17-pt1-PgH756-4.pdf
31. Letter from Captain Carroll in Alaska to his wife, 24 March 1942, Carroll Family Archive.
32. Letter, Carroll to his wife, 24 March 1942.
33. Letter, Carroll to his wife, 24 March 1942.
34. Bauer, A. and Bauer, A.H., 'Day to Day Resistance to Slavery', *The Journal of Negro History*, 27.4 (October 1942), pp.401–402.
35. See: Bauer, A. and Bauer, A.H., 'Day to Day Resistance to Slavery', pp.388–419.
36. See: Kelly, R., '"We Are Not What We Seem": Rethinking Black Working-Class Opposition in the Jim Crow South', *The Journal of American History*, 80.1 (June 1993), pp.75–112.
37. 'Memorandum for the Chief of Staff regarding Employment of Negro Man Power in War, November 10, 1925', President's Official Files 4245-G: Office of Production Management: Commission on Fair Employment Practices: War Department, 1943; Archives of the Franklin D. Roosevelt Library. Cited in U.S. Army War College, 'The Army War College Studies Black Soldiers,' *SHEC: Resources for Teachers*, https://shec.ashp.cuny.edu/items/show/808 (accessed 18 April 2025).
38. Letter from Capt. Carroll in Alaska to his wife, 24 March 1942, Carroll Family Archive.
39. See the notes of Allan Morrison, a former *Stars and Stripes* reporter, in Roberts, M.L., *What Soldiers Do: Sex and the American GI in World War II France* (Chicago University Press, Chicago: 2013), p.208.
40. Lilly, R.J., *Taken By Force: Rape and American GIs in Europe during World War II* (Palgrave Macmillan, 2007), pp.6–9.
41. Letter, Carroll to his wife, 24 March 1942.
42. Certificate of Service, Carroll, Edward G., 23 July 1945, Carroll Family Archive.

43. Bradley, S., *Photo History of the Black 95th Engineer General Service Regiment in World War II: vol 2*, (Railway Station Press, Virginia, 2017), p.3.
44. Edward Carroll, Personal Memoir, Carroll Family Archive.
45. See: 'The Liverpool Blitz', The Imperial War Museum, https://www.iwm.org.uk/history/the-liverpool-blitz (accessed 31 March 2025).
46. Edward Carroll, Letter to his parents, 14 December 1943, 'Activities of Chaplain', 'Exhibit B', Intercepted Letter, NARA, RG 498, File: 291.2 Race – Negroes and Colored Troops.
47. Letter from Phenola Carroll in Washington to Captain Carroll, 10 October 1943, Carroll Family Archive.
48. Letter from Phenola Carroll in Washington to Captain Carroll, 10 October 1943, Carroll Family Archive.
49. Photograph of the Jersey Beach Hotel, Ridley Photographic Collection (1966), Library of Wales, https://archives.library.wales/index.php/jersey-beach-hotel-port-talbot (accessed 27 March 2025).
50. 'Activities of Chaplain', 'Exhibit A', Capt. John A. Welsh Witness Statement, NARA, RG 498, File: 291.2 Race – Negroes and Colored Troops.
51. 'Activities of Chaplain', Capt. John A. Welsh Witness Statement.
52. 'Activities of Chaplain', Capt. John A. Welsh Witness Statement.
53. 'Activities of Chaplain', Capt. John A. Welsh Witness Statement.
54. 'Activities of Chaplain', Capt. John A. Welsh Witness Statement.
55. Edward Carroll, Letter to his parents, 14 December 1943, 'Activities of Chaplain', 'Exhibit B'.
56. Letter from J.B. Allison, Port Intelligence Officer to Chief of Training & Security, SOS, APO 871, US Army, 'Activities of Chaplain', 21 December 1943, NARA, RG 498, File: 291.2 Race – Negroes and Colored Troops.
57. Letter from J.B. Allison, Port Intelligence Officer to Chief of Training & Security, SOS, APO 871.
58. Letter from J.B. Allison, Port Intelligence Officer to Chief of Training & Security, SOS, APO 871.

59. Letter from J.B. Allison, Port Intelligence Officer to Chief of Training & Security, SOS, APO 871.
60. Letter from J.B. Allison, Port Intelligence Officer to Chief of Training & Security, SOS, APO 871.
61. Edward Carroll, Personal Memoir, Carroll Family Archive.
62. Letter from Reverend Bannister, P.E., Mumbles Methodist Church, to Reverend Carroll, 17 January 1944, Carroll Family Archive c/o of Edward Carroll Junior.
63. Letter from H & S Company, 95th Engineers to Reverend Carroll, 2 March 1944, Carrol Family Archive.
64. Letter from H & S Company, 95th Engineers to Reverend Carroll.
65. Letter from Betty and Wyndham of Morriston, Wales to Edward, 4 March 1944, Carroll Family Archive.
66. Correspondence between Author and Edward Carroll Junior, 30 December 2023.
67. For example, see the story of the African American 320th Barrage Balloon Battalion in Hervieux, L., *Forgotten: The Untold Story of D-Day's Black Heroes, At Home and At War* (HarperCollins, 2015).
68. Newspaper Report, 'Chaplain Death Toll is 24; 3,400 Serving Overseas', *Stars & Stripes*, 31 July 1944.
69. Carroll, Reverend, Edward, Personal Memoir, Carroll Family Archive.
70. Carroll, Reverend, Edward, Personal Memoir.
71. Carroll, Reverend, Edward, Personal Memoir.
72. Carroll, Reverend, Edward, Personal Memoir.
73. Rubin, N., 'D-Day 75 years later: You didn't have to shoot a rifle to shape history', *The Detroit News*, 6 June 2019, https://eu.detroitnews.com/story/news/local/detroit-city/2019/06/06/d-day-75-years-allied-soldiers-normandy/1339002001/ (accessed 8 April 2025).
74. Rubin, N., 'D-Day 75 years later', *The Detroit News.*
75. Carroll, Reverend, Edward, Personal Memoir.
76. Captain Reverend Edward Carroll, Research notes for Fern Babcock Grant, Carroll Family Archive.
77. Carroll, Research Notes.

78. For more on the WW2 German chaplains, see: Bergen, D.L., *Between God and Hitler: Military Chaplains in Nazi Germany* (Cambridge University Press, 2023).
79. Report on the 'The Army Chaplain in the European Theatre', General Board, US Forces, European Theatre 1946, p.13, https://mcoecbamcoepwprd01.blob.core.usgovcloudapi.net/library/Documents/Hardcopy/paper/D731.1_E8_No.68.pdf (accessed 7 July 2025).
80. Captain Reverend Edward Carroll, Certificate of Service, US Army, 23 July 1943, Carroll Family Archive.
81. See: Biondi, M., 'How New York changes the story of the Civil Rights Movement', *Afro-Americans in New York Life and History* (2007), 31.2.
82. See: Yale University Online Exhibitions, 'Early Black Students at Yale', Edward Gonzales Carroll, https://onlineexhibits.library.yale.edu/s/early-black-yale-students/item/20534#?cv=&c=&m=&s=&xywh=0%2C0%2C499%2C499 (accessed 1 May 2025).
83. See: Massey, M., 'Morgan State students played prominent Civil Rights role with sit-down protests', *CBS News*, 8 February 2023, https://www.cbsnews.com/baltimore/news/morgan-state-students-played-prominent-civil-rights-role-with-sit-down-protests/ (accessed 2 May 2025).
84. For example, see: '500 attend Methodist Conference in city', *Baltimore Afro-American*, 18 February 1961, p.7, https://msa.maryland.gov/megafile/ecpdata/webroot/msaref14/msa_sc5458_000045_000295/pdf/msa_afro_1961_01-0071.pdf (accessed 2 May 2025).
85. See: '101,777 Registered: Hail Register To-Vote Drive As Success In Baltimore', *Baltimore Afro-American*, 27 September 1958, p.1, https://msa.maryland.gov/megafile/ehttps://bostonlocaltv.org/catalog/V_C0PBOB24Q4SS72M (accessed 13 February 2025). cpdata/webroot/msaref14/msa_sc5458_000045_000250/pdf/msa_afro_1958_01_bc_late_edition-0566.pdf (accessed 2 May 2025).
86. See: Guzmán, S., 'A Quiet Force for Change', *Meetinghouse* magazine, Summer 2021, pp.15–19, https://issuu.com/

friendsseminary/docs/meetinghouse_summer21/16 (accessed 1 May 2025).

87. Husock, H., 'Boston: The Problem That Won't Go Away', *The New York Times*, 25 November 1979, p.8, https://www.nytimes.com/1979/11/25/archives/boston-the-problem-that-wont-go-away-boston.html#:~:text=Although%20they%20make%20up%20only,of%20racial%20tension%20on%20Boston (accessed 13 February 2025).
88. WGBH Boston, 'Clergy Plead For Racial Peace', *Ten O'Clock News*, Broadcast 29 October 1979,
89. See: Letter from Edward G. Carroll, former Bishop of the Boston Area United Methodist Church, to John D. O'Bryant, Boston School Committee member, 30 October 1980, https://openarchives.umb.edu/digital/collection/p15774coll33/id/72/ (accessed 6 May 2025).
90. Hervieux, L., *Forgotten*, p.5.

Chapter Six

1. See; Zeiger, S., *Entangling Alliances: Foreign War Brides and American Soldiers in the Twentieth Century* (New York University Press, 2010).
2. See Virden, J. *Good-bye, Piccadilly: British War Brides in America* (Urbarna: University of Illinois Press, 1996).
3. Edmead, P., 'Time On My Hands', Personal Memoir, Edmead Family Archive.
4. Marriage Certificate, Louis Edmead and Patricia Venn, 12 April 1947, Edmead Family Archive.
5. Patricia Edmead Memoir.
6. See: Todd, S., 'Poverty and Aspiration: Young Women's Entry to Employment in Inter-war England', *Twentieth Century British History*, 15.2, pp.119–142.
7. Patricia Edmead Memoir.
8. Brooklyn Historical Society, *Caribbean Immigrants in Brooklyn: an American story* (New York University Press, 2014), p.15, https://static.bklynlibrary.org/prod/public/documents/brooklyn-

collection/connections/PS%20233%202017%20Young%20 Scholars1.pdf (accessed 25 August 2025).
9. Marriage Certificate, Louis Edmead and Patricia Venn.
10. New York Evening College Certificate, Edmead Family Archive.
11. See: Aiello, T., '"Not Too Far Removed From Slavery": Police Brutality and Rights Activism in Valdosta, Georgia, 1945–55', *Journal of Civil and Human Rights*, 5.2 (2019), pp.34–67.
12. US Army Discharge Papers, Louis Edmead, 14 November 1945, Edmead Family Archive.
13. Penny, J. Luftwaffe Operations Over Bristol: 1940/1944, Bristol Branch of the Historical Association, 1995, p.1, https://bristolha.wordpress.com/wp-content/uploads/2019/09/bha085.pdf (accessed 21 February 2025).
14. Penny, Luftwaffe Operations over Bristol, p.1.
15. Postans, A, 'World War II bomb experts to oversee Premier Inn demolition amid fears of unexploded devices', *Bristol Post*, 25 October 2024, https://www.bristolpost.co.uk/news/bristol-news/world-war-ii-bomb-experts-9661425 (accessed 22 January 2025).
16. Patricia Edmead Memoir.
17. Patricia Edmead Memoir.
18. Unit History, 1944th QM Truck Company (Avn), January 1942 – September 1944, US Air Force Historical Research Agency, IRIS 00028950.
19. Dresser, M and Fleming, P., *Bristol: Ethnic Minorities and the City 1000-2001* (Phillimore, 2007), p.135.
20. See: Richardson, D., *The Bristol Slave Traders: A Collective Portrait* (Bristol Historical Association, 1985).
21. See: Chapter 3, 'For Blacks or Dogs', in Olusoga, D., *Black and British: A Forgotten History* (Macmillan, 2016).
22. Dresser and Fleming, *Bristol: Ethnic Minorities*, p.136.
23. Edmead, P., 'A Wartime Sunday', BBC WW2 People's War contribution, 22 August 2005, https://www.bbc.co.uk/history/ww2peopleswar/stories/12/a5258612.shtml (accessed 28 January 2025).

24. Wynn, NA, '"Race War": Black Americans and West Indians in Britain During the Second World War', *Immigrants & Minorities*, 24.3, November 2006, pp.324–346.
25. Edmead, P., 'Time On My Hands', a personal family memoir, courtesy of Kerry Edmead (son).
26. Edmead, P., BBC WW2 People's War, 2005.
27. For a contemporary view of Black GIs and the jitterbug and British women, see: 'Britain's Brown Babies: Illegitimate tots a tough problem for England', *Ebony*, November 1946, pp.19–23, https://archive.org/details/sim_ebony_1946-11_2_1/page/19/mode/1up?view=theater (accessed 25 November 2024).
28. Romano, R.C., *Race Mixing: Black-White Marriage in Postwar America* (Harvard University Press, 2003), p.24.
29. Letter from the Base Censor Office No 4, APO 871, US Army Special Report on Negro Troops, 1-15 March 1944, NARA, RG 498, File: 291.2 Race – Negroes and Colored Troops.
30. Base Censor Office No 4, APO 871, US Army Special Report on Negro Troops, 1-15 March 1944, Letter from an officer in the 999 QM Salvage Collection Company, APO 230 (Bristol, England) March 1942, NARA, RG 498, File: 291.2 Race – Negroes and Colored Troops.
31. Bristol local quoted in Reynolds, D., *Rich Relations: The American Occupation of Britain, 1942–1945* (Phoenix Press, 2000), p.311.
32. See the *Chicago Defender* advertisement, 'America's Hard-Hitting Columnists', *The Crisis*, August 1943, p 226.
33. Hachey, T., 'Walter White and the American Negro Soldier in World War II: A Diplomatic Dilemma for Britain', *Phylon*, 39.3 (1978), pp.241–249, p.246.
34. Byrne, E., 'Love, Jealousy and Riots: How Bristol welcomed the Americans during WW2', Bristol Post, 23 June 2019, https://www.bristolpost.co.uk/news/bristol-news/love-jealousy-riots-how-bristol-3006514 (accessed 24 January 2024).
35. 'Children Entertained', *Western Daily Press*, 20 October 1943, featured in the Yanks in Bristol website, https://yanksinbristol.co.uk/bristolian-us-relations/ (accessed 6 February 2025).

36. Olusoga, *Black and British*, p.479.
37. Letter from Louis to Patricia, 17 May 1944, Edmead Family Archive.
38. Wynn, N.A., '"Race War": Black American GIs in Bristol and Gloucestershire During World War II', *Bristol Radical Pamphleteer No 7* (Bristol Radical History Group, 2008), p.9.
39. Wynn,NA, 'Race War', (2008), p.11.
40. 'Army Not Yet Content With Bristol Probe', *Jackson Advocate*, 26 August 1944, p.6.
41. Reynolds, *Rich Relations*, pp.310–311.
42. Patricia Edmead, Memoir.
43. Patricia Edmead, Memoir.
44. Patricia Edmead, Memoir.
45. Letter from Louis to Patricia, 1 September 1943, Edmead Family Archive.
46. Rose, SO, 'Sex, Citizenship, and the Nation in World War II Britain', *The American Historical Review*, 103.4 (1998), pp.1147–1176, p.1152.
47. Byrne, E., 'Love, Jealousy and Riots: How Bristol Welcomed the Americans during WW2', *Bristol Post*, 23 June 2019, https://www.bristolpost.co.uk/news/bristol-news/love-jealousy-riots-how-bristol-3006514 (accessed 19 June 2025).
48. Byrne, E., 'Love, Jealousy and Riots' (2019).
49. MacInnes, C.M., *Bristol at War* (London Museum Press, 1962), pp.162–163.
50. MacInnes, *Bristol at War*, p.163.
51. See, 'Vicar's Wife Insults Our Allies', *Sunday Pictorial*, 6 September 1942, from the Yanks in Bristol website, https://yanksinbristol.co.uk/bristolian-us-relations/ (accessed 6 February 2024).
52. 1944th Unit History, January 42 – September 1944.
53. Letter from Louis Edmead to Patricia Venn, 1944 (postmark smudged), Edmead Family Archive.
54. Letter from Louis Edmead to Patricia Venn, 1944 (postmark smudged), Edmead Family Archive.
55. Patricia Edmead Memoir.

56. Research Interview with Patricia Edmead (nee Venn), Jonathan Beamish for the feature documentary *Terry's GI Dad*, https://local-colour.co.uk/Terrysgidad (accessed 10 July 2025).
57. Quoted in Langhamer, C., *The English in Love: The Intimate Story of an Emotional Revolution* (Oxford University Press, 2013), p.73.
58. Patricia Edmead Memoir.
59. See: Facebook, Britain's 'Brown Babies', https://www.facebook.com/groups/464383327655779 (accessed 24 February 2025).
60. Bland, L., *Britain's 'Brown Babies': The stories of children born to Black GIs and white women in the Second World War* (Manchester University Press, 2019), p.112.
61. 'The Problem of Marriage in the ETO', ETO Administrative History Collection, File ADM 518, p.3.
62. 'Anglo-U.S. Marriages', *Western Daily Press*, 15 May 1944, cited in the Yanks in Bristol website, https://yanksinbristol.co.uk/bristolian-us-relations/ (accessed 6 February 2024).
63. Davenport, O., 'US race prejudice dooms 1000 British Babies', *Reynolds News*, 9 February 1947.
64. Romano, R.C., *Race Mixing*, p.26.
65. Wynn, N.A., 'Race War', (2008), p.11.
66. Romano, R.C., *Race Mixing*, p.26.
67. Memo from the Air Ministry to the Foreign Office, May 1944, Quoted in Virden, J., *British War Brides in America,* p.40.
68. Smith, G., *When Jim Crow Met John Bull, Black American Soldiers in World War II Britain* (Tauris, 1987), p.206.
69. Foreign Secretary Oral Answers, 'British Subject USA Sentence', Hansard, 11 February 1948, https://hansard.parliament.uk/Commons/1948-02-11/debates/82bbb14c-77ea-45d6-a809-35c9e76da3fc/BritishSubjectUsa(Sentence (accessed 29 May 2025).
70. Formby, G., 'Our Fanny's Gone All Yankee' (Van Dusan Publishing, 1944), Regal Zonophone MR3795.
71. Enlisted Record and Report of Separation, Honorable Discharge Form, Louis A. Edmead, 14 November 1945, Edmead Family Archive.

72. Patricia Edmead Memoir.
73. Smith, G., *When Jim Crow Met John Bull*, p.204.
74. Patricia Edmead Memoir.
75. Louis Edmead letter to Patricia, 25 August 1945, Edmead Family Archive.
76. 'British Girl Stows Away to Marry Yank Soldier', *The Home Nugget*, Alaska, 28 November 1945, p.1.
77. 'Brides' Hour for West Girls', *Western Daily Press*, 31 July 1945, from the Yanks in Bristol website, https://yanksinbristol.co.uk/bristolian-us-relations/ (accessed 6 February 2024).
78. Letter from Louis to Patricia from New York, 9 September 1945, Edmead Family Archive.
79. 1944th Unit History, January 1942 – September 1944.
80. See: Mann Bond, H., The Education of the Negro in the American Social Order (Octogan, 1934), p.114.
81. Ottman, T.M., 'World War 2', New York State Military Museum and Veterans Research Center, https://museum.dmna.ny.gov/unit-history/conflict/world-war-2-1939-1945#:~:text=New%20York%20State's%20higher%20education,discrimination%20in%20private%20college%20admissions, (accessed 20 January 2025).
82. See the U.S. National Archives, 'Servicemen's Readjustment Act (1944)', https://www.archives.gov/milestone-documents/servicemens-readjustment-act (accessed 20 January 2025).
83. Turner, S and Bound, J (2003), 'Closing the Gap or Widening the Divide: The Effects of the G.I. Bill and World War II on the Educational Outcomes of Black Americans', *The Journal of Economic History*, *63*(1), pp.145–177, p.172. http://www.jstor.org/stable/3132498 (accessed 20 January 2025).
84. Bryan Greene, Interview with Author via FaceTime, 12 November 2024.
85. Johnson, H., (1947), 'The Negro Veteran Fights for Freedom!', *Political Affairs*, p.430.
86. Herbold, H., 'Never a Level Playing Field: Blacks and the GI Bill, *The Journal of Blacks in Higher Education*, 6 (winter 1994–1995), pp.104–108.

87. National Archives, GI Bill.
88. Patricia Edmead Memoir.
89. 'Digest of the G.I. BILL OF RIGHTS', *Chicago Sun*, 1946, Edmead Family Archive.
90. Letter from Louis to Patricia, Posted in New York, September 1946, Edmead Family Archive.
91. Bolton, P., 'Education: Historical statistics', House of Commons Library, SN/SG/4252, November 2012, https://researchbriefings.files.parliament.uk/documents/SN04252/SN04252.pdf (accessed 4 February 2025).
92. Letter from Patricia to Louis, 21 November 1946, Edmead Family Archive.
93. 'Notice of Authorisation of Training and Subsistence Allowance', US Embassy, London, 3 March 1949, Edmead Family Archive.
94. Mettler, Suzanne, *Soldiers to Citizens: The G. I. Bill and the Making of the Greatest Generation* (Oxford University Press, 2005), pp.141–142.
95. NBC News, 'American Vets: Benefits, Race and Inequality', Broadcast 28 February 2023, https://www.nbcnews.com/now/video/older-black-veterans-battle-for-gi-education-housing-compensation-and-disability-payments-164145221979 (accessed 4 February 2025).
96. Letter from Louis to Patricia, Posted New York, 15 December 1945, Edmead Family Archive.
97. Letter from Louis to Patricia, Posted New York, 15 December 1945, Edmead Family Archive.
98. 'CRIME RIDDEN N.Y. SENDS OUT 'ARSENAL' CARS', *Chicago Daily Tribune*, 20 November 1945, p.17.
99. Jou, C., 'Neither Welcomed, Nor Refused: Race and Restaurants in Postwar New York City', *Journal of Urban History*, 40.2 (March 2014).
100. See: Biondi, M., *To Stand and Fight: The Struggle for Civil Rights in Postwar New York* (Harvard University Press, 2003).
101. Letter from Louis to Patricia, Posted New York, 1 October 1946, Edmead Family Archive.

102. Letter from Louis to Patricia, Posted New York, 11 January 1947, Edmead Family Archive.
103. Patricia Edmead Memoir.

Chapter Seven

1. See: Deans. J. '*Foyles War* returns victorious, with nearly 6 million viewers', *The Guardian*, 12 April 2010, https://www.theguardian.com/media/2010/apr/12/foyles-war-ratings-billie-piper (accessed 8 May 2024).
2. *Foyle's War*, Series 6, Episode 2, 'Killing Time', First Broadcast on ITV, 18 April 2010.
3. Eley, G., 'Finding the People's War: Film, British Collective Memory, and World War II', *The American Historical Review*, 106.3 (2001), pp.818–838, p.818.
4. See: Roberts, A, *Hitler and Churchill: Secrets of Leadership* (Weidfenfeld & Nicolson, 2003).
5. Colley, T., 'War, Brexit and national identity', Kings College London News Centre, 3 September 2019, https://www.kcl.ac.uk/news/war-brexit-and-national-identity See also, Colley, T., *Always at War: British Public Narratives of War* (University of Michigan Press, 2019).
6. See: Smith, G., *When Jim Crow Met John Bull: Black Soldiers in World War II Britain* (Tauris, 1987) and Reynolds, D., *Rich Relations: The American Occupation of Britain 1942–45* (Phoenix Press, 2000).
7. Werran, K., *An American Uprising in Second World War England: Mutiny in the Duchy* (Pen & Sword, 2020).
8. Page, A., *We Prepare the Way, From Eglin Field to Eschborn: The Story of the 923rd Engineer Regiment during the Second World War* (Suffolk Archives, 2023).
9. Webb, S., *Fighting for the United States, Executed in Britain: US Soldiers Court-Martialled in WWII* (Pen & Sword, 2021).
10. Werran, K., *Black Yanks: Defending Leroy Henry in D-Day Britain* (Pen & Sword, Yorkshire, 2024).

11. Parker, LA, *1944 We Were Here: African American GIs in Dorset*, https://www.louisaadjoaparker.com/blinking-in-the-light-1 (accessed 16 June 2025).
12. Brown Babies Facebook Site: https://www.facebook.com/groups/1884765031760098/ (accessed 19 June 2025).
13. Mixed Museum Online Exhibition, 'Brown Babies', https://mixedmuseum.org.uk/brown-babies/ (accessed 17 July 2025).
14. Royal Television Society, 'Why is the Second World War so popular on Television?', 6 May 2015, https://rts.org.uk/article/why-second-world-war-so-popular-television#:~:text=%22We're%20a%20commercial%20broadcaster,and%20offer%20a%20varied%20diet.%22&text=With%20so%20many%20facets%20to,magnitude%2C%20intensity%20and%20impact.%22 (accessed 24 June 2025).
15. *Foyles War*, Series 6, Episode 2, 'Killing Time', First Broadcast on ITV, 18 April 2010.
16. ITV, *Foyles War*, Series 6, Episode 2, 'Killing Time', First Broadcast 18 April 2010.
17. See: Movie trailer for *The Railway Children Return*, 2022, https://youtu.be/g6IsUeWO2Yw (accessed 7 May 2025).
18. Channel 4, *Churchill: Britain's Secret Apartheid*, First broadcast 19 October 2024, https://www.channel4.com/programmes/churchill-britains-secret-apartheid (accessed 7 May 2025).
19. BBC, *Black and British*, Episode 4, 'The Homecoming', Broadcast 30 November 2016, https://www.bbc.co.uk/iplayer/episode/b084ndpt/black-and-british-a-forgotten-history-4-the-homecoming (accessed 9 May 2025).
20. Brian Lawrenson, born Liverpool, 30 May 1944, Interview with author via Zoom, 4 July 2025.
21. Channel 4, *Britain's Secret War Babies*, Broadcast 17 August 2022, https://www.channel4.com/programmes/britains-secret-war-babies (accessed 7 May 2025).
22. BBC, *DNA Family Secrets*, Broadcast 2 March 2021, YouTube clip https://www.youtube.com/watch?v=oMB3JjpTpZ4, Full episode on BBC iPlayer https://www.bbc.co.uk/iplayer/episode/m000sth9/dna-family-secrets-series-1-episode-1 (accessed 9 May 2025).

23. Yet to be Released Feature Documentary, Terry's GI Dad, https://local-colour.co.uk/Terrysgidad (accessed 7 July 2025).
24. Interview with Professor Lucy Bland, in *WWII 'Brown Babies': A Hidden History*, A National Trust Podcast, 2024, https://www.youtube.com/watch?v=4uD-2THvRbw (accessed 28 March 2024).
25. Interview with Chamion Caballero, in *WWII 'Brown Babies': A Hidden History*, A National Trust Podcast, 2024, https://www.youtube.com/watch?v=4uD-2THvRbw, (accessed 28 March 2024).
26. See, 'Britain's Brown Babies: Illegitimate tots a tough problem for England', *Ebony*, November 1946, pp. 19–23, https://archive.org/details/sim_ebony_1946-11_2_1/page/19/mode/1up?view=theater, (accessed 25 November 2024).
27. Brian Lawrenson, born Liverpool, 30 May 1944, Interview with author via Zoom, 4 July 2025.
28. Brian Lawrenson, Interview with author.
29. Kidd, W., 'What about another war memorial', *Leicester Mercury*, 17 February 1964, *Leicester Mercury* Archives, University of Leicester.
30. BBC News, 'World War Two: Memorial to Battle of Bamber Bridge finished', 27 June 2022, https://www.bbc.co.uk/news/uk-england-lancashire-61950464 (accessed 15 May 2025).
31. BBC News, 'D-Day: African American soldiers remembered for war efforts', 6 June 2019, https://www.bbc.co.uk/news/uk-wales-48550522 (accessed 15 May 2025).
32. See: Hervieux, L., 'Remembering the Black GIs in Wales', 28 September 2016, http://www.lindahervieux.com/blog-and-news/2016/10/2/remembers-the-black-gis-in-wales (accessed 20 May 2025).
33. Netflix, *The Six Triple Eight*, Movie trailer, https://www.netflix.com/gb/title/81590591?source=35 (accessed 14 May 2025).
34. See: King Edward's School Birmingham, 'US Ambassador presents plaque to commemorate the 6888th Battalion', https://kes.org.uk/us-ambassador-presents-plaque-to-commemorate-6888th-battalion/ (accessed 15 May 2025).

35. Hervieux, L., *Forgotten: The Untold Story of D-Day's Black Heroes, At Home and At War* (Harper Collins, 2015).
36. Wynn, NA, *The African American Experience during World War II* (Rowman & Littlefield, 2011), pxiii.
37. Litwack, L.F., *How Free is Free: The Long Death of Jim Crow* (Harvard University Press, 2009), p.75.
38. 'Along the NAACP Battlefront', *The Crisis*, September 1946, p.276, https://books.google.co.uk/books?id=J1sEAAAAMBAJ&pg=PA276&dq=veterans&hl=en&sa=X&ved=0ahUKEwiosr-Eur7NAhUqBMAKHXJCDMo4FBDoAQg3MAc#v=onepage&q=veterans&f=false (accessed 20 June 2025).
39. Fairclough, A., *Better Day Coming, Blacks and Equality: 1890–2000* (Penguin, 2001), p.208.
40. See: Newman, M., *The Civil Rights Movement* (Edinburgh University Press, 2004), pp.43–50 and Greene, B., 'After Victory in World War II, Black Veterans Continued the Fight for Freedom at Home', *Smithsonian Magazine*, 30 August 2021.
41. Brooks, J.E., 'Winning the Peace: Georgia Veterans and the Struggle to Define the Political Legacy of World War II', in Feldman, G., *Before Brown: Civil Rights and White Backlash in the Modern South* (University of Alabama Press, 2004), p.239.
42. Katznelson, I., *When Affirmative Action Was White: An Untold History of Racial Inequality in Twentieth-Century America* (W.W. Norton & Company, 2005).
43. Banks, S.L., 'Higher Education and the Poor', *The Crisis* magazine, November 1974, pp.311–312, https://books.google.co.uk/books?id=cNg3VXWmrSAC&pg=PA312&dq=gi+bill&hl=en&sa=X&ved=0ahUKEwi_5LbX177NAhWIJMAKHf37AOk4ChDoAQgjMAI#v=onepage&q=gi%20bill&f=false (accessed 23 June 2025).
44. Stone, T.L., *Courage Has No Color: The True Story Of The Triple Nickles: America's First Black Paratroopers* (Candlewick, 2013), p.97.
45. Biggs, B., Gavin: *A Biography of General James M. Gavin* (Archon, 1980), pp.74–77.

46. United States Congressional Record, 85th Congress, First Session, 103.12, 22–30 August 1957, Strom Thurmond 'filibuster' speech, https://www.senate.gov/artandhistory/history/resources/pdf/Thurmond_filibuster_1957.pdf (accessed 29 August 2025).
47. Thurmond, S., *The Faith We Have Not Kept* (Viewpoint Books, 1968), pp.160–161.
48. Gavin, J.M., *Crisis Now: Crisis in the Cities, Crisis in Vietnam, A Commitment To Change* (Random House, 1968), p.117.
49. McKenzie, J. *On Time, On Target: The World War II Memoir of a Paratrooper in the 82d Airborne* (Presidio Press, 2000), p.226.
50. See: McGuire, P., 'Desegregation of the Armed Forces: Black protest, Leadership and World War II', *The Journal of Negro History*, 68.2 (1983), pp.147–158.
51. ONS, Ethnic Group, England and Wales: Census 2021, 29 November 2022, https://www.ons.gov.uk/peoplepopulationandcommunity/culturalidentity/ethnicity/bulletins/ethnicgroupenglandandwales/census2021#ethnic-groups-within-households (accessed 20 May 2022).
52. For more on the growth of 'mixed-race Britain', see, Adekoya, R., *BiRacial Britain: A Different Way of Looking at Race* (Constable, 2021) and Kaufmann, E., *Whiteshift: Populism, Immigration and the Future of White Majorities* (Penguin, 2019).
53. Dunlap-Berg, B., 'Black Clergy, Laity Share Perspective's on Churches Future', *United Methodist Insight*, 11 April 2023, https://um-insight.net/in-the-church/umc-future/black-clergy-laity-share-perspectives-on-church's-future/ (accessed 20 May 2025).
54. Mohdin, A., 'Institutional racism blocks progress of Black clergy in Church of England, report finds', *The Guardian*, 6 November 2024, https://www.theguardian.com/world/2024/nov/06/institutional-racism-blocks-progress-of-black-clergy-in-church-of-england-report-finds (accessed 20 May 2025).
55. School of Public Health, University of Illinois Chicago, Law Enforcement Epidemiology Project, 'U.S. Data on Police Shootings and Violence', https://policeepi.uic.edu/u-s-data-on-police-shootings-and-violence/, (accessed 16 May 2025).

56. BBC News, 'George Floyd: What happened in the final moments of his life', 16 July 2020, https://www.bbc.co.uk/news/world-us-canada-52861726, (accessed 20 May 2025).
57. Bor, J. et al, 'Police killings and their spillover effects on the mental health of black Americans: a population-based, quasi-experimental study', The Lancet, 392.10144, p.302–310, 28 July 2018.
58. Dodd, V., 'Black people seven times more likely to die after police restraint in Britain, figures show', *The Guardian*, 19 February 2023, https://www.theguardian.com/uk-news/2023/feb/19/black-people-seven-times-more-likely-to-die-after-police-restraint-in-britain-figures-show (accessed 20 May 2024).
59. Greene, B., 'After Victory in World War II, Black Veterans Continued the Fight for Freedom at Home', *Smithsonian Magazine*, 30 August 2021, https://www.smithsonianmag.com/history/summer-1946-saw-black-wwii-vets-fight-freedom-home-180978538/ (accessed 17 July 2025).

Further Reading

Adekoya, R., *BiRacial Britain: A Different Way of Looking at Race* (Constable, 2021).

Aiello, T., "Not Too Far Removed From Slavery": Police Brutality and Rights Activism in Valdosta, Georgia, 1945–55', *Journal of Human and Civil Rights*, 5.2 (2019), pp.34–67.

Barksdale, S., 'Prelude to a Revolution: African American Veterans, Double Consciousness, and Civil Rights, 1940-1955', PhD Thesis, University of North Carolina, 2014.

Bauer, A and Bauer, A.H., 'Day to Day Resistance to Slavery', *The Journal of Negro History*, 27.4 (October 1942), pp.388–419.

Beazley, B., *Peelers to Pandas: An illustrated History of the Leicester City Police* (Breedon Books, 2001).

Bennett, G.H., *Destination Normandy; Three American Regiments on D-Day* (Stackpole Books, 2007).

Bergen, D.L., *Between God and Hitler: Military Chaplains in Nazi Germany* (Cambridge University Press, 2023).

Berry, A., *And Suddenly They Were Gone: An Oral and Pictorial History of The 82d Airborne Division in England, February – September 1944* (Overlord, 2015).

Biggs, B., Gavin: *A Biography of General James M. Gavin* (Archon, 1980), pp.74–77.

Bland, L., *Britain's 'Brown Babies': The stories of children born to Black GIs and white women during the Second World War* (Manchester University Press, 2019).

Bland, L., 'Interracial Relationships and the "Brown Baby Question": Black GIs, White British Women, and Their Mixed-Race Offspring in World War II', *Journal of the History of Sexuality*, 26.3 (2017).

Bristol, D.W. and Stur, H.M., (eds), *Integrating the US Military: Race, Gender, and Sexual Orientation Since World War II* (John Hopkins University Press, Baltimore: 2017).

Brooklyn Historical Society, *Caribbean Immigrants in Brooklyn: an American story* (New York University Press, 2014).

Brooks, J.E., 'Winning the Peace: Georgia Veterans and the Struggle to Define the Political Legacy of World War II', in Feldman, G., *Before Brown: Civil Rights and White Backlash in the Modern South* (University of Alabama Press, 2004).

Carswell, J. Johnson, R., and Kirrane, S., *Ours to Defend: Leicestershire People Remember the Home Front* (Leicester Oral History Archive, 1989).

Colley, T., *Always at War: British Public Narratives of War* (University of Michigan Press, 2019).

Cook, H., *The Long Sexual Revolution: English Women, Sex, and Contraception 1800–1975* (Oxford University Press, 2004), p.103.

Covais, J.S., *Battery! C Lenton Sartain and the Airborne GIs of the 319th Glider Field Artillery* (Create Space, 2010).

Davis, M.L., *The Methodist Unification: Christianity and the Politics of Race in the Jim Crow Era* (New York University Press, New York, 2008).

Dresser, M., and Fleming, P., *Bristol: Ethnic Minorities and the city 1000-2001* (Phillimore, 2007).

Eley, G., 'Finding the People's War: Film, British Collective Memory, and World War II', *The American Historical Review*, 106.3 (2001), pp.818–838.

Equal Justice Initiative, *Lynching in America: Confronting the Legacy of Racial Terror, Third Edition*, (Montgomery, Alabama, 2017), https://lynchinginamerica.eji.org/report/ (accessed 25 March 2024).

Evans, J. 'The Origins of Tallahassee's Racial Disturbance Plan: Segregation, Racial Tensions, and Violence During World War II', *The Florida Historical Quarterly*, 79.3 (2000), pp.346–364.

Fairclough, A., *Better Day Coming: Blacks and Equality* 1890–2000 (Penguin, 2001).

Farrell, S., 'Not Just Farms Anymore: The Effects of World War II on Mississippi's Economy', Mississippi History Now (2001), https://www.mshistorynow.mdah.ms.gov/issue/the-effects-of-world-war-II-on-mississippis-economy (accessed 30 April 2024).

Finkle, L., 'The Conservative Aims of Militant Rhetoric: Black Protest During World War II', *The Journal of American History*, 60.3 (December 1973), pp.692–713.

Freeman, R., *The Friendly Invasion* (Lavenham Press, 1992).

Gardiner, J., *'Over Here'; The GIs in Wartime Britain* (Collins & Brown, 1992).

Gavin, J.M., *Crisis Now: Crisis in the Cities, Crisis in Vietnam, A Commitment To Change* (Random House, 1968).

Gordon, L.A., 'Mahatma Gandhi's Dialogues with Americans', *Economic and Political Weekly*, 37.4 (26 January – 1 February 2002), pp.337–352.

Gough, Allison, J. 'Messing Up Another Country's Customs: The Exportation of American Racism During World War II', *World History Connected,* October 2007, http://worldhistoryconnected.press.illinois.edu/5.1/gough.html (accessed 17 May 2025).

Greenberg, C.L., Moore, J.M. and Mjagkij (eds), *To Ask for an Equal Chance: African Americans in the Great Depression* (Rowman & Littlefield, 2011).

Guidry, P.F., *Treasures in My Heart: A true WWII love story* (iUniverse, 2004).

Hachey, T., 'Walter White and the American Negro Soldier in World War II: A Diplomatic Dilemma for Britain', *Python*, 39.3 (1978), pp.241–249.

Hart, J.F., 'The Changing Distribution of the American Negro', *Annals of the Association of American Geographers*, 50.3 (September 1960), pp.242–266.

Hegseth, P., *The War on Warriors: Behind the Betrayal of the Men Who Keep Us Free* (Fox Books: 2024).

Heltzel, P.G., 'Building the Beloved City: Howard Thurman and Martin Luther King Jr.', in *Resurrection City: A Theology of Improvisation* (William B. Eerdmans Publishing Company, 2012).

Herbold, H., 'Never a Level Playing Field: Blacks and the GI Bill', *The Journal of Blacks in Education*, 6 (Winter 1994–1995), pp.104–108.

Hervieux, L., *Forgotten: The Untold Story of D-Day's Black Heroes, at Home and at War* (Harper Collins, 2015).

Holyoak, V., *But for these things: Leicester and its people in WWII* (Matador, 2014).

Huddle, MA (ed), *Roi Ottley's World War II: The Lost Diary of an African American Journalist* (University of Kansas Press, 2011).

Jou, C., 'Neither Welcomed, Nor Refused: Race and Restaurants in Postwar New York City', *Journal of Urban History*, 40.2 (March 2014).

Katznelson, I., *When Affirmative Action Was White: An Untold History of Racial Inequality in Twentieth-Century America* (NW.W. Norton & Company, 2005).

Kaufmann, E., *Whiteshift: Populism, Immigration and the Future of White Majorities* (Penguin, 2019).

Kelly, R., 'We Are Not What We Seem: Rethinking Black Working-Class Opposition in the Jim Crow South', *The Journal of American History*, 80.1 (June 1993), pp.75–112.

King, M.L., *Junior, Stride Towards Freedom: The Montgomery Story* (Harper & Row, 1958).

Kruse, K.M., and Tuck, S., (eds), *Fog of War: The Second World War and the Civil Rights Movement* (Oxford University Press, 2012).

Langhamer, C., The English in Love: An Intimate Story of an Emotional Revolution (Oxford University Press, 2013).

Latty, Y., *We Were There: Voices of African American Veterans from World War II to the War in Iraq* (Amistad, 2005).

Lee, U., *The Employment of Negro Troops* (US Army Center of Military History, 2001).

Lilly, R.J., *Taken By Force: Rape and American GIs in Europe during World War II* (Palgrave Macmillan, 2007).

Litwack, L.F., *How Free is Free, The Long Death of Jim Crow* (Harvard University Press, 2009).

LoFaro, G., *Sword of St. Michael: The 82nd Airborne Division in World War II* (De Capo, 2011).

Longmate, N., *The G.I.'s: The Americans in Britain, 1942–45* (Hutchinson of London, 1975).

MacInnes, C.M., *Bristol at War* (London Museum Press, 1962).

Mann Bond, H., *The Education of the Negro in the American Social Order* (Octogan, 1934).

Martin, H.M., *Soldier: The Memoirs of Matthew B. Ridgway* (Harper & Brothers, 1956).

McGregor, M., *Integration of the Armed Forces; 1940-65* (US Defense Committee, 1979).

McGuire, P., 'Desegregation of the Armed Forces: Black protest, Leadership and World War II', *The Journal of Negro History*, 68.2 (1983), pp.147–158.

McGuire, P., *Taps for a Jim Crow Army; Letters from Black Soldiers in World War II* (ABC-CLIO, 1983).

McKenzie, John D., *On Time On Target, The World War II Memoir of a Paratrooper in the 82nd Airborne* (Presidio Press, 2000).

Meier, A. and Bracey, J.H., 'The NAACP as a Reform Movement, 1905–1965: "To Reach the Conscience of America"', *The Journal of Southern History*, 59.1 (February 1993), pp.3–30.

Mershon, S. and Schlossman, S., *Foxholes and Color Lines: Desegregating the U.S. Armed Forces* (John Hopkins University Press, 1988).

Mettler, Suzanne, *Soldiers to Citizens: The G. I. Bill and the Making of the Greatest Generation* (Oxford University Press, 2005), pp.141–142.

Millgate, H.D., *Got Any Gum Chum? GIs in Wartime Britain, 1942–1945* (The History Press, 2009).

Miller, D.L., *Masters of the Air: America's Bomber Boys Who Fought The Air-War Against Nazi Germany* (Simon & Schuster, 2006).

Mormino, G.R., 'Gi Joe Meets Jim Crow: Racial Violence and Reform in World War II Florida', *The Florida Historical Quarterly*, 73.1 (1994), pp.23–42.

Moskos, C., 'From Citizens' Army to Social Laboratory', *The Wilson Quarterly*, 17.1, (winter 1993).

Motley, M.P., *The Invisible Soldier; The Experiences of the Black Soldier, World War II* (Wayne State University Press, 1987).

Nash, D. and Reader, D., *Leicester in the Twentieth Century* (Alan Sutton Publishing, 1993).

Newman, M., *The Civil Rights Movement* (Edinburgh University Press, 2004).

Nordyke, P., *All American All the Way: The Combat History of the 82nd Airborne Division in World War II* (Zenith, 2005).

Olusoga, D., *Black and British: A Forgotten History* (Pan, 2016).

Osur, Alan M., 'Blacks in the Army Air Forces During World War II: The Problem of Race Relations' (Office of Air Force History, 1977) p.131, https://apps.dtic.mil/sti/tr/pdf/ADA036585.pdf (accessed 19 June 2025).

Page, A., *We Prepare The Way. From Eglin Field to Eschborn: The Story of the 923rd Engineer Regiment during the Second World War* (Suffolk Archives, 2023).

Palmer, R.R., Bell, IW and Keast, W.R., *The Army Ground Forces: The Procurement and Training of Ground Combat Troops* (Center of Military History, 1991).

Piehler, G.K., *A Religious History of the American GI in World War II* (University of Nebraska Press, 2016).

Reynolds, D., *Rich Relations: The American Occupation of Britain 1942–45* (Phoenix Press, 2000).

Reynolds, D., 'The Churchill Government and the Black American Troops in Britain during World War II', *Transactions of the Royal Historical Society*, vol 35 (1985), pp.113–133.

Richardson, D., *The Bristol Slave Traders: A Collective Portrait* (Bristol Historical Association, 1985).

Roberts, A., *Hitler and Churchill: Secrets of Leadership* (Weidfenfeld & Nicolson, 2003).

Roberts, M.L., What Soldiers Do: Sex and the American GI in World War II France (University of Chicago Press, 2013).

Rogerson, D., *The Battle of Bamber Bridge: The True Story* (Purple Parrot, 2022).

Romano, R.C., *Race Mixing: Black-White Marriage in Postwar America* (Harvard University Press, 2003).

Rowe, M., 'Sex, "race" and riot in Liverpool, 1919', *Immigrants & Minorities: Historical Studies in Ethnicity, Migration and Diaspora*, vol 19, (2000).

Ruddy, A.J., *To the Last Round; The Leicestershire and Rutland Home Guard 1940–1945* (Breedon Books, 2007).

Sanders, T., *The Last Good War: The Faces And Voices of World War II* (Welcome, 2010).

Schaffer, G., 'Fighting Racism: Black soldiers and workers in Britain during the Second World War', *Immigrants and Minorites*, 28.2–3, pp.246–265.

Schiffman, J., 'The Education of Negro Soldiers in World War II', *The Journal of Negro Education*, 18.1 (winter, 1949).

Sherwood, M., 'Walter White and the British: A lost opportunity', *Contributions to Black Studies: A Journal of African and Afro-American Studies*, vol 9 (1992), pp.216–226.

Shute, N., *The Chequer Board* (Heinemann, 1947).

Simpson, J., *'Aliens' in Unreliable Sources: How the Twentieth Century was Reported* (Macmillan, 2010).

Slate, N., 'The drama of nonviolence: Theatre as education in the American civil rights movement', *Ride: The Journal of Applied Theatre and Performance* (2022), 27.1, pp.73–87.

Smith, G., *When Jim Crow Met John Bull; Black Soldiers in World War II Britain* (Tauris, 1987).

Smith, H.L., *Britain in the Second World War: A Social History* (Manchester University Press, 1996).

Stone, T.L., *Courage Has No Color: The True Story Of The Triple Nickels America's First Black Paratroopers* (Candlewick).

Thurmond, S., *The Faith We Have Not Kept* (Viewpoint Books, 1968).

Todd, S., 'Poverty and Aspiration: Young Women's Entry to Employment in Inter-war England', *Twentieth Century British History*, 15.2, pp.119–142.

Turner, S. and Bound, J. (2003), 'Closing the Gap or Widening the Divide: The Effects of the G.I. Bill and World War II on the Educational Outcomes of Black Americans', *The Journal of Economic History*, 63(1), pp.145–177.

Virden, J. *Good-Bye, Piccadilly: British War Brides in America* (Urbarna: University of Illinois Press, 1996).

Walck, P., 'Mutiny at Bamber Bridge: How the World War II Press Reported Racial Unrest among U.S. Troops and Why It Remains in British Memory', *American Journalism*, 37.3 (2020).

Ward, J.M., Defending White Democracy: The Making of a Segregationist Movement and the Remaking of Racial Politics, 1936–1965 (University of North Carolina Press 2011).

Webb, S., *Fighting For the United States, Executed in Britain: US Soldiers Court Martialled in WWII* (Pen & Sword, 2021).

Werran, K., *An American Uprising in Second World War England: Mutiny in the Duchy* (Pen & Sword, 2020).

Werran, K., *Black Yanks: Defending Leroy Henry in D-Day Britain* (Pen & Sword, 2024).

White, George Junior, '"I Am Teaching Some of The Boys:" Chaplain Robert Boston Dokes and Army Testing of Black Soldiers in World War II', *The Journal of Negro Education*, 81.3 (summer 2012), pp.200–217.

Williams, M.V., *Medgar Evers: Mississippi Martyr* (University of Arkansas Press, 2011).

Wills, D., *Put on Your Boots and Parachutes! The United States 82nd Airborne Division* (Deryk Wills, 1992).

Wood, A.L., *Lynching and Spectacle: Witnessing Racial Violence in America, 1890–1940* (North Carolina Press, 2009).

Wynn, N., 'Race War: Black Americans and West Indians in Britain During the Second World War', *Immigrants & Minorities*, 24.3, November 2006, pp.324–346.

Wynn, N., The African American Experience during World War II (Rowman & Littlefield, 2010).

Zeiger, S., *Entangling Alliances: Foreign War Brides and American Soldiers in the Twentieth Century* (New York University Press, 2010).

Further Viewing: British Television Programmes and Movie Trailers

BBC, *Black and British*, Episode 4, 'The Homecoming', Broadcast 30 November 2016, https://www.bbc.co.uk/iplayer/episode/b084ndpt/

black-and-british-a-forgotten-history-4-the-homecoming (accessed 9 May 2025).

BBC, *DNA Family Secrets*, Broadcast 2 March 2021, YouTube clip https://www.youtube.com/watch?v=oMB3JjpTpZ4, Full episode on BBC iPlayer, https://www.bbc.co.uk/iplayer/episode/m000sth9/dna-family-secrets-series-1-episode-1 (accessed 9 May 2025).

Channel 4, *Churchill: Britain's Secret Apartheid*, First broadcast 19 October 2024, https://www.channel4.com/programmes/churchill-britains-secret-apartheid (accessed 7 May 2025).

Channel 4, *Britain's Secret War Babies*, Broadcast 17 August 2022, https://www.channel4.com/programmes/britains-secret-war-babies (accessed 7 May 2025).

Netflix, *The Six Triple Eight*, Movie trailer, https://www.netflix.com/gb/title/81590591?source=35 (accessed 14 May 2025).

The Railway Children Return, 2022, Movie trailer, https://youtu.be/g6IsUeWO2Yw (accessed 7 May 2025).

Index